Genealogical and Biographical Account of the family of Bolton: in England and America. Deduced from an early period, and continued down to the present time.

Robert Bolton, Robert Bolton

From the author to his
friend,

Mrs A Stevens

New York Oct 16 1873

GENEALOGICAL

AND

BIOGRAPHICAL ACCOUNT OF THE FAMILY

OF

BOLTON:

IN

ENGLAND AND AMERICA.

DEDUCED FROM AN EARLY PERIOD, AND CONTINUED DOWN TO
THE PRESENT TIME.

COLLECTED CHIEFLY FROM ORIGINAL PAPERS AND RECORDS:

WITH AN APPENDIX.

BY

ROBERT BOLTON, A.M.,

AUTHOR OF THE "HISTORY OF WESTCHESTER COUNTY;" ALSO "HISTORY OF THE PROTESTANT EPIS-
COPAL CHURCH IN THE COUNTY OF WESTCHESTER," "GUIDE TO NEW-ROCHELLE,"
A MEMBER OF THE PROTESTANT EPISCOPAL SOCIETY, AND OF THE
NEW-YORK AND GEORGIA HISTORICAL SOCIETIES.

"Those only deserve to be remembered by posterity who treasure up the history of their
ancestry."—BURKE.

"I must not give up my attachment to Genealogy, and every thing relating to it, because
it is the greatest spur to noble and gallant actions."—Rev. MARK NOBLE.

New-York:

JOHN A. GRAY, PRINTER, STEREOTYPER, AND BINDER,

FIRE-PROOF BUILDINGS,

CORNER OF FRANKFORT AND JACOB STREETS.

1862.

1192541

TO

JAMES ROBERT BOLTON, Esq.

Of San Francisco,

THE FOLLOWING

GENEALOGICAL MEMOIR

IS AFFECTIONATELY INSCRIBED

BY HIS COUSIN,

ROBERT BOLTON

Bedford, Westchester County 24th January, 1862

PREFACE.

————◆•————

MEMOIRS of eminent men may be considered as essential materials for the composition of History, and afford us not only a pleasing amusement, but the most instructive lessons. No study, perhaps, can be better calculated to impress on the minds of youth an early love of virtue, and a desire of being useful to mankind in general, or devoting themselves particularly to the service of God or their country, for while we are contemplating the characters and actions of our pious ancestors, the generous spark of emulation is kindled in our own breast, and we ardently seek the opportunity of imitating such illustrious examples. To do justice to the characters of men of such distinguished piety, to whom we are so much indebted, is not only an act of gratitude, but a pleasing, a generous task.

Though this family has been eminently conspicuous from having given so many ministers to the Church of England, one of whom it has been justly remarked, was "celebrated for his singular learning and piety," there has not been a single attempt to collect and arrange any kind of memorial of it either in England or America. Hence it is easy for every one to see, that when the author undertook such a task, he had much to do.

The greatest attention has been paid in examining the numerous works of the historian, topographer, genealogist and antiquarian, and many distant parts of both England and the United States have been visited by the author or his friends to inspect authentic records; yet unhappily, researches of this kind, can seldom be complete or entirely without mistake. Those only who know the fatigue of collecting materials, and classing them for books of this sort, after a period of full twenty-five years has been spent in constantly watching, searching and waiting for facts, can form a proper judgment of such a laborious undertaking.

The author's progress in investigating the genealogy of his family was greatly aided by a beloved father, who, one of nature's noblemen and an indefatigable antiquarian, first commenced the inquiry, imbued his son with a taste for the same, and fully intended to have completed it before his death. To his preserving hand the family are greatly indebted for many MS. materials which otherwise would have been lost.

It would be unpardonable not to mention likewise, with the greatest gratitude and respect, the obligations due to those who have contributed to the compilation of these memoirs, by permitting an inspection of records and other curious papers, as the Rev T Rushton, vicar of Blackburn, Lanc ; Rev Frederick Calder, officiating minister, and master of the endowed grammar-school, of Chesterfield, Derbyshire ; Rev. Mr Hawley, incumbent of Wales and Thorpe Salvin, Yorkshire ; Rev Mr. Appleton, vicar of Worksop, Nottinghamshire, Rev. Mr Eastwood, curate of Eckington, Derbyshire, Rev Mr Smith of Killamarsh, Derbyshire, Rev Charles H. Ramsden, minister of Shirland, Derbyshire ; Rev J Thomas, Librarian and Keeper of the Records, Archiepiscopal Palace, Lambeth ; Rev Benjamin Dorr, D D, rector of Christ Church, Philadelphia, Pennsylvania ; to the following gentlemen, for the promptness with which they have responded to my inquiries in visiting distant places, and sending numerous extracts from the registers, etc , Perrot Fenton, Esq , Proctor in Doctors' Commons, London , William Robinson, Esq , of Lancaster, late Deputy Sheriff of Lancashire , Mr Thomas Hinchliffe, of Sheffield, Yorkshire ; Samuel Mitchell, Esq , of The Mount, near Sheffield, John Holland, Esq , of Sheffield , Joseph Jessop, Esq , of Sheffield , John Edward Dibb, Esq , Deputy Registrar, Wakefield, Yorkshire , Messrs. Hudson and Buckle of the York Registry, York , Charles T. W Parry, Esq , of the District Registry, Chester , W Brooks Gates, Esq , District Registry, Northampton ; Frederick Dawes Danvers, Esq., Duchy of Lancaster Office, Lancaster Place, London , R Holmes, Esq , of the MS department of the British Museum, London , Joseph Hunter, Esq , Historian of Hallamshire, Rolls Office, London , Charles Roberts, Esq , of the Public Record Office, Rolls House, Chancery Lane, London, W. C ; Mr Samuel Cooper, Parish Clerk of Chesterfield, Derby; E Dresser Rogers, Esq , Bridge House Chambers, London , Joseph G Cogswell, LL.D , Astor Library, New-York, and his assistants ; J K Tefft, Esq , of Savannah, Georgia , Samuel G. Drake, Esq , of Boston ; Lloyd P Smith of the Philadelphia Library, Robert Habersham, Esq , of Savannah, Georgia

In conclusion, the author must acknowledge the valuable assistance he has also derived from the work of a beloved brother, entitled, *"Footsteps of the Flock*, Memorials of the Rev Robert Bolton, Rector of Pelham, United States, and Chaplain to the Earl of Ducie, and of Mrs Bolton "* This precious memento of their venerated parents was chiefly derived from their diaries extending over a period of forty years

The numerous wood-cuts of arms interspersed throughout the genealogies were from drawings by the late Rev. Robert Bolton, taken from the originals in the Visitations of Lancashire in the British Museum, while the residences and tombs are from drawings taken on the spot by the author   They were cut by Mr Williams, a well-known engraver, of No. 60 Fulton Street, New-York

CONTENTS.

——————•◆•——————

PART I.

SECTION I.

PART II.

SECTION I.

SECTION III

SECTION IV.

PART III.

SECTION I

SECTION II

SECTION III.

SECTION IV.

SECTION V.

SECTION VI

Genealogical and Historical Memoirs

OF THE

BOLTON FAMILY.

PART I.

SECTION I.

FAMILY ANTIQUITY.

THE Bolton Family is of an ancient British stock, the genealogy of which has been traced up to the Conquest. At this time it was in possession of great landed estates both in Yorkshire and Lancashire; in the former, Bolton juxta Bowland. Manors of Remington[a] and Midhope;[b] in the latter, the Lordships of both Great and Little Bolton, and also Bolton le Sands.

The parish of Bolton juxta Bowland,[c] sometimes called Bolton West, in order to distinguish it from Bolton East, or Bolton Canons, is thus surveyed in Domesday :

᙮In BODELTONE 7 RAGHIL, 7 HOLME VIII., CAR AD GLD.

---

[a] In Domesday, Renitone, Remstone, now Remington, in Ribblesdale parish of Gisburn "In 1316 the Manor of Remington belonged to Michael Bolton and others." Whitaker's Craven

[b] "This manor was parcel of the great possessions of the Boltons, and passed into the Lister family by marriage with a co-heiress of that most ancient name temp Edward II" Ditto.

[c] "The church of Gisburn was visited by Dodsworth, May 3d, 1621, when the windows contained with other things, Gules, a chevron between three mullets pierced, or, two bolts feathered downward in chief—crest, a buck's head, argent attired, or, for Boulton" Ditto.

"Bodelton, or Bothelton, the ancient orthography of all the towns which bear this name," says Whitaker, "is evidently from Boel, mansio, implying, probably, that it was the principal residence of some Saxon thane." "The ancient Saxon orthography of Great Bolton, says Baines, is Boltune or Bolrune, a town adjoining to a principal mansion or manor-house."[d] "Ton or Tun," observes another writer, "is derived from the Saxon ıun, a *hedge* or *wall*, and this seems to be from 'ðun,' a hill, the houses being anciently built on *hills* for the sake of defence and protection in times of war. This thane, whose *chief residence* was on a *hill*, was doubtless Edwin Earl of Mercia, who was seized of the manor of Bodelton before the Conquest, and even held it five years after. "In the later Saxon times," says Whitaker, Bodeltone, or **Boꝣꞇune** (the town of the principal mansion) was the property of Earl Edwin, whose large possessions in the north were among the last estates in the kingdom which, after the Conquest, were permitted to remain in the hands of their former owners"[e] "This nobleman was son of Leofwine, and brother of Leofric, Earls of Mercia."[f] From the Saxon proprietors, therefore, the Boltons descend; for, according to Sir William Dugdale, Oughtred de Bolton,[g] Lord of Bolton, by Bowland,[h] in 1135, was the lineal representative of the Saxon Earls of Mercia. "Oughtred and his immediate descendants," says Burke, "the Lords of Bolton, held the office of Bow-bearer in the Royal Forests of Bow-

---

d Edward Baines' *History of the County of Lancashire*

e It was before the Domesday survey that this nobleman had incurred the forfeiture, and his lands in Craven, consisting of lxxvii carucates, are accordingly surveyed under the head of TERRA REGIS, called the Fee of Earl Edwin

⊙In *BODELTONE*. comes Eduuin h̄b̄ . vi . car træ ad gld

Whitaker's *Deanery of Craven*, p 209   See Dugdale's *Warwickshire*, first edition, p. 87.

f See Ormerod's *History of Cheshire*, vol i , p 6

g See Dugdale's *Warwickshire*, 1st edition, p 87.   Outred, doubtless, the Anglo-Saxon personal, whence Utred or Uhtred

h Bowland Forest is situated in the counties of York, West Riding, and Lancaster, and parishes of Slaidburn and Whalley, has an area of 20,700 acres, greater part of which is enclosed   In the time of Henry VIII , Sir ―― Darcy Knt High Steward and Master Forester of Bowland Forest, for destruction of red deer summoned several parties before the Court of Swainmote and Woodenote in Yorkshire land[i] and Gilsland, (which were portions of the demesnes of the Earls of Mercia) for ten successive generations" John de Bolton, Lord of Bolton, was fifth in descent from Oughtred, and held the office of Bow-bearer in 1312.

The spelling of the name, with a slight variation, was continued a century or more after the Conquest, for in the time of Stephen, Abbot of Sallay, A.D 1154, Elias de Bothelton held lands in the parish of Bolton juxta Bowland of fendo de la Leya. In the reign of Henry III, Richard de Bonhilton is named of the village of Bonhilton in Yorkshire.[j] The Testa de Nevill', of the reign of Edward II, contains the name of Robert de Bolrun as holding six acres of land at Bolrun.[k] According to Segar, Bolton in Yorkshire was an ancient barony by tenure in the time of Henry II., and the Scroops of Bolton, Masham and Upsal, are in a direct line all descended from the Barons Bolton of Bolton, though the style hath been altered like many others.[l] Robert de Boulton, Earl of Boulton, in Yorkshire, is mentioned as a liberal benefactor to the repairs of that noble edifice, the York Minster, in the west tower of which he is represented armed, cap a pie, in a coat of mail of that time.[m] In 1311 Robertus de Boulton held one

---

The great forests of Lancashire were peopled by an indigenous race of wild cattle, some of which are still to be seen in the park at Gisburn.

[i] In the Harl MSS , 891, are depicted the arms of the Boultons of Boulton in Bowland, al) a fg[t]., bol 3 k arg., i e a chev sa between 3 mullets of the last *Flowers' Visitation of Lancashire* in 1567   Arms of the Earls of Mercia—sa an eagle displayed, or   Bolton's of Bolton, sa a falcon argent, beaked, belled, membered, and jessed, or

[j] Whitaker's *Craven*

[k] "*Testa de Nevill*', fol 110, (818.) In the 'Placita de Quo Warranto,' p 385 occurs the following· 'Posteaven' burgen's p' dee ville et dant dno Regi decem marcas p exit eazdem, etc —hinc a die scr' Mich in tres sept[r] s p pl Robti Payen, Lambti le spens, Robti le Ken, Robti Catherton, *Robti de Bohun* and Lambti de Bulk, 35 Edward I 1307"

[l] Segar's preface, 25   *Extinct Peerage of England*, by Solomon Bolton, 1769 "This Barony and castle is between Askrig and Middleham in the north of Yorkshire and north side of the Ouse," (p 30)

[m] "The first stone of the nave was laid with great state in 1291, and was finished 1330   The materials for building the nave were supplied by Robert de Vavasour and Robert de Boulton, Earl of Boulton, the former of whom gave the stone, the latter the timber   The memory of these noble benefactors is preserved by statues at the east and west end of the cathedral '—*Saturday Magazine*, Jan'y 19 1833

messuage and seventy-two acres of land in Yarpesthorpe of the King in capite by military service, and one tofto, four bovates, and twenty acres in Appleton.[n]

At Great Bolton or Bolton le Moors in Salford Hundred, Lancashire, the Boltons had been long seated. In 1291, 20th Edward I., Christiana, wife of Thomas, son of Matilda de Bolton, brought her writ of dower at Lancaster on the octaves of the Holy Trinity against John, Archbishop of York, and Edmund, the King's brother, for a tenement in Bolton, and recovered her right [o]

In 1487, Robert Bolton, of Bolton on the Moors, claimed, with others, the tolls and customs of the Fair and Court Leet holden at that place.[p] By a calendar of pleadings in the *Ducatus Lancastriæ*, 5th and 6th of Philip and Mary, 1558, we find Sir Peter Leighe, Knt, and two other justices of the peace plaintiffs in a suit against Robert Bolton and two other defendants for a disturbance of tithe collection and interruption of levy at Bolton.[q] In 1574, Robert Bolton and others, inhabitants of Bolton on the Moors, claimed a messuage and lands situated in Tokholes, Blackburn, Lancashire, for maintaining the grammar-school at Bolton.[r]

The Manor of Little Bolton, mentioned in the charter of Roger de Mareshey, was also held by the family of Bolton, even after the death of Ranulph de Blundeville. William de Bothelton, says the *Testa de Nevill*, held a bovate of land in chief of our Lord the King in fee farm; his heir is in wardship of our Lord the King. Roger de Bothelton holds one

---

[n] *Calendarium Rutalorum Patentium*, 72 Secunda Patten' de domo 5° Regis Edwardi secundi In 1338, Thomas, son of Robertus de Boulton, died, possessed of lands at Apelton, in Rydale, York *Inquisitiones Post Mortem*, vol ii No 2 In 1350, Robert de Boulton died, seised of lands in Castel Levington Manor, Tampton Manor, Newbye and Ridale in the same county. Ditto, vol. ii No. 35 William de Gurnays and Thomas de Boulton gave two oxgangs of land at Yarum, Yorkshire, of the fee of Su de Grey Knight, who exempted the nuns of Wilberfoss from doing foreign service, or suits of Court, or other secular service in the same, and Robert de Boulton gave one oxgang at Yarum, adjoining to that given by William de Gurnay *Monasticon Eboracense* by John Burton, p 1118

[o] *Plita de Jurates et Assisz*, etc , fo 20, MSS , in the Charter House, Lancaster.

[p] *Ducatus Lancastriæ*, Pars secunda, vol ii No. 24.

[q] *Ducatus Lancastriæ*, Pars secunda, vol viii No 14, p 305

[r] *Ducatus Lancastriæ*, Pars secunda, vol xlv No 11

carucate of the heir of Ranulph Fitz Roger by the service of the twelfth part of one knight's fee.[s] In Birche's MS., a feodarium, drawn up in the time of Henry, Duke of Lancaster,[t] Richard de Bolton is said to hold Little Bolton, in Thanage, by the service of sixteen shillings per annum. Roger de Bolton is said to hold of our lord, the Duke of Lancaster. the sixteenth part of a knight's fee in Little Bolton, in Salford, which his ancestors formerly held of the Earl Ferrers as of the King[u] In 20th of Henry VII., 1504, Roger de Bolton was seised of this manor,[v] and in 1st and 2d Philip and Mary, 1554–5, William de Bolton had messuages and lands both in Great and Little Bolton.[w] Also 2d of Queen Elizabeth, 1559, Robert Bolton died seized of messuages, a mill and lands, etc , both in Great and Little Bolton ;[x] and 21st of the same reign, 1578, Robert Bolton, his son, died, possessed of messuages and lands in Little Bolton Manor,[y] while still later, 2d of James I., 1604, Robert Bolton died seised of messuages and lands at Little Bolton,[z] and 10th of James I., 1612, Peter Bolton died possessed of messuages, mill, and lands at Bolton [a]

---

[s] *Testa de Nevill*, fol. 405 In Kirby's Inquest, taken 35 Edward I , 1306, the parish of Wensley is thus surveyed WEST BOLTON ET PARVA BOLTON, "Sunt in eisdem villis 6 carucatæ terræ et dein quæ faciunt feodum unius militis , de quibus Henricus de Bothes et *Elena de Bolton*, tenent 2 bovates terræ de magistro sancti Leonardi et idem Magister de Preston in puram ille mosquem " *Whitaker's Hist of Richmondshire*, vol 1 p 369 In Wensley dale, an extensive tract on the Ure, are Bolton-hall and the remains of Bolton Castle, which, for a time, was the prison of Mary Queen of Scots

[t] Henry, created Duke of Lanc 1345, died 1360, was son of Henry and grandson of Crouchback, Earl of Lancaster, son of Henry III

[u] *Matt Gregson's History of Lanc* The Earls of Derby were also descended from the Saxon proprietors, William de Ferrers, 6th Earl of Derby, who died in 1246, mar. Agnes, sister and one of the co-heirs of Ranulph de Meschines, Earl of Chester, great grandson of Ranulph de Meschines, Earl of Chester, and Lucia, daughter of Algar, Earl of Mercia The lands between the rivers Ribble and Mersey, possessed by the Earls of Chester, descended to the Ferrers, Earls of Derby

[v] *Ducatus Lancastriæ*, Pars prima, *Calend Inquisitionem Post Mortem*, vol ii No 13, p 4 See Duchy Rec vol 1. No 14

[w] Ditto, vol x No. 8, p 38.

[x] Ditto, vol. xi No 54, p 44

[y] Ditto, vol. xiv. No 15, p 51

[z] Ditto, vol xix. No 16, p 70

[a] Ditto, vol xxiii No. 17, p 83

"Bodeltone, or Bolton le Sands, Lonsdale Hundred, according to the Domesday survey, consisted of four carucates in the Manor of Halton   On the foundation of the Priory at Lancaster, Roger de Poictou gave the church of Boelton, with the tithes of the Lordship, and half a carucate of land; and several transactions of a family of the local name, who are mentioned in the *Testa de Nevill*, occur in the registry or chartulary of that institution.[b] In 3d of John, 1201, William de Boulton paid five marks for confirmation of 6 bovates of land in Boulton, which he had from the King when Earl of Moreton, and held by the service of ten shillings per annum.[c] About this time lived Sarra de Bothelton, whose marriage was in the donation of the King,[d] and in 19th Henry III , 1234, the King received the homage of Elyas, son and heir of Saroth de Boulton for two bovates of land in Boulton, which Saroth had held in chief of the King[e] An inquisition in the *Testa de Nevill* states that Canel de Bothelton, and Dawe and Annays, and Thomas, and Gilbert, and Godie, and Simon, held two carucates and a half of land in Bothelton[f] These persons seem to have belonged to the same family. In 46th Henry III , 1261, a son of Godie, Henry, "filius Godyche de Bothelton," died, possessed of land in Bothelton; by a deed without date, Adam, son of Gilbert de Bouelton, gave land in Bouelton to his daughter Helewise, who conferred it upon the Priory of Lancaster.[g] The same Adam, son of Gilbert " de Bailton," gave during the shrievalty of Sir Robert Lathom a quantity of land, to Thomas, the son of Adam de Coupmanraia; and Edmund Crouchback, in 1273, gave the Benedictines of Lancaster, liberty to enter into and hold the lands and tenements of

---

[b] Matt Gregson's *Hist of Lanc*   A carucate of the Normans, or family manse, or hide of the Saxons, or what we call a ploughland, was as much arable land as with one plough and beasts sufficient belonging to it, could be tilled and ordered the whole year about, having also meadow and pasture for the cattle, and houses also for them, and for the men and their households, who managed it   Carucate, 100 acres, viz. 6 score to the hundred, 4 virgats made a carucat. 8 bovates or oxgangs went to a carucat—acres unequal

[c] *Rot Cancell* , 3   Johan V.   1st nova oblata.

[d] *Testa de Nevill*, fol. 371

[e] *Rot Fin* 19 Henry III m 11

[f] *Testa de Nevill*, fol 407

[g] *Regist S Mariæ Lanc* MS fol 25

Thomas de Coupmanwra in the township of Boulton, saving the services due to him.[h]   The Manor of Bolton, however, was appurtenant to the church which, in 1267, was perpetually annexed to the archdeaconry of Richmond."[i]

BOLTON REBUS.

---

[h] *Registr. S. Mariæ Lane.* MS. fol. 38.

[i] *Dugdale Monas. Anglic.* ii. p. 999, n. 5.   See also Edward Baines' *Hist. Lanc.* "Stephen, Earl of Britain, gave to St. Mary's Abbey, York, the church of Boelton," *Drake's Hist. and Antiq. of York,* M.A.I., 390, p. 354.   "Richard de Rullos granted to the same the church of Bolton super Swale and two oxgangs of land there."   Ditto, R. M. 274.   Pl' ita cor' D'me Rege apud Lincoln, etc.   Per assisam et jur' anno 7 Ed 2d (1313) Joh'nes Nevill de Snartford recup[d] seisin suam de manio de Scotelthorp et XL., lib. p. champa versus ROBTUM DE BOLTON et al.   Abbreviatio Placitorum, Ed. II. No. 77, p. 541.

SECTION II.

ARMS OF THE BOLTONS.

ARMS OF THE BOLTONS OF BOLTON.

Sable, a falcon, close, argent, beak'd, membered, jessed, and bell'd, or, charged on the breast with a trefoil slipp'd proper.

It is a maxim with heralds, that the more simple a coat of arms, the more ancient it is; this is too obvious to need any other proof in support of it, than the repetition of the maxim; which eminently applies to the arms of Bolton. The crest of this coat is a falcon close, argent, charged on the breast with a trefoil slipped vert, beaked and belled, or.

The figure in the shield or escutcheon is thus described by Guillim: "This fowl hath her talons or pounces inwardly crooked like a hook, and is called, in Latin, *Falco*, (saith *Calepine.*) *Non quod falcatis unguibus, sed quod rostro, etc., talis tota falcata, sit ad rapinam;* because it hath both talons, beak, and all made hooked for to prey. *Upton* calleth her *Alietus*, saying, Alietus, (*ut dicit Glossa super Deuteron,* 14,) *idem est quod Falco.* "This bird (according to the same Author) is very bold and hardy, and of great stomack; for she encountreth and grapleth with fowls much greater than her-self, invading and assailing them with her brest and feet." "This coat may therefore represent some bearer who was ready and serviceable for high affairs." It is obviously derived from the chase, and plainly denotes the possession of an appropriate hereditary office. "These birds," (hawks,) says Strutt, "were considered as ensigns of nobility, and no action could be reck-oned more dishonorable to a man of rank than to give up his hawk." "The period of the introduction of hawking into England cannot be clearly determined; but, about the middle of the eighth century, Winifred, or Boniface, Archbishop of Mons, who was himself a native of England, presented to Ethelbert, King of Kent, one hawk and two falcons; and a king of the Mercians requested the same Winifred to send to him two falcons that had been trained to kill cranes. In the succeeding century, the sport was very highly esteemed by the Anglo-Saxon nobility." "No persons but such as were of the highest rank were permitted under the Norman govern-ment, to keep hawks, as appears from a clause inserted in the Forest Charter." "The books of hawking assign to the differ-ent ranks of persons the sorts of hawks proper to be used by them; and they are placed under the following order:

The eagle, the vulture, and the merloun for an emperor.

The ger-faulcon and the tercel of the ger-faulcon for a king.

The faulcon gentle and the tercel gentle for a prince.

The faulcon of a rock for a duke.

The faulcon peregrine for an earl.

The bastard for a baron.

The sacre and the sacret for a knight.

The lanere and the laneret for an esquire.

The marlyon for a lady.

The hobby for a young man.

The gos-hawk for a yeoman.

The tercel for a poor man.

The sparrow-hawk for a priest.

The musket for a holy water clerk.

The kesterel for a knave or servant."

There are two kinds of hawk borne in armory, the gos-hawk or falcon, which is the large sort, and the spar-hawk or sparrow-hawk, the smaller sort.

He beareth sable a falcon, close, argent, beaked, membered, jessed, and belled, or, charged on the breast with a trefoil slipped proper by the name of Bolton. This coat was confirmed and granted by William Camden, Clarencieux, by patent, dated August 26th, 1615, to Thomas Bolton of Woodbridge, in Suffolk, Esq., descended from the Boltons of Bolton, in Lancashire.

Bolton (Suffolk, 1615,) quarterly; first and fourth, sa a falcon, close, ar. beaked and belled, or; second and third, gu. three wolves' heads, erased, or, a trefoil, slipped in the centre. Crest, a falcon, close, ar. charged on the breast with a trefoil, slipped vert, beaked, and belled, or.[k] These arms and crest are depicted in *Flowers' Visitation of Lancashire*, A.D. 1567; and were also borne by the Rev. Samuel Bolton, D.D., Master of Christ Church College, Cambridge, in 1654.

Bolton, (Yorkshire and Lancashire,) arg on a chev gu three lions, passant guardant, or, (another, arg.)—Crest, a buck's head, erased arg. attired, or, gorged with a chaplet, vert, pierced through the neck with an arrow of the second. Motto, *Vi et virtute*. By strength and valor.

Bolton or Boulton, crest, a horse courant, saddled and bridled, another at full speed.

Bolton, (Sir William, Lord Mayor of London, in 1667,) sa. a hawk, ar.

Bolton, az. three arrows, in pale, fesseways, or, points to the dexter.—Crest, on a wreath, a tun, erect, pp'r. transpierced by an arrow, fesseways, or. (Borne by Sergeant Bolton, who died 1787.)

Bolton, (Yorkshire,) argent, three door-bolts, gu.

Boulton, of Little Boulton, ar. 3 bolts, sa. feathered down-

---

[k] The silver falcon, charged on the breast with a trefoil, on a field of sable, (diamond,) denoted not only the rank of the bearer, but that he also possessed the sole right to hawk in a certain territory of woody grounds and pastures, while the three wolves' heads erased betokened the jurisdiction and authority the forester possessed to kill wolves therein "The treyfoile (says Peacham) is the Herald of the Spring, and the first grass that appeareth, hereupon it was the embleme of *Hope*, etc"

ward. (Borne by Robert Boulton of Little Boulton, A.D. 1567. Harl. MSS. 891, p. 59.)

Boulton of Boulton, ar. a chev. sa. between three mullets (or rowels of spurs) of the second, the arms of Boulton of Boulton, in Bowland aly a fg*, bol. 3 k. (*Flowers' Visitation*, Harl. MSS. 891, p. 59.)

Boulton, gu. a chev. between three mullets (or rowels of spurs) pierced, ar. two bolts, or, feathered downward in chief. Crest, a buck's head, ar. attired, or. (Borne by John de Bolton, bow-bearer of Bowland Forest.)

Bolton, (Mt. Bolton, County of Waterford,) a family which formerly possessed considerable estates in Yorkshire, but went over to Ireland under the banner of Cromwell; it is now represented by John Bolton, Esq., Major of 7th Dragoon Guards, son of John Bolton, Esq., grandson of Charles Bolton, Esq., and great grandson of John Bolton of Mount Bolton, Esq., whose second son was the late General Sir Robert Bolton, G C.H. Arms and crest, arg on a chev. gu. three lines passant guardant, or.—Crest, a buck's head erased, arg. attired, or, gorged with a chaplet vert, pierced through the neck with an arrow of the second.

Bolton, (Brookhouse, Blackburn, Lanc.,) sa. a falcon, close, ar. beaked, jessed, membered, and belled, or.—Crest. a falcon, ar. beaked, jessed, membered, and belled, or. (Borne by Samuel Bolton, D.D., 1660, son of Robert Bolton, B.D., of Brookhouse, Blackburn, Lancashire.)

Bolton, (London,) sa. a gos-hawk, ar. armed, jessed, and belled, or.

Bolton, (Bolton, Lancashire,) sa. a hawk, argent.—Crest, a hawk, belled, ar.

Bolton, az. a tun, with a bird-bolt through it, ppr.

Bolton, (Burston, Norfolk,) gu. on a bend, engr. ar. three leopards' faces of the field.

Bolton, ar. on a bend, gu three leopards' faces, or.

Bolton, sa. a falcon, ar. beaked, jessed, membered, and belled, or, charged on the breast with a trefoil, slipped, ppr. (Granted to Thomas Bolton of Woodbridge, Suffolk, Aug. 26, 1615.)

Sa, a falcon, ar. beaked, jessed, membered, and belled, or,

charged on the breast with a trefoil, slipped, ppr. by the name of Bolton. Guillim says, this coat was confirmed and granted by William Camden Clarencieux, by patent, dated August 26th, 1615, to Thomas Bolton of Woodbridge, Suffolk, Esq., descended of the Boltons of Bolton, in Lancashire.

Bolton, of Stixwold and Moulton, Lincoln and Oxenden, Northampton, az. three bird-bolts, or.—Crest, a bolt, gu. in a tun, or Motto, *Dux vitæ ratio.*

Bolton, ar. a chev. gu.

Bolton, ar. a fesse, sa between three pellets of the last.

Bolton, or, on a chev. gu. three lions, passant, guardant, ar.

Bolton, of Waterford, Ireland, arg. on a bend gules, three leopards' faces, or.—Crest, a stag's head erased, arg. pierced through the nose with an arrow.

Bolton, or Boulton, az. on a chev. gu. a lion's head, or.

Bolton, ar. a lion rampant, az. fretty of the field.

Bolton, ar. on a chev. gu. three leopards' heads of the field.

Bolton, or Boulton, ar. on a chev. gu. three leopards' faces, or. (Another of the field.)

Bolton, or Boulton, ar. on a bend gu. three leopards' faces of the field, between two beacons, az.—Crest, a boar's head and neck, ar. bristled, az. pierced through the mouth with an arrow, or, feathered and barbed, ar. (See *Visitation of Lanc.* 1613, by Richard St. George, Norroy.)

Boulton, (Suffolk,) ar. on a chev. gu. a leopard's face of the field.

Boulton, (Norfolk,) gu. on a bend engr. ar. three leopards' faces of the field.

Boulton, (Yorkshire and Norfolk,) ar. on a bend, engr. gu. three leopards' faces of the field.—Crest, on a holly-bush, vert, fructed gu. a hawk, rising ppr.

Boulton, sa. a hawk, ar. on a canton, or, a crab gu. quartering, az. a chev. between two fleurs-de-lis in chief, and a crab in base, or.—Crest, on a wreath, a hawk, ar. collared, legged, and belled, gu. the wings expanded, the dexter foot supporting a shield, az. charged with a fleur-de-lis, or. (Borne by H. Boulton, Esq., of Gibbon Grove, Leatherhead, Surrey, 1823.)

SECTION III.

OUGHTRED DE BOLTON, temp. Henry I., held Manor of Bowland, Lanc., 1135.

ELIAS DE BOTHELTON, 1154, of Bothelton juxta Bowland, Yorkshire.

RICHARD DE BONHILTON, 1156, of Bonhilton, Yorkshire.

WILLIAM DE BOULTON, 1201, of Boulton, Lanc.

GALF DE BOULTON, 1213, rector of the Prior Moiety Church of St. Mary, York.

ELYAS, son and heir of SAROTH DE BOULTON, 1224, of Boulton, Lanc.

HENRY, son of GODYCHE BOTHELTON, 1261, of Bothelton.

SIMON, son of MICHAEL DE BOLTON, 1265, of Bolton.

THOMAS DE BOULTON, 1268, Justice of Chester.

THOMAS DE BOULTON, Sheriff of Lincolnshire, 1271.

HENRY DE BOUELTON and JOAN, his wife, 1276, of Fountains, Yorkshire

ROGER DE BOTHELTON, 1291, of Bothelton, Lanc.

CHRISTIANA, wife of THOMAS BOLTON, son of MATILDA BOLTON, 1291, of Bolton, Lanc.

ADAM, son of GILBERT DE BOUELTON, 1273, of Bouelton, Lanc

JOHN DE BOLTON, 1300, Bow-bearer of the Royal Forest of Bowland in Lanc. He was (according to Sir Wm. Dugdale) the lineal representative of the Saxon Earls of Mercia

ROBERT DE BOLRUN, circ. 1300, of Bolrun, Yorkshire.

WILLIAM DE BOLRUN, circ. 1300, of Bolrun, Yorkshire.

ROBERT DE BOLRUN, 1307, tenant in capite Lonesdale. Lanc

WILLIAM DE BOTHELTON, circ. 1300, of Bothelton.

ROBERT DE BOLTON and THOMAS, his son, 1311, of Yarpes-thorpe, Yorkshire.

THOMAS DE BOLTON, 1314, a citizen of York.

JOHN BOLTON, buried in the Christ Church, in the Percy chantry, York. '✠ Hic jacet JOHN BOLTON, carpentarius'

WILLIAM BOLTON, buried in St. Martin's Church, Conyng, St. York. '✠ Orate pro animabus Alain Hyle = WILLIELMI BOLTON et AGNETIS.'

ROBERTUS DE BOLTON, 1310, held lands in Appleton, Yarpes-thorpe, Hoton, Calton, Sandburne, and Bolton, Yorkshire

JOHN DE BOLTON, 1316, one of the joint Lords of the Manor of Bolton Also Patron of the Church of Bolton juxta Bow-land, in 1304.

THOMAS DE BOLTON, 1322, of Hoton, Yorkshire.

JOHN DE BOLTON, 1326, and KATHARINE, his wife, of Cawle-ton, Yorkshire

CARIEL DE BOTHELTON, 1327, DAWE, AUNAYS, THOMAS, GIL-BERT, GODIC, and SIMON of Bothelton.

HENRY DE BOLTON, 1326, one of the representatives in Par-liament for the city of York. Mr. Torre gives a fourth, which he says, was founded in Percy's chantry, in Castlegate, at the altar of St. Mary, the Virgin, to pray for the souls of HENRY BOLTON and others. (*Drake's Hist. of York.*)

STEPHANUS DE BOLTON, temp. Edward III., of Northumber-land.

THOMAS DE BOLTON, temp. Edward III., of Gaynesburgh, Yorkshire.

D'ns JOHN DE BOLTON, instit. rector of the Church of Boul-ton juxta Bowland, 9th Dec., 1330, creatus officialis. Rich-mondæ Archiad. vacante 11 Feb. 1343. JOHN DE BOULTON, patron.

UTRED BOLTON, a learned man, who flourished under King Richard II.; a friend of Wickliffe, and author of *Pro Veris Monachis.*

THOMAS DE BOLTON, perpetual Vicar of Rochdale, 1331

HENRY DE BOLTON, 1334-9, Mayor of the city of York.

STEPHEN DE BOLTON, Jan. 1339, Phr. Cav. Inc. of S. Bo-tolph, Barton Segrave.

ROBERT DE BOULTON, 1338-1344, and THOMAS, his son, of Apelton Rydale, Yorkshire.

ROGER DE BOLTON, 1345, held the sixteenth part of a knight's fee in Little Bolton, which his ancestors formerly held of Earl Ferrers.

RICHARD DE BOLTON held Little Bolton in Thanage, 1345

ROBERT DE BOLTON and ALICIA, his wife, "feofaverunt Ricum fil THOME DE BOLTON, 1350, of Castle Levyngton Manor, Yorkshire."

ROBERT DE BOLTON, one of the Commissioners for taking the Ninths, fourteenth year of Edward III., (1340,) for the Church of Blakeburn in the Wapentake of Blakeburn, Lanc.

HENRY DE BOLTON, ditto.

THOMAS DE BOULTON of Hoton Colswayn, Yorkshire, 1351.

WILLIAM DE BOLTON, between 1361 and 1372, Incumb. of St. John's Stotesbury, Northamptonshire.

ROBERT DE BOLTON, Incumbent of St. Michael's Birgbrook, in the Deanery of Hadden, 22 March, 1376

JOHN DE BOLTON, 1387, Bailiff of the city of York.

JOHN DE BOLTON, 1390, a member of the Common Council of the city of York.

Sir JOHN DE BOLTON was one of the knights who represented the chivalry of England, at the tournament held at Inglevere in Picardy, 1390.

THOMAS DE BOLTON, 16th Sept. 1394, elected Abbot of Whalley Abbey, Lancashire.

WILLIAM DE BOLTON, Cl. 22 Dec. 1397, Incumb. of Church Holy Trinity, Tassley.

THOMAS BOLTON, Feb. 1401, Incumb. of St. Michael's Church, Birgbrook, Northamptonshire.

JOHN DE BOLTON, 1406, Gloucester.

THOMAS BOLTON, Abbot of Whitby, York, obiit 1413.

Dom. WILLIAM BOLTON, Pbr., 5th Aug. 1419, Incumb. St. Leonard, Hardwick, in the Hundred of Orlingbury, Northampton.

THOMAS BOLTON, 1427, Bishop of Worcester.

ROBERT BOLTON, 1438, Rector.

JOHN BOLTON, 1420, Rector of All Saints in the Pavement, York.

ROGER DE BOLTON, 1433, Knottesford, Lanc.

Friar WILLIAM BRAHAM, alias BOLTON, Prior of Helagh, 1475

Sir THOMAS DE BOULTON resided at Horton Pagnale near Doncaster, in 1442.

ROBERT BOLTON, 1487, of Bolton upon the Moors, Lanc

ROGER DE BOLTON, 1504, of Bolton.

WILLIAM BOLTON, from 1509 to 1512, Prior of St Bartholomew's, Lord of the Manor of Stanmere Magna. His device, a *bolt* and *tun*, was lately to be seen in some parts of the park wall. Canonbury-house is said to have been made use of as a country residence by the Priors of St. Bartholomew. (*Lyson's Environs of London*, vol. iii. 302.) He is portrayed upon a sable with his brethren in the collection of Sir Robert Cotton.

Dom. NICHOLAS BOLTON, Cap. 6th of June, 1517, Incumb. St. Peter Clopton in Oundle Deanery, Northampton.

THOMAS BOLTON, Fr., 29th April, 1527, Abbot of Sallay, Craven, Yorkshire.

ROGER BOLTON, 1526, Islam, Lanc.

THOMAS BOLTON and AGNES, his wife, 1537, of Chippying, Lanc

ROBERT and ADAM BOLTON, 1539, claimed title to lease-hold lands and tenements called the Blackfelds and the Mosschays, Abram, Lanc.

WILLIAM BOLTON of Salforth, 1541

RICHARD BOLTON, 1546, Blackburneshire, Wapentake.

WILLIAM BOLTON leased of the Monastery of Birkenhead a farm in Newsham of the yearly value of fifteen shillings.

ROBERT BOLTON, 1545, leased the same farm in Newsham, by indenture of the Court of Augmentation for twenty-one years.

ROBERT BOLTON, 1547, held a messuage or tenement called Laugherhowse and a close called the Moe Erthe, Abraham, Lanc.

WILLIAM BOLTON, 1546, claimed land, called Goreye Acre, Burnedeyn, in Bolton, Lanc

ADAM BOLTON, 1550, claimed a pasture, called Newerthe, Abraham, Lanc.

WILLIAM BOLTON, 1550, of Lytyll Bolton, Lanc

JAMES BOLTON, 1551, claimed a messuage and lands at West Walton, Derby Manor, Lanc.

WILLIAM BOLTON, installed Prebendary of Lincoln, Nov. 8th, 1477.

WILLIAM BOLTON, Prebendary of London, April 3d, 1481, vice Morton, resigned.

ROBERT BOLTON, 1516, fellow of King's College and vice provost of Cambridge.

WILLIAM BOLTON died possessed of the Prebendary of Bullingham, in 1528.

ROBERT BOLTON, 1552, claimed lands and tenement at Abram. Lanc.

JOHN BOLTON, 1553, of Bolton, in Craven, York.

JULIAN, daughter of WILLIAM DE BOLTON, relict of William, son of Gilbert de Melmorby.

HUGH DE BOLTON.

JAMES BOLTON, 1554, Vicar of Bolton on the Moors, presented by the Bishop of Chester   Died 1556.

EDWARD BOLTON, 1554, '5, '6, '7, Furneys Manor, Lanc.

THOMAS BOLTON, 1554, Mayor of Liverpool, "otherwise Lyverpole Manor," Lanc.

ADAM BOLTON, 1554, claimed messuages and lands at Abraham and Hyndley, Lanc.

ROBERT BOLTON, 1554, of Lytle Bolton, Lanc.

ROBERT BOLTON, admitted to Corpus Christi College, Cambridge, 1557, M.A. 1570.

ROBERT BOLTON, 1558, '9, of Bolton, Lanc

ROBERT BOLTON, 1557, held grant of Rents and Farms in Mellynge, in parish of Halsoo, and in Liverpool, in the parish of Walton, Lanc., of the Monastery of Birkenhead, Chester.

ADAM BOLTON, 1558, in right of marriage, claimed messuage and lands in West Laughton Manor, Lanc.

LEONARD BOLTON, 1558, Deputy Bailiff of Furness Liberties, Lanc

JAMES BOLTON, 1560, and ISABEL, his wife, claimed divers lands and tenements in Rochdale Parish, Lanc.

JAMES BOLTON, 1560, and Catharine, his wife, daughter of John Singleton, claimed lands and messuages at Salisbury, Chnynglehall, Lanc.

EDWARD BOLTON, 1561, claimed messuages and lands, house and appurtenances at Cleyton, Lanc.

2

JFFFREY BOLTON, 1560, farmer and tenant of Bogger and Southend, in Island of Waney, in Furness, Lanc.

THOMAS BOLTON, 1561, Bailiff of Higham Ferrers, Lanc.

WILLIAM BOLTON, 1561, of Ruse Mill, Furness, Lanc.

JAMES BOLTON, 1562, and KATHARINE, his wife, late wife of John Towneley, claimed goods and chattels at Towneley hall, Dutton, Salburie, Lanc.

JOHN BOLTON, 1562, and ELIZABETH, his wife, late wife of Thomas Boydell, claimed a house, tenement, and appurtenances at Penyngton, Lanc.

JAMES BOLTON, 1563, claimed moiety of a customary messuage and tenement, West Derbye Manor, Lanc.

JANE BOLTON, 1563, late wife of Edmund of Barton, upon Irwell, Lanc.

RICHARD BOLTON, 1563, and ELIZABETH, his daughter, lessees of James Hassall, and ELIZABETH, his wife, of a messuage and lands at Cleyton, Lanc.

JOHN BOLTON, 1565, and JOHAN, his wife, claimed messuage at Acrington Manor, Lanc.

ROBERT BOLTON, 1567, married AGNES, daughter of Nicholas Rushton.

WILLIAM BOLTON, 1572, of Lancashire.

THOMAS BOLTON, 1569, Leyland Manor, Lanc.

JOHN BOLTON, 1570, Dalton Furness, Lanc.

ROBLRT BOLTON, 1571, of Bolton on the Moors, claimed a messuage and lands at Tokholes, Blackburn, for maintaining the grammar-school at Bolton.

WILLIAM BOLTON, 1572, defendant for lands called Great Tobotham, Lanc.

EDWARD BOLTON, son of FRANCIS, 1575, of the Manor of Bragdyshall and Maldenham in Burston, Norfolk.

ROBERT BOLTON, 1576, claimed close of land called the Holme, Little Bolton, Lanc.

THOMAS BOLTON, 1577, of Northamptonshire.

ROBERT BOLTON, 1582, claimed lands at Abraham, Lanc.

RICHARD BOLTON, 1582, of Lancashire.

THOMAS BOLTON, 1582, claimed tenement and appurtenances called Tytripp, Furness Manor, Lanc.

JOHN BOLTON, 1582, of Liverpool, Lanc.

NICHOLAS BOLTON, 1585, of Walton in le Dale, Lanc.

LAWRENCE BOLTON, 1585, claimed messuage and lands at Dalton, Furness Manor, Lanc.

EDMUND BOLTON, 1585, lands and appurtenances at Lytell Bolton, Lanc.

JOHN BOLTON, temp Queen Elizabeth, and JOHAN, his wife, of Leeke, County of Stafford.

THOMAS BOLTON of Norfolk, temp. Queen Elizabeth.

THOMAS BOLTON of Suffolk, temp. Queen Elizabeth.

ROGER BOLTON of Audley, Stafford, temp Queen Elizabeth.

WILLIAM BOLTON and his wife ALICE of the same place.

JOHN BOULTON of Cumberland, temp. Queen Elizabeth.

PARNELL BOULTON, widow of THOMAS of Heywood Hall, Disse and Burston, in County of Norfolk.

ROBERT BOULTON of London, Middlesex.

MARGARET BOLTON, 1586, claimed a messuage and lands at Blackburne, Lanc.

GEORGE BOLTON, 1590, claimed messuage and lands called Barnevere, Garston Parish, Lanc.

HENRY BOLTON, 1591, claimed messuage and lands West Darby Manor, Lanc.

RICHARD BOLTON, 1591, claimed capital messuage, called Single hall, land and appurtenances at Whittingham and Houghton, Lanc.

THOMAS BOLTON, 1593, claimed a messuage in Manchester, Furness Manor, Lanc.

RICHARD BOLTON, 1594, claimed messuage and land at Farnworth, also messuage and lands called Hall Hayes, Ribchester, Lanc.

JOHN BOLTON, 1595, claimed land called Brichland and a tenement called Tonghill, Pleasington, Lanc.

JOHN BOLTON, 1596, Dalton, Furness Manor, Lanc.

RICHARD BOLTON, 1594, of Lancashire.

KATHARINE BOLTON, 1596, widow of PETER, claimed a yearly rent upon a certain messuage and lands at Whitstone, Piescott Parish, Knowsley Sutton, Lanc.

WILLIAM BOULTON of Christ's College, Proctor of Cambridge, 1596.

AMBROSE BOLTON, 1599, of Yorkshire.

ROBÈRT BOLTON, 1599, claimed with others a messuage and land, West Derby Manor, Lanc.

RI'CUS BOLTON, 1600, de Chippin, one of the freeholders of Blackburn, Lanc.

JOHN BOLTON, 1600, of Little Bolton, Lanc., married BRIDGET, daughter of Hugh Shakerly.

EDMUND BOULTON or BOLTON, 1610, a retainer to the great George Villiers, Duke of Buckingham, under whom he probably enjoyed some office. Author of the *Elements of Armories*, London, 1610, 4to, and a poem entitled *Prosopopœia Basilica*, upon the translation of the body of Mary, Queen of Scots, from Peterborough to Westminster, in 1612, now remaining in MS. in the Cottonian Library, where is also another MS, by the same author, entitled *Agon Heroicus*, 'or concerning Arms and Armories.' *Life of Henry II.; Nero Cæsar, or Monarchie Depraved*, London, 1624, fol.; *Hypercritica, or a Rule of Judgment for writing or reading our Histories;* published by Dr. Hall, at the end of *Trivet's Annals*, Oxon. 1772, 8vo. *Vindiciæ Britannicæ*, unpublished. *Life of the Emperor Tiberius.* The time of his death is not known.

JOHN BOLTON, *Life of Christopher Cartwright*, London, 1610, 4to.

HENRY BOULTON of Stixwold, Lincolnshire, 1615.

ADAM BOLTON, 1634, of Yorkshire.

ADAM BOLTON was instituted Vicar of Blackburn, Lanc., June 20th, 1628. Presented by George, Archbishop of Canterbury, (Rector of Blackburn.) He died in 1646, leaving by his wife ANN, one son, SAMUEL BOLTON

ADAM BOULTON, 1646, of Blackburn, Minister of the Third Classis of Lancashire, embracing the parishes of Blackburn, Whalley, Chipping, and Ribble Chester.

NICHOLAS BOULTON, Dorchester, Mass, admitted member of the Church, 1644, freeman 1644. Died 17 May, 1683

JOHN BOLTON of Bridgewater, Mass., 1680, son or grandson of Nicholas of Dorchester.

WILLIAM BOLTON of Newbury, Mass.

JOHN BOLTON, admitted to Corpus Christi College, Cambridge, 1655, B A 1680.

WILLIAM BOULTON, killed at Bolton in the Moors, May 28th, 1644, by Prince Rupert.

SAMUEL BOULTON, *Medicina Magica tamen Physica*, London, 1656 and 1665, 8vo.

ROBERT BOLTON, Divine and Author, Broughton, Northampton; died 1671. See Camden's *Hist. of England*, epitomized and continued by Tymms.

SIR RICHARD BOLTON, *Statutes of Ireland*, Dublin, 1621, fol. *Justice of Peace for Ireland*, Dublin, 1683, fol., new edition, enlarged and corrected by Michael Travers, 1750, 4to.

STEPHEN DE BOLTON, 1673, of Warwick.

JOHN BOLTON, admitted to Corpus Christi College, Cambridge, 1677, B.D 1739.

Sir WILLIAM BOLTON, Knight, married ADA, one of the three daughters and co-heirs of William Hobson.

ROBERT BOLTON, (BOLRON,) January, 1676, resided at Shippen Hall, four miles from Leeds, and quarter of a mile from Barnboro, in the parish of Barwick, in Elmet, West Riding of Yorkshire. In 1676, he was sworn into a secret association of the papists The oath having been administered by one William Rushton, a papist priest, in the chapel of Barnboro Hall, the seat of Sir Thomas Gascoigne. On the 17th of October, 1679, he was sent by order of the Council to search the papists living in Yorkshire, Lancaster, Durham, and Northumberland. He was the author of *The Papist's Bloody Oath of Secrecy*, Dec. 16th, 1680. Printed, Stationer's Hall, London, 1680, folio.

WILLIAM BOLTON, *Sermons*, 1683, 4to, etc.

THEOPHILUS BOLTON, D.D., Archbishop of Cashel, was born at Burrishead, in the County of Mayo, about 1678, graduated at Trinity College, Dublin, was ordained deacon in 1702, priest in 1703, became Prebendary of St. Patrick's, Dublin, in 1707, Chancellor of that Cathedral in 1714, Vicar General of the Diocese of Dublin in 1720, Vicar of Ferriglas, near Dublin, in the same year; Precentor of Christ Church, Dublin, in 1722; Bishop of Clonfert, in the same year; Bishop of Elphin, in 1724; Archbishop of Cashel, in 1729, to which Diocese he bequeathed his valuable library. He died in January, 1744, and was buried at St. Werburgh's Church in Dublin.

WILLIAM BOULTON, of Newberry, Mass., died 27th March, 1697.

RICHARD BOULTON, a physician at Chester in the beginning of the eighteenth century. He was of Brazennose College, Oxford, and published several works. Among his publications are: *A Treatise concerning the Heart, Heat of the Blood, and Use of the Lungs*, London, 1698, 8vo; *An Answer to Dr. Leigh's Remarks upon the Same*, London, 1698, 8vo; *The Works of the Hon. Robert Boyle epitomized*, London, 1699, 4 vols. 8vo; *System of Rational and Practical Chirurgery*, London, 1699, 1713, 8vo.

"ROBERT BOLTON, LL.D., an English Divine, born 1697, son of a London merchant, educated at Kensington and Wadham College, Oxford. Ordained 1719, and in 1722 chosen senior fellow of Dulwich College. Preacher at the Roll's Chapel. He was preferred to the Deanery of Carlisle, February 1st, 1734–5, and then Vicar of St. Mary's, Reading; wrote several tracts against card-playing and travelling on Lord's Day. He was very tall, thin, and dark-complexioned, a good scholar and active parish priest, and an amiable man. He died in London, Nov. 26th, 1765, but was buried in the church porch of St. Mary's, Reading." He published nine *Letters to a Lady and to an Officer against Card Playing and Travelling on the Lord's Day*, 1748–57, 8vo; *The Employment of Time*, three essays on, 1750, 8vo, London, 1754; *The Ghost of Ernest*, 1757, 8vo; *Letters and Tracts on the Choice of Company*, etc., 1761, 8vo.

—— BOULTON. *Vindication of the Complete History of Magick, Sorcery, and Witchcraft*, 1722, 8vo.

MATTHEW BOULTON, born at Birmingham, Sept. 3d, 1728, son of Mr. MATTHEW BOULTON, manufacturer, and was educated principally at Deretend, in the Academy of Rev. Mr. Ansted. He was a celebrated engineer and improver of steam-engines. He died A D. 1809.

STEPHEN BOLTON, 1737, of Corpus Christi College, Proctor of Cambridge.

FRANCIS BOLTON, 1746, an officer in the Welsh Fusileers; buried at Harrow on the Hill, Middlesex.

STEPHEN BOLTON, 1750, Rector of Stalbridge, Dorset.

RICHARD BOLTON, 1750, buried at Newington Butts.

SOLOMON BOLTON, 1769, author of *The Extinct Peerage of England*, London, printed 1769, 8vo, pp. 315. "The author of this work, the late SOLOMON BOLTON, was a man of judgment and abilities, many of whose writings have met with a favorable reception from the public."

THOMAS BOLTON entered the South-Carolina line in Capt. James Mitchell's Company of the Continental Corps, during the Revolutionary War.

JAMES BOLTON, of Stannary, near Halifax, April 1st, 1796, author of *Felices Britannicæ*, Leeds and Hud. 1785–90, 4to; *A History of British Proper Ferns*, etc., 1795, 8vo; *Fungusses about Halifax*, London, 1788–91, 4 vols. 4to; 'Plants of Halifax,' in *Watson's History Parish of Halifax*, London, 1775, 4to; *Harmonia Ruralis*, or an Essay towards a Natural History of British Song Birds; London, 1794–96, 2 vols. 4to.

JOSEPH BOLTON, 1783, Clericus, buried in Hammersmith Cemetery.

D'ARCY BOULTON, *Sketch of Upper Canada*, 1805, 4to.

WILLIAM BOLTON, 1815, Captain R.N., Companion of the Most Hon. Mil. Order of the Bath.

SAMUEL BOLTON, of Great Bealings, near Woodbridge, Suffolk, god-child to Lord Nelson, and was with him at the battle of Trafalgar as aid-de-camp. After the death of Nelson, he bought a commission in the army, and served in Jamaica, W. I., in the Thirty-ninth Light Infantry.

THOMAS BOLTON, Clericus, late of Hollesley, near Woodbridge, Suffolk, now at or near Norwich.

GEORGE BOLTON, author of a work on Fire-arms.

GEORGE BOLTON, author of *Practice of Criminal Courts*, 1835, 12mo.

REBUS OF WILLIAM BOLTON, (PRIOR OF ST. BARTHOLOMEW'S, LONDON.)

SECTION IV.

EARLIEST GENEALOGIES OF THE BOLTONS.

OUGHTREDE[1] DE BOLTON, temp. Henry I., held the Manor of Bowland, in Lancashire, had a son

ELIAS[2], whose son was

RICHARD[3], 30th Henry III., who had

I. JOHN[4],

II. NICHOLAS[4],

JOHN[4], son of RICHARD, left

I JOHN[5],

II. CATHARINE[5], wife of John Mantell.

JOHN[5], son of JOHN, left

I. RICHARD[6].

II. CATHARINE[6], wife of Simon Pudsey, temp. Edward II., now represented by Mary Litteldale of Bolton Hall, Skipton, Yorkshire.

III. IBOTA[6], wife of Henry Cliderall.

IV. CHRISTIANA[6], wife of Alan Ryton.

RICHARD[6], son of JOHN, had

JOHN DE BOLTON,[7] son and heir of s. p. vix 5 Edward III.[a]

JOHN LISTER, of Derby, 6 Edward II., 1312, married ISABEL, daughter and heir of JOHN DE BOLTON, bow-bearer of Bowland.

---

[a] Whitaker's *Deanery of Craven*, p 101

MS. Harl. 1987, fol 84.

ELLES fil WILLI DE BOULTON dedi, etc   HEN fil JOHIS DE HULTON, etc,
testibus RICO fil DAVID DE HULTON, RICO RATLIFE de lever chevelers
ROBTO DEL BRADSHAW, ROGERO DE BOLTON, Wᵒ. DE BRUSTER, dat. 23
E. 1ᵒ.

HEN DE BOULTON dedit, etc, testibus RICO DE WORKESDELEY, ADAM
DE RATCLIVE, JOHE DE HULTON, HEN. DE WORKESDELEY, dat 16, E. 2

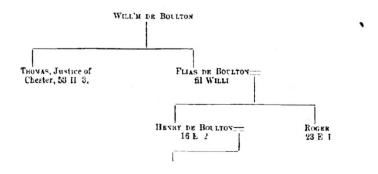

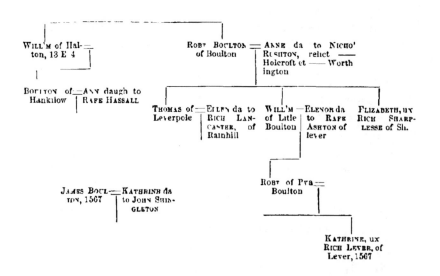

In Dei nom   Amen   Ego Rob'tus Bolton armiger, die Lune fæ post fist s'ci Mathei Apli & Evanj Ao Dni 1432 sanes, etc, in hunc modum meum sondo testament   Imprimis lego aorum, etc, corpus meum ad seperhend in Eccla, Ste Marie de Berkynge coram altari sci Jacobis (oi) Executores suos constituit Elizabetham uxorum suam, Thomam Boltone cl'icum fratrum suum (etc)

Hic est ultima voluntas mei Robti Boltone armigeri fact ap^d Berkynge die Lune, etc, post fest sci Mathei Apli Ao Dni 1432.   Hunc volo quod Elizabetha uxoi mea habeat omnia huas & tenta mea in Castor, Berkynge, Buremondeston, Nedham, Ladenhum, & alibi in Com, Suff, (etc) ad totam vitam ejusd Elizabetha. Sta 9^d post secessum ejusd Elizabetha omnia pedia remaneant Michaeli filio meo Thuro de corpore suo ligettime pi'creatis & pr'deflectu palis exitus remavere, etc —Probat 20 Oct 1432.

Rob'tus Bolton, arm. and test. 1432.   Elizabetha, Extrix.
Thomas Bolton, Cl'icus, frater et lexton Rob'ti
Michael fil Robti, Joh'es fil Eliz.
Edmundus fil Eliz.

Bolton of Suffolk.   Robert Bolton, 1432.   Ar. of Barking.

Thomas[1] Bolton, brother of Robert, Clericus.

Michael[2] Bolton, son of Robert, left two sons,

I. John,

II. Edmund.

Pedigrees MS. from Sir Jno. Blois, p. 82, or Acct. of Salt fames, MS. from Sir Jno. Blois, p. ditto.

Bolton from Norris's MS. Collections from Sir Arm. Wodehouse's MS., p. 80.

Edward[1] Bolton of Boyland in Norfolk, Esq., married Benedict, daughter and heir of Wm. Lancaster of Catywall in Suffolk, Esq.   He left two sons and a daughter

I Thomas[2] Bolton.

II. William[2] Bolton of Boyland married Eliz., sister and heir to William Curson, Clerk, son and heir to W. Bolle Curson.

III. Constance[2].

William[2] of Boyland left two sons and four daughters.

I. Francis[3] Bolton of Burston in Norfolk, Esq., son and heir, married Ann, daughter of John Pickerell of London, gent., by Anne, his wife, daughter and co-heir of Toms. Fyfield, Esq., gent.

II. Antony[3], second son of William.

III. Alice[3], married to Thomas Peclowe.

IV Elizabeth[3], widow to Edward Colbye of Banham, gent.

V. Susan[3].

VI Constance[3].

Francis[3] Bolton of Burston left one son and four daughters.

I. Edward[4], son and heir.

II. Ruth[4].

III. Eliz[4].

IV. Susan[4].

V. Judith[4].

The Harl. MSS. No. 1496.

Hugh[1] Bolton of Little Bolton in Com. of Lancaster, a younger son, married a daughter of Hassall of Hanklow, in Com. Chester, and left issue,

Randolph[2] Bolton of Hanklow in County of Chester, eldest son, married Elizabeth, daughter of —— Grosvenor of Belleport, in County of Sallop, and had issue.

I. William[3] Bolton.

II. Ralph[3] Bolton.

III. Jane[3].

IV. Margery[3], wife to —— Bates.

V. Randolph[3] Bolton, third son.

In Harl. MSS. No. 6159, another copy of the *Visitation* of 1567, written and augmented in 1598, by William Smith, Rouge Dragon, "a work," stated in the *Harl Catalogue*, to be "carefully executed, but unfinished." The arms are all nearly colored

Robt Bolton married Agnes Rushton, daughter of Nicholas Rushton, gent.

In Harl MSS No 1549, f 108. Descents registered at the Visitation of 1613, by Richard St. George, Norroy.

BOLTON OF BOLTON,
spell also BOULTON.

ROBERT BOLTON of
Little Bolton.

In Harl. MSS. No. 1096, f. 130.
Sir WILLIAM BOLTON of London, Knt. Lord Mayor, A°.
1667.

In Harl. MSS. No. 2086, William Flower, Norroy, *Visitation of Lancashire* in 1567. This MS. is neatly written in the
hand of the celebrated Glover, Somerset Herald, who accompanied his father-in-law, Flower, in the visitation. It has
some continuations in other hands.

"KATHERINE, daughter of ROBERT BOLTON of Little Bolton
in Com. of Lancashire, gent., married Richard Lever of Little
Lever, issue RICH. THOS. BOLTON, married Betts, etc., and ELI-
ZABETH, daughter of ROBERT BOLTON, in Com. Lanc., gent.,
married Richard Sharples of Sharples in Lancashire."

In Harl. MSS. No. 891, f. 59, another copy of the *Visitation*
of 1567, written narratively, are the following arms:

BOULTON OF BOULTON in Dow-
land, aly a fig'. bol 3 k.

BOULTON of Little
Boulton.

In Harl. MSS. No. 1468, f. 12, another copy of William Flower, Norroy, *Visitation*, in 1567, are the following arms:

Three lions.

In Harl. MSS. No. 1096.

LAWRENCE[1] BOLTON of Bolton in Litmore, Co. Lanc., who had

I. JOHN[2] BOLTON of Totten[m] in Co. of Midd[x], who left

SIMON[3] BOLTON de Tott[m], who married Jane, daughter of Ab[m]. Okeman of Tott[m], and left issue.

I. JOHN[4] of Tott[m], who married Elizabeth, daughter[2] of Hunt, who left one son,

JOHN[5] BOLTON.

II. ABRAHAM[4] BOLTON of London married Ellen Edwards.

III. THOMAS[4] BOLTON of Hornsey.

IV. JANE[4].

V. MARY[4].

VI. MARGARET[4].

VII. ANN[4].

VIII. ELIZABETH[4].

IX. SUSAN[4].

SIR WM. BOLTON OF LONDON, Knt.,
Lord Mayor, A°. 1667.

(Hawk.)

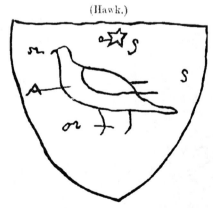

In Harl. MSS. No. 1476, see also additional MSS. Nos. 5822 and 5533.

"This arms and crest, as it is here depicted, is the coat armor of Bolton of Bolton Hall in Lanc., but stands in the house of Wm. Bolton in Warwick, set up by his grandfather, Peter Bolton, out of which house he conceiveth his ancestors descendeth."

PETER BOLTON[1] married Mary ——, and had issue,

WILLIAM[2] BOLTON of the town of Warwick, who married Alice, daughter of John Massam of Coventry, and left

WILLIAM[3] BOLTON of Cornhill, grocer, living 1633, married Mary, daughter of Stephen Burton of London, grocer, and had

I. STEPHEN[4] BOLTON, sonne and heir, living 1633, 27 years of age.

II. WILLIAM[4] BOLTON.

III. NICHOLAS[4] BOLTON.

IV. JOHN[4] BOLTON.

V. HELEN[4], wife to Elisha Robt. Silkman.

VI. MARTHA[4].

VII. MARY[4].

VIII. ELIZA.[4]

In additional MSS. No. 5533.

Bolton of London descended of Lancashire.

THOMAS[1] BOLTON of London, grocer, and his brother,

WILLIAM[1] BOLTON of London, 1634, married first daughter of —— Burton of London; 2d, married a daughter of —— Tomes of Gloucestershire. Left issue by first wife, two sons and a daughter,

I. Stephen[2] Bolton, eldest son, married Frances, daughter of Wm. Christmass of London.

II. William[2] Bolton, second son, married ——, daughter of Alderman Bide of London.

III. A daughter[3], married to Elisha Rob'tns Silkman of London.

Burton.

Tomes.

This coat on a monument in Black-friars, in the cloisters.

In additional MSS., 5533.

Wm. Bolton of London, 1634.

PART II.

SECTION I.

THE EARLY HISTORY OF THE BOLTONS IN THE WAPENTAKE OR PARISH OF BLACKBURN.

TOWARDS the close of the thirteenth century, we find a family of the Boltons seated in the Parish of Blackburn,[a] Lancashire; for about 1290, Henry de Lascy,[b] Earl of Lincoln and Constable of Chester, granted the waste of Bilyngton to Henry, son of Robert de Bolton[c] The name of Richard de

---

[a] In the Domesday survey, entitled "Blackeburn Hundred," and still later "Wapentagium de Blackburnshire," and "Blackeburnshire Wapentac," but it is now recognized as one of the seven Hundreds of Lancashire "Orme, the Saxon," says Whitaker, "was the ancient proprietor before the conquest of Blackburn and adjoining parts of Yorkshire" In Saxon times says Baines, "King Edward the Confessor held Blackburn, as appears from the Domesday survey" "In 1160, Henry de Blackburne held the church and manor of Blackburne, as they had been held by those of his predecessors Gamaliel, Gilbert, and John Henry had two sons, Richard and Adam, between whom the property was divided in equal moieties, and Roger, the son of Adam, assigned his moiety to John de Lacy, Earl of Lincoln and Constable of Chester, who granted it to the Abbot and monks of the Locus Benedictus of Stanlaw, the parent of Whalley Abbey" " The Rectory of Blackburn," together, unquestionably, with half the manorial rights, as well as half the ancient manorial demesnes of the town of Blackburn, continued part of the possessions of the Abbey of Whalley until the year 1537, when, on the attainder of Abbot Paslew, they passed to the Crown, and were given, inter alia, to the Archbishop of Canterbury, along with the advowson of the vicarage, in exchange for other manors and advowsons belonging to that see, in the year 1547 See *Notitia Cestriensis*, vol ii. part i p 130, note 16

[b] Henry de Lascy or Lacy was the son of Edmund de Laci, second Earl of Lincoln, a descendant of the Meschines's Earls of Chester and Lincoln, and Algar, Earl of Mercia Henry de Lascy died in 1312 See Burke's *Extinct and Dormant Peerages.*

[c] "Titulus de Bilyngton X COPIA CARTE QUAM COMES LANCASTRIE FECIT HENRICO DE BOLTON DE VASTO DE BILYNGTON. Hen-

Bolton appears as witness to the grant. In 15th of Edward III., 1341, (on the Saturday next after the festival of St. Hilary,) among the parishioners of the "Wapen de Blakeburn," who found upon their oath the true value of the ninth of corn, wool, and lambs of the "Ecclesia de Blakeburn," were Henry and Robert de Bolton,[d] sons, probably, of the preceding Henry de Bolton. How long they had held lands here, there remain no means to enable us to determine; that they belonged, however, to the same ancient stock as the Boltons of Great and Little Bolton, is quite certain from the similarity of their armorial bearings and Christian names,[e] and likewise from the fact that the chase of Blackburnshire[f] embraced the royal forest and manor of Bowland, where the Boltons, as descendants of the Saxon Thanes, had been resi-

---

ricus de Lascy, comes Lincoln, et constabularius Cestric, omnibz ad quos presens scriptum puenerit salutem in dño   Noueritis nos concessisse, dedisse, et hac presenti carta mea confirmasse Henr filio Roberti de Bolton sexaginta acras simul iacentes de vasto nostro de Bilyngton, et sexdecim acias in territorio ciusdem cum ptinentijs quam idem Henr prius de nobis tenuit   Tenend et habend de nobis et heredibz nostris dicto Henr et heredibz suis libere quiete bene et in pace imppetuum   Reddendo inde annuatim nobis et heredibz nostris xxv solidos et iiij denarios argenti ad festum sancti Egidij p omnibz seruicijs, et consuetudinibz et demandis   Et nos predictus Henr de Lascy et heredes nostri totam predictam terram cum suis ptinentijs dicto Henrico filio Roberti de Bolton et heredibz suis contra omnes homines imppetuum warantizabimus   In cuius rei testimonium huic presenti scripto sigillum nostrum apponi fecimus   Testibz, dñis Johanne de Bek, Willmo le Vauasour, Ada de Hoghton, Ada de Blakeburn, militibz, Gilberto de Clifton tunc senescallo nostro, magistro Henr de Clayton, Alex de Keuerdal, Willmo del Hakkyng, Ric de Bolton, et alijs"   See 'Titulus de Bilvngton,' *Coucher Book of Whalley Abbey*, ed by W A Hulton, Esq, vol iv p 945   The names of both Henry de Bolton and Richard de Bolton occur frequently in the 'Titulus de Bilyngton'   The township of Billington is situated on the opposite side of the river Calder to the Abbey of Whalley   It is a chapelry of Blackburn Parish, five and a half miles N N E from Blackburn   See *Coucher Book of Whalley Abbey*, ed by W A Hulton, Esq, vol iv p 937.   Printed for Chetham Society.

    [d] *Inquisitiones Nonarum in curia Scaccarii Com Lanc.* temp Regis Edward III p 33

    [e] The name of ROBERT, as has been seen, is a very prominent one among the BOLTONS   "Robert," says Lower, "is a Teutonic personal name of great antiquity, introduced into England about the time of the Conquest   As Rotbertus, it is frequently found in Domesday"

    [f] The four forests of Blackburnshire were as follows: Bowland (called Boeland in reign of Henry I,) Trawden, Pendle, and Rossendale with Accrington   "In the times of our Saxon ancestors," says Baines, "as at a much later period, the forest

dent from time immemorial as bow-bearers and falconers.[g]
For a long period antecedent to the Reformation, the family
held, as tenants at will, a house, a garden, and several acres
of land, called the *Brookhouse*,[h] from St. Mary's Abbey,

---

of Bowland was distinguished for archery, and hence the name Bow-land One of
its principal offices was the bow-bearer or chief steward, called, in the patent of
Henry IV , granted to Sir James Harrington, the Forester" "Richard de Radclif
was seneschall et meistre forestre de Blakeburnschir et de Bowland temp Edward
III " Bowland, in the time of Edward III , was considered partly in Lancashire and
partly in Yorkshire In fact, many of the parishes in Yorkshire were within the
chase of Blackburnshire, which "consisted of woody grounds and pastures, privi-
leged for wild beasts and fowls of forest, chase, and warren to rest and abide in,
under the protection of the king for his pleasure " The Blackburn men were celebrated for their skill in archery   "In the battle of Floddenfield, (9 Sept 1213,)
so memorable in the history of Lancashire, the bravery of the *Blackburn* and *Bolton* men, who fought under Sir Edmund Stanley, is celebrated in language which
conveys a strong impression of their courage and prowess ·

> W[th] fellowes fearce and fresh for feight,
> W[ch] Halton fields did turne in foores,
> W[th] Lusti ladds hever and light
> From *Blakborne* and *Bolton* in ye Moores "
>
> (Baines' *Lanc*)

g The armorial bearings of the Boltons plainly denote the possession of an appropriate hereditary office, with a privilege of free chase, etc , for example, the silver falcon belled and jessed of gold. The stag's head erased, attired of gold, gorged
with a green chaplet, and pierced through the neck with a golden arrow. The
wolf's head erased. The bird-bolt and the mullet or rowel of spur.

h So called from its proximity to the black-burn or brook, sometimes styled black
water or yellow stream As early as 1616 it is denominated *Bruchouse*. This property was probably a portion of the ancient glebe, as we are informed by the following extract taken from the survey of 1537. "*Blackburn*. Memorandu, that
the[r] is noe temperall land within the towne of Blackburne but all glebe " See
Couchei Book of Whalley Abbey, by W. A. Hulton, Esq Appendix, 1224 Brookhouse was visited by the author in 1834 It was a very respectable mansion, some-
what verging to decay, stood low and very much exposed, and presented the appearance of having been used as a double tenement In 1860 this venerable struc-
ture was pulled down to make way for other buildings. Nich del Bruche and
Mary, his wife, were pensioners of Whalley Abbey, temp Edward III "The
value of the ecclesiastical lands of Blackburn Rectory was taken by commission
26 Henry III 1534. "Decanatus De Blakebourne—Sp'ualia Pertinen Mon' P' D' M
D' C' C Comitatu Lanc.' BLAKEBOURNE RECTORIA, etc." See *Valoi Ecclesiasticus*,
or Liber Regis, vol v pp 227-230. "The parish church was erected in 596, soon
after the introduction of Christianity into England At the time of the Domesday
survey, this church, dedicated to St Mary, had 2 bovates of land in Blackburn and
2 carucates in Whalley, free of all customs " (Baine's *Hist. Lanc*)

Whalley,[1] and continued in possession under Thomas Cranmer, Archbishop of Canterbury, (the first Protestant rector of Blackburn,) who was invested by Henry VIII. in the Whalley moiety of the Manor of Blackburn.

The following extracts are taken from a survey of the Abbey possessions in 1537. "*The survey then taken the* xxix*th day of June in the* xxix*th year of the raine of our suffreine Lord King Henery the Eighth.*"

1192541

Remesgreus w'th the p'ish of Blackbure, Tennäts at Will.

James Boulton, Willi, Edward Boulton, and Robte Boulton houldeth the moyety of a tenement & a garden, and xx acres of arable land, pasture, and medow, called the Rames green,[j] and payeth by the year	0	7	4
Willii Boulton houldeth ye other moytie of ye said tenement, garden, and xx acres of arable land, past., and medow, and payeth by the year	0	7	4
Richard Bolton[k] houldeth a house, a garden, iiij acr. of arable land, ij acres of medow, vij of pasture, and payeth yearly	0	15	0
Robte Boulton and Willi. Boulton, his brother, houldeth 2 acres and a halfe of medow, called Newfied, withe ye gate or pasteridg of two cowes or 2 beasts within Wourple hill, by the year v[s]	0	5	0

[1] Whalley was founded (says Leland) by the ancestors of the Lacies Earls of Lincoln, translated from Stanlaw, Cheshire, 1206, 25th Edward I, Order of Cistercian Monks—value £551 4s. 6d. The first Abbot was Gregory Northbury, who died on the day of St Vincent, 1309 On the 16th of September, 1394, *Thomas de Bolton* was elected Abbot The last Abbot was John Paslew, executed for his share in the Pilgrimage of Grace, March 12th, 1537

[j] Rhoms, rambs or ramps (wild onions) in Saxon. In 35 of Edward III, Henry Duke of Lancaster, gave monks of Whalley 2 cottages, 7 acres of land, 183 acres of pasture, and 200 acres of wood, called Rommesgreue, all lying in chase of Blakeburn. See *Coucher Book of Whalley Abbey*, ed by W. A Hulton, Esq, Appendix, 1154; also 1223, and *Monasticon Anglia*, tom i "Memorandu, their is a wood called Romes-green-wood, which is well replenished with ould okes," etc *Coucher Book of Whalley Abbey*, p 1223

[k] Richard Bolton, in 1546, held a messuage and lands in Blackburnshire, Wapentake (*Ducatus Lanc*, Pars Secunda, vol xiv No 1, p 181) Among the freeholders in Blackburn, A D. 1600, is "Ricus Bolton de Chippin den[d]" (Brit Mus Harl MSS. 2042, fol. 9.

Item James Boulton, his porcō of wast ground
on Worple hils, and payeth by the year .   . 0 5 0

" The Survey taken their."

Little Harwod in the p'ish of Black- burne, Tennats at Will

Roger Boulton houldeth a house, a garden,
xvj acres of arab land, xvj of pasture, and
four acres of medow, called Bankehey,[1] and
payeth yearly   .   .   .   . 1 18 11[m]

In 5th of Elizabeth A.D. 1562, James Bolton and Katherine, his wife, late wife of John Towneley, were plaintiffs in a suit to recover goods and chattels of John Towneley, deceased, at Salburie,[n] Blackburn,[o] and the same year John Bolton and

---

[1] Bank-hey is now the property of the Burial Board of Blackburn, forty acres of which has been inclosed for a cemetery

[m] *" Coucher Book* or *Chartulary of Whalley Abbey,* edited by W A Hulton, Esq , vol iv Printed for Chetham Society, Appendix, 1222–1224 This document is a literal copy of the survey of the Abbey possessions, furnished by Sir Charles G. Young, Garter, from the fifth volume of De Kuerden's MSS , relating to the County of Lancaster, preserved in the library of the College of Arms, and referred to in the Editor's preface It appears to have been taken soon after the dissolution of the Abbey " (See *Coucher Book,* vol iv Appendix, 1183) The survey was ordered by the Augmentation Court, erected 27 Henry VIII 1535 "It belonged to this Court to order, survey, and govern, sell, let all manors, lands, tenements, etc , formerly belonging to priories, and since their dissolution to the crown, etc , and all persons holding any leases, etc , by former grants from the convents came into this Court, produced their deeds, and upon examination of the validity thereof, had the same allowed them " (Fuller's *Ch Hist of Britain,* vol. ii) The indexes of the Augmentation Office afford no reference to the name of Bolton in connection with Blackburn, (Lanc) Nor are the Court Rolls of the Manor to be found there The following " Particulars for Grants " refer to the name of Bolton in relation to lands, etc , in Lancashire, being parcel of the possessions of the Monastery of Birkenhead, (Ches)

Particulars for Grants

Robert Bolton 4, 5, Philip and Mary,
" Rents and Farms in
" Mellynge in the parish of
" Halsoo and in Liverpool
" in the parish of Walton (Lanc)
" parcel of the possessions of the
" Monastery of Birkenhead, (Ches)

A farm in Newsham of the yearly value of 15s is represented in the body of the Record, as leased to William Bolton A note adjoining the entry states that it was leased to Robert Bolton by Indenture under the seal of the Court of Augmentation, 10th March, 37 Hen VIII , for 21 years

[u] Salisbury is one of the towns of Blackburn Parish

[o] *Duc Lanc* Pars Secunda, Cal of Pleadings, vol xiv No 14.

Elizabeth, his wife, claimed a house and tenement at Penyngton, (Pleasington,) Blackburn parish.[p] The year following Richard Bolton and Elizabeth, his daughter, as lessees of John Hassall, etc., claimed a messuage and tenement at Clayton in Blackburn parish.[q] In 29th Elizabeth, (1586,) Margaret Bolton held a messuage and lands at Blackburn,[r] and in 38th of the same reign (1595) John Bolton claimed land called Brichland and a tenement styled Tonghill, at Pleasington, in the same parish.[s]

The Boltons were also for a long period possessed of lands at Little Harwood, (styled Lyttyll Harewood, in 1554,) situated a few fields only from Brookhouse. The following is a literal copy of the "Inventory of the effects of William Boulton[t] of Banncke-hey, (probably son of Roger of Bankehey in 1537,) taken in 1594."

"*The* xii *of March Anno Regin. Elizabeth* xxxvi. 1594. *An Inventory of all the Goods and Cattles* w[ch] *we[r] latly Will Boultown of Banncke hey in Lyttl Harwood, in the County of Lanne: prsed according to the trew valuewe of the same goods by four honeste and dessent p'sons, whos names are her under wryten.* JAMES RYGHT—JOHN COWBRAND—WILL CLAYTON—JOHN PELL.

Imprimis in Oxon kyne Younge Beasts and Horses	51	9	4
It. in Waynes: Whelles: plouges: haroes: yoakes, teames, and all implements of husbandry	2	13	8
It. in Oats and Barly	20	0	0
It. in Hay. turfes and coles	3	13	4
It. in Meall and Malte		10	0
It in Sheepe	10	0	0
It. in bedding and bed cloathes	10	0	0
It. in table cloathes		6	8
It money in his Chyste and all debts owing unto him. . . .	c14	16	2
It. in brass and pewdar	3	13	4
It. in Cirkes. and chyte	3	13	

---

[p] *Duc Lanc* Pars Secunda, Cal of Pleadings, vol xiv No 13.

[q] Ditto, vol. xviii. No. 35

[r] Ditto, vol cm No 1 See Will of Margaret Bolton Appendix.

[s] *Duc. Lanc* Pars Sec. vol cxxxii No 11.

[t] The following entry occurs in the minute-books of the Blackburn Free Grammar School; "Wm. Bolton a Gov[r]. Mortuus, 1594"

It. in bords and cubboards	20	0
It. in bedstocks	33	4
It. in beaste and bacon	26	8
It in wooden vessell	26	8
It in henes and geese	5	0
It. in butter and Chease	6	8
It in Spininge whelles and sacks and winders .	15	8
It. in haynas and load sadles	6	8
It one Swine	13	4
It. all swine troughes, etc	16	0
It. in sives and rydles		16
It. in shovles and ginnons	6	3
It in flaxe	19	0
It. in woollen cloathe	4	0
It in sycles, &c.	2	6
It. in wye Ropes		20
It. in pychforkes and rakes		12
It. in all lower ger about the fyre	26	0
It. in all his apparell for his body	44	0

Som totalis[u] . . . . CC.XXXVI. XII "

In 15th of James I., (1617,) George Boulton, son of William and Governor of Blackburn Free Grammar School, died seised of messuages and lands at Little Harwood,[v] and in 1619, William Bolton died possessed of messuages and lands in the same place.[w] In 1683, William, son of Henry Bolton (great-great-great-grandfather of the late Thomas and Henry Bolton of Blackburn) was born at Little Harwood.[x]

---

[u] Ext from District Registry, Court of Probate, Chester.

[v] *Duc. Lanc* Pars Prima, Cal Inq. Post Mortem, vol. xxi. No 19, p. 77 George Boulton was Gov[r] of Blackburn Free Grammar School in 1598 See Appendix for Minute-Books of that school. George de Boulton de Bank was buried in St Mary's Church, Blackburn, A D 1617 See Appendix for Parochial Registers

[w] *Duc Lanc* P P Cal Inq Post Mortem, vol xxii No 17, p 80.

[x] See Letter of Henry Bolton in Appendix.

SECTION II.

FROM the foregoing sections, it appears that the Bolton Family, which is one of remote antiquity, bears one of the earliest British surnames upon record, familiar now for more than seven hundred years in both the counties of Yorkshire and Lancashire, originally adopted, according to well-authenticated evidence, from the principal place of residence of their progenitors, the Saxon Thanes of Mercia; and that in the year 1135, it was represented by

OUGHTREDE DE BOLTON[1], Lord of Bolton by Bowland, according to Dugdale, the lineal representative of the Saxon Earls of Mercia, who held the office of *bow-bearer* and *falconer* in the Royal Forests of Bowland and Gilsland. He had issue two sons, namely:

I. ELIAS DE BOLTON[2], juxta Bowland, living in 1134, the father of Richard de Bolton, 30th Henry III., (1246,) held advowson of Bolton juxta Bowland, whose descendants, as Lords of Bolton, were *bow-bearers* of *Bowland* and *Gilsland* for five successive generations. This branch of the family is now represented by the Boltons of Mt Bolton, Waterford, Ireland, and West-Tanfield, Yorkshire, etc.

II. RICHARD DE BOLTON[2], held in 1156 Little Bolton, in Thanage, by the service of 16s. per annum, and had a son,

WILLIAM DE BOLTON[3], who, in 1201, paid 5 marks for confirmation of 6 bovates of land in Bolton, which he had from the King, and held by the service of 10s. per annum. Also held a bovate of land in Bolton in chief of the King. He espoused Sarra or Saroth, whose marriage was in direction of the King; had issue two sons,

I. ELIAS DE BOLTON[4], his successor.

II. THOMAS DE BOLTON[4], Justice of Chester, 53 Henry III.[y]

ELIAS DE BOLTON[4], successor of his father. In 1234 Henry III received the homage of Elyas, son and heir of Saroth de Bolton, which Saroth held in chief of the King. In the *Visitation* of Flower, Norroy, he is styled "Elles fil Willie de Boulton." He had issue

I. HENRY DE BOLTON[5], his successor,

II. ROGER DE BOLTON[5], supposed ancestor of the Boltons of Little Bolton; held sixteenth part of a Knight's fee for lands in Little Bolton, in Salford, which his ancestors formerly held of Earl Ferrers. He was living 23 Edward I.[z]

HENRY DE BOLTON[5], successor to Elias, was living 16 Edward II, and left with other issue,

GILBERT DE BOLTON[6], who held 2 carucates and a half of land in Bolton, and left a son,

ADAM DE BOLTON[7], who gave a quantity of land in Bolton to Thomas, son of Adam Coupmanrara; had with other sons,

ROBERT DE BOLTON[8], living in 1290, was father of

I. HENRY DE BOLTON[9], one of the assessors for taking the "ninths" of the church of Blackburn in 1341, and owner of lands in Billington.

II. ROBERT DE BOLTON[9], also one of the assessors or venditors for taking the "ninths" of the church of Blackburn in 1341, left issue

I. ROBERT BOLTON[10] of Bolton, living in 1487.

II. WILLIAM BOLTON[10], living in 1473.

ROBERT BOLTON[10] of Bolton left issue

I. ROBERT BOLTON[11] of Bolton, living in 1539.

II. ADAM BOLTON[11], living in 1539, whose son was

RICHARD BOLTON[12], held in 1537 Brookhouse, a garden, four

---

[y] Concordia facto Aº 1268 coram D'mis Tho de Boulton tunc Justic' Cestr' etc (Brit. Mus Harl MSS. 2042, fol 9.)

[z] Roger de Bolton, his descendant, was possessed of lands at Knottesford in 1433, as appears by the following. "Hug Burayne ded Rog'o de Bolton terr in Knottesford, 12 Henry VI" (Brit Mus. Harl fol 102, f; see also Harl 2077 fol 102, d.)

acres of arable land, two acres of meadow, and seven of pasture, situated in Remesgreeve, within the parish of Blackburn, as tenant at will (by the annual payment of 15s.) of St. Mary's Abbey Whalley. He was living in 1545, and left issue,

I. ADAM BOLTON[13], who succeeded his father in possession of Brookhouse and adjoining lands as tenant at will of the Archbishop of Canterbury.

II. GYLES BOLTON[13], Governor of the Free Grammar School. Blackburn, in 1590.

III. ROBERT BOLTON[13], one of the original Governors of the Blackburn Free Grammar School in 1567.

ARMS OF JOHN DE BOLTON, LORD OF BOLTON, AND BOW-BEARER OF BOWLAND FOREST.

SECTION III.

"These were honoured Men in their Generations"
(Ecclus 44 · 71)

In 1570 Adam Bolton[13], the son of Richard[12], was in possession of the Brookhouse property, and here his younger son, Robert Bolton, the accomplished scholar, was born on Whit-Sunday, A.D. 1572. Fuller, the historian, speaking of the latter, says: "Though Mr Bolton's parents were not overflowing with wealth, they had a competent estate, as I am informed by credible intelligence, wherein their family had comfortably continued a long time in good repute."[a]

Adam Bolton was appointed one of the original Governors of the Blackburn Free Grammar School under the charter of Queen Elizabeth, in 1567.[b] His death is recorded in the Minute Book of the Governors, as having taken place in 1593.[c]

The issue of Adam Bolton[13] and Elizabeth, his wife, who died in 1610, were six sons—daughters unknown.

I. Adam Bolton[14], who succeeded to his father's lands in 1593. Edward Bagshawe, in his *Life and Death of Robert Bolton*, (a younger brother of Adam,) written in May, 1632, says: "In the middest of these his studies," at Lincoln Colledge, Oxford, "his father died, and then his means failed, for all his father's lands fell to his elder brother now living."[d]

Adam Bolton died at Brookhouse in 1639, and was buried in the church of Blackburn, leaving an only daughter, Eliza-

[a] Fuller's *Worthies of England*, by Nuttall, vol ii 207

[b] By this charter, "Her Majesty was pleased to ordain that there should be for ever in the village and parish of Blackburn, fifty men of the more discreet and honest of the inhabitants or freeholders to be the Governors of the possessions belonging to the school," etc. (Baines' *Hist of Lanc.*)

[c] See Appendix for Extracts of Minute-Books of Governors

[d] Mr. Bolton's last and learned work, by Edward Bagshawe. 4th edition. Printed 1639

beth, who was baptized in St Mary's church, Blackburn, Monday, September 2d, 1605. His will bears date the 28th of February, 1639, and was proved 3d of April, 1640.

THE WILL OF ADAM BOLTON OF BROOKHOUSE. 1639

In the Name of God. Amen The eight and twentieth daie of Februarie, in the year of our Lord God one thousand six hundred thirtie-nine, Adam Bolton of Brookhouse, in the Townshipp of Blackborne, in the Countie of Lancaster, yeoman, secke in bodie, but of good and p'fect memorie—praised be God—made his Will nuncupative in these words, implyinge the same or like effect, that is to say—First and principally, I comm'd my soul into the hands of Almightie God, trustinge and undoubtedlie believinge through the merities and bloud shoeding of his most blessed sonne Jesus Christ, my onely Saviour and Redeemer, to be one of the number of those to whom that joyfull sentence shall be pronounced, videlicet—Come yee blessed of my Father, possesse yee a Kingdome prepared for you from the beginninge of the worlde—and my bodie to bee buried in the Church of Blackborne aforesaid, at the discretion of mine Executor. Also my will and minde is, and I doe give and bequeath unto my Daughter, Elizabeth Bolton, all my goods whatsoever, in as much as I can, wch by law and right doe to mee belonge; and I doe constitute, ordaine, make, nominat, and appoynt, my said Daughter, Elizabeth Bolton, my true and lawfull Executrix, to execute and p'forme this my said Will and Testament, according to the trust and confidence in her reposed.

Witnesses hereof   Gyles Bolton,   Richard Bradley

On the eighth day of April, 1640, the Will of Adam Bolton, late of Brookhouse, in Blackburn, in the County of Lancaster, yeoman, deceased was proved in the Bishop's Consistory Court of Chester, by Elizabeth Bolton, the sole Executrix therein named, she having been first sworn duly to administer.[e]

II. Gyles Bolton[14] of Brookhouse, second son of Adam and Elizabeth Bolton, was also one of the Governors of the Free Grammar School in 1625, and continued to hold that office until 1641.[f] I find nothing mentioned of him after this; neither is the time of his death known. His children were

I. Adam Bolton[15], baptized in St. Mary's Church, in Blackburn, April 3d, 1602. This gentleman was likewise a Governor of the Free Grammar School in 1647, and died intestate A.D. 1666. On the 5th of April, 1667 letters of administra-

---

[e] Extracted from the District Registry of Her Majesty's Court of Probate a Chester.

tion of the effects of "Adam Bolton, late of Brookhouse, in the parish of Blackburn, deceased," were granted by the Consistory Court of Chester unto Robert Bolton.[g]

II. ROBERT BOLTON[15] of Brookhouse, administrator of the effects of his brother Adam in 1667. The time of his death is not known. He left two sons,

1. GILES BOLTON[16], baptized in St Mary's church in Blackburn, Feb'y 9, 1622.

2. JOHN BOLTON[16], baptized in ditto, 1632

III. THOMAS BOLTON[15] of Brookhouse, third son of Gyles, baptized in St. Mary's church, Blackburn, April 13, 1606, and buried April, 1653.

IV. JOHN BOLTON[15] of Brookhouse, fourth son of Gyles, baptized in St. Mary's church, April 12, 1616. He appears to have been Clerk of Blackburn in 1658, and was chosen a Governor of the Free Grammar School in 1662, and bestowed upon that institution a gratuity of 10s. the same year. In the Minute-Book of the Governors he is styled "John Boulton of Brookhouse, gentleman." He died in 1688[h], and had issue two sons and two daughters,

1. JOHN BOLTON[16], of whom in Part III.

2. ELIZABETH BOLTON, baptized in St. Mary's church, May 28th, 1654.

3. ESTHER BOLTON, baptized in St. Mary's church, Sept. 11, 1661.

4. ROBERT BOLTON[16], buried 1680, styled in the Registers, "Robert, son of John Bolton, of Blackburn, clerk."

V. JAMES BOLTON[15] of Brookhouse, fifth son of Gyles, baptized in St Mary's church, April 7th, 1626.

III. THOMAS BOLTON[14] of Brookhouse, third son of Adam and Elizabeth Bolton, was buried Dec. 17th, 1622. It is very probable that Thomas and Robert Bolton, twins, baptized Feb. 16th, 1615, were his sons. Robert was buried March 5th, 1615, and Thomas, January 14th, 1616. His wife appears to have been buried Sept. 7th, 1617.

---

[f] Minute-Book of Governors of B F G. S. See Appendix.

[g] Chester Registry Court of Probate, Chester See Appendix

[h] After 1688 the Boltons cease to be named in connection with *Brookhouse* in the Parochial Registers.

IV. JAMES BOLTON[14] of Blackburn, fourth son of Adam and Elizabeth Bolton, was buried October, 1635, leaving issue,

I. JAMES BOLTON[15].

II. JOSEPH BOLTON[15].

III. Rev. ADAM BOLTON[15], vicar of Blackburn, appointed by Archbishop Abbott, June 20th, 1628; buried at Blackburn in 1646. "The will of the Rev. Adam Bolton, late of Blackburn, clerk," bears date 24th of September, 1646, and was proved the same year.[1] Whether he was the Mr. Adam Boulton of Blackburn (minister of the third Classis of Lancashire, embracing parishes of Blackburn, Whalley, Chipping, and Ribble Chester,) in 1646, I am unable to determine. By his wife, Ann Farrington, he had issue,

1. SAMUEL BOLTON[16]. There is a strong presumption that this individual was the celebrated Samuel Bolton, D D., Master of Christ's College, Cambridge, notwithstanding the assertion of Wood and other historians, that he is not known to have been of the same family as Robert Bolton, the divine.

"Samuel Bolton, D D. This excellent divine (says Brook) was born in the year 1606, and educated in the University of Cambridge. He afterwards became minister of St. Martin's church, Ludgate street, London, where he continued about three years. Upon his removal from this situation, he was chosen minister at St. Saviour's, Southwark, where he continued seven years, and then removed to St. Andrew's, Holborn At each of these places his ministry was made a blessing to many souls. He was nominated one of the additional members in the Assembly of Divines. Upon the death of Dr. Bainbrigge, he was chosen master of Christ's College, Cambridge, which he governed with great wisdom and prudence the rest of his days. Having strong desires to win souls to Christ, though he was Master of a College, and had no ministerial charge of his own, he preached gratuitously every Lord's day for many years. In the year 1648, a minister of his name, and probably the same person, attended the Earl of Holland upon the scaffold, when he was beheaded in the palace-yard, Westminster.[2]

[1] See Appendix for extracts from will of Rev. Adam Bolton, in Chester Registry

[2] Whitlocke's *Mem.* p 387, edit. 1702.

"During his last sickness, which was long and painful, he exercised great patience, and often said, though the providence of God was dark towards him, he had light and comfort within. A little before he died, he said to a person moving him in bed: 'Let me alone; let me lie quietly. I have as much comfort as my heart can hold.' The last time Mr. Calamy visited him, he was anxious to be with Christ, saying: 'O this vile body of mine! when will it give way, that my soul may get out and go to my God—when will it be consumed, that I may mount up to heaven?' When he perceived any symptoms of his approaching dissolution, he rejoiced exceedingly, calling them 'the little crevices through which his soul peeped.' He died, greatly lamented, October 15th, 1654, aged forty-eight years, and was buried in St. Martin's church, mentioned above. He gave orders, in his last will and testament, to be interred as a private Christian, and not with the outward pomp of a doctor; 'because,' as he observed, 'he hoped to rise in the day of judgment, and appear before God, not as a *doctor*, but as an *humble Christian*.' Numerous elogies were published on his death.

"Dr. Bolton was a person of good parts and considerable learning, a burning and shining light in his day, and a man of great piety and excellent ministerial abilities. He was orthodox in his judgment, philanthropic in his spirit, and a celebrated interpreter of Scripture. He studied, not only to *preach* the word, but to *live* as he preached. His life was an excellent comment on his doctrine. He was the voice of God. crying aloud to those around him, by his exemplary life, as well as his holy doctrine. He was a man of much prayer, reading, meditation, and temptation—the four things which, in the opinion of Luther, make a preacher. He was assaulted with manifold temptations, and very probably with more than many hundreds of his brethren. He labored under the buffetings of Satan, that, being himself tempted, he might be better able to comfort those who were tempted. The words from which Mr. Calamy preached his funeral sermon had often been a source of great joy to his soul: 'Who shall change our vile body, that it may be fashioned like unto his glorious body, according to the mighty working whereby he is able even to subdue all things to himself.' "[k]

There is a portrait of him prefixed to his *Treatises*, 1657, copied 4to, W. Faithorne ; engraved by F. H. Van Horn. Encircling the portrait is the following Latin inscription : " VERA EFFIGIS SAMUELIS BOLTON, S. S. THEOL. D. NVPER COLL. C. CANTAB. MAG." Beneath the picture is the following coat of arms, in the shape of a seal. Quarterly first and fourth sa. a falcon close ar. beaked, membered, jessed and belled, or, second and third, gu. three wolves' heads erased, or.—Crest on a wreath, surmounting the helmet and mantling of an esquire, a falcon as in arms. Also the following inscription : " Qui obiit Oct'brs. 1654, ætat 48. F. H. Van Horn."[l]

His Works—1. *A Vindication of the Rights of Law and the Liberties of Grace*, 1645. 2. *The Arraignment of Error*, 1646. 3. *The Sinfulness of Sin*, held forth in a sermon preached to the Honorable House of Commons upon the late solemn Day of Humiliation, March 25th, 1646. 4. *The Guard of the Tree of Life :* a Sacramental Discourse, 12mo, 1647. 5. *The Dead Saint speaking to Saints and Sinners*, 1657. 6. *A Tossed Ship making for a Safe Harbor, or a Word in Season to a Sinking Kingdom, in Sermons for Days of Humiliation*, from Matt. xiv. 22 to 28, small 8vo, 1644. 7. *The Wedding Garment*.

SEAL OF REV. SAMUEL BOLTON, D.D. 1651.

---

[k] Calamy's Funeral Sermon for Dr. Bolton—*Clark's Lives*, part i. p. 43–17. There is no will of Dr. Bolton to be found in the Registry at Peterborough, which includes Northamptonshire and the University of Cambridge, nor Doctors' Commons, London. " Samuel Bolton, S.T.P., Master of Christ's College ; he died in October, 1654." " In 1651, Samuel Bolton, S.T.P., Master of Christ's College, was Vice-Chancellor of Cambridge." *Le Neve Fasti*, continued by Hardy.

[l] There is another print of Dr. Bolton, with the following arms and crest—sa. a falcon arg. close beaked, jessed and belled or.—Crest, a falcon as in arms.

2. JOHN BOLTON[16], buried January, 1630.

3. HANNAH BOLTON, baptized August, 1629.

4. ELIZABETH BOLTON, baptized November 27th, 1631, buried March, 1634.

5. SARAH BOLTON, baptized April 6th, 1634.

6. ELIZABETH BOLTON, baptized February 14th, 1635.

4. MARGERY BOLTON, of Blackburn, married —— Whalley.

5. ALICE BOLTON, of Blackburn, married —— Edge.

6. MARGARET BOLTON, of Blackburn, married Henry Tomlinson.

7. ABIGAIL BOLTON, of Blackburn.

V. JOHN BOLTON[14], of Blackburn, fifth son of Adam and Elizabeth Bolton, was buried March, 1635. He had issue,

I. JOHN BOLTON[15], buried October 10th, 1608.

II. HENRY BOLTON[15], baptized July 12th, 1608, had a son Henry Bolton[6], baptized November 10th, 1633, of Little Harwood, the father of William Bolton[7], baptized April 4th, 1683, the great grandfather of Henry Bolton[20] of Blackburn, born in 1747, died 1827, leaving two sons, Thomas[21] and Henry Bolton,[21] residing at Blackburn in 1834.

III. ROBERT BOLTON[15], baptized March 1st, 1609; buried June, 1610.

IV. ROBERT BOLTON[15], baptized June 4th, 1610.

V. WILLIAM BOLTON[15], baptized November 1st, 1616.

BROOKHOUSE, BLACKBURN, (erected prior to 1537.) From an original sketch made by the author in 1834.

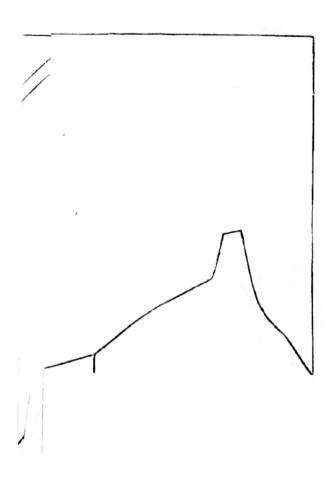

2. JOHN BOLTON[16], buried January, 1630.

3. HANNAH BOLTON, baptized August, 1629.

4. ELIZABETH BOLTON, baptized November 27th, 1631, buried March, 1634.

5. SARAH BOLTON, baptized April 6th, 1634.

6. ELIZABETH BOLTON, baptized February 14th, 1635.

4. MARGERY BOLTON, of Blackburn, married —— Whalley.

5. ALICE BOLTON, of Blackburn, married —— Edge.

6. MARGARET BOLTON, of Blackburn, married Henry Tomlinson.

7. ABIGAIL BOLTON, of Blackburn.

V. JOHN BOLTON[14], of Blackburn, fifth son of Adam and Elizabeth Bolton, was buried March, 1635. He had issue,

I. JOHN BOLTON[15], buried October 10th, 1608.

II. HENRY BOLTON[15], baptized July 12th, 1608, had a son Henry Bolton[6], baptized November 10th, 1633, of Little Harwood, the father of William Bolton[7], baptized April 4th, 1683, the great grandfather of Henry Bolton[20] of Blackburn, born in 1747, died 1827, leaving two sons, Thomas[21] and Henry Bolton,[21] residing at Blackburn in 1834.

III. ROBERT BOLTON[15], baptized March 1st, 1609; buried June, 1610.

IV. ROBERT BOLTON[15], baptized June 4th, 1610.

V. WILLIAM BOLTON[15], baptized November 1st, 1616.

BROOKHOUSE, BLACKBURN, (erected prior to 1557.)   From an original sketch made by the author in 1834.

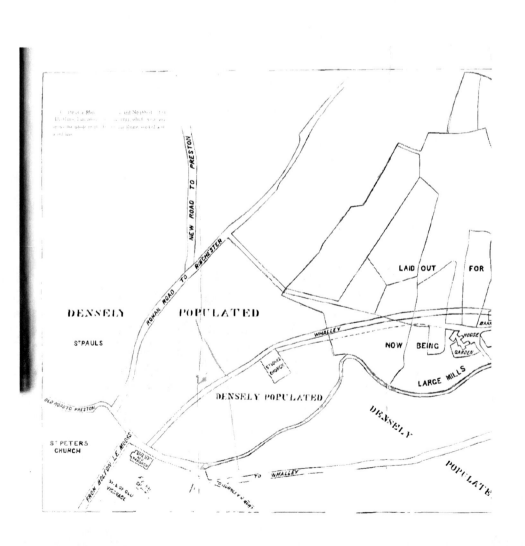

NEW ROAD TO PRESTON

ROMAN ROAD TO RIBCHESTER

DENSELY   POPULATED

St PAULS

LAID OUT   FOR

WHALLEY

NOW   BEING   HOUSE
GARDEN

St JUDE'S
CHURCH

LARGE MILLS

OLD ROAD TO PRESTON

DENSELY POPULATED

DENSELY

St PETERS
CHURCH

FROM BOLTON LE MOORS

SITE OF OLD
VICARAGE

TO WHALLEY

POPULATED

VI. Robert Bolton[14], sixth son of Adam[13] and Elizabeth Bolton, was born at Brookhouse on Whitsunday, 1572, and educated at the Free Grammar School, Blackburn,[o] where he greatly distinguished himself by his close application and successful attention to study.

"In 1590, he was entered a student of Lincoln College, Oxford, being then in his eighteenth year, and placed under the care of Mr. John Randal, a man of considerable reputation in the University, from whose example in learning he made rapid advancement. 'In the midst of these his studies his father died, and then his means failed, for all his father's lands fell to his elder brother.'[p] But his want of means proved an advancement unto him; for not having whence to buy books, he borrowed the best authors of his tutor, read over, abridged into note-books, and returned them. In a short time his progress in Greek was so amazing that he was able to discourse in that language with as great facility as in his native tongue, and even in his disputations, with as much readiness and ease as in Latin. From Lincoln he removed to Brazen Nose College, with a view to a fellowship, and took his degree of B.A on the 2d of December, 1596; but, being poor and in indifferent circumstances, he waited a long time, receiving in the mean while assistance and encouragement from Dr. Richard

---

[o] Then taught by a Mr. Yates, supposed ancestor of the Yates, partner of the first Sir Robert Peel

[p] "He was borne at *Blackburn*, says Bagshawe, a towne of good note in *Lancashire*, on Whitsunday, *Anno Domini* 1572. His parents being not of any great meanes, yet finding in him a great towardliness for learning, destinated him to bee a Scholler, and strugled with their estate to furnish him with necessaries in that kind apprehending the advantage of a snigular Schoole-Master that was then in the Towne. (Mr Yates) Hee plied his book so well, that in short time he became the best scholler in the Schoole," etc. "He continued long at Schoole, and came not to the University till about the twentieth yeare of his age He was placed at *Oxford* in *Lincolne Colledge*, under the tuition of Mr *Randall*, a man of no great note then, but afterward became a learned Divine and godly Preacher at *London*. In that Colledge he fell close to the studies of Logicke and Philosophie, and by reason of that groundwork of learning he got at schoole and maturity of years, he quickly got the start of those of his owne time, and grew into fame in that House In the middest of these his studies his Father died, and then his meanes failed, for all his Father's lands fell to his elder brother now living" (Edward Bagshawe's *Life and Death of Mr Bolton*, prefixed to Mr Bolton's *Foure Last Things* 4th ed London 1639.)

4

Brett, a noted giver and an eminent scholar of Lincoln College.

"At length, in 1602, with great difficulty and some disappointments, he was elected fellow, and proceeded M.A. on the 30th of July.

"His great reputation now getting abroad, he was successively elected lecturer in logic and also in moral and natural philosophy in his own College. As another proof of the estimation in which he was held, he was chosen to be one of the disputants before King James in natural philosophy, when that learned monarch first visited the University of Oxford

"To his other attainments, it is said, that he added eminence in metaphysics, mathematics, and the divinity of the schoolmen

"Notwithstanding all his ornamental and useful accomplishments, he was still destitute of the one thing needful: he had no serious concern for his soul, but loved plays and cards, was a horrible swearer, Sabbath-breaker, and familiar associate of the wicked.

"During his residence at Oxford, he became intimately acquainted with one Anderton, formerly his school-fellow, but now a learned popish priest[q], who, taking advantage of his mean circumstances, persuaded him into a reconciliation to the Church of Rome, and to accompany him to one of the English seminaries in Flanders, where, said he, 'you shall have gold enough.' The time and place of embarking were accordingly appointed, but Anderton disappointing him, he renounced the object altogether, and returned to his College. Here, by the instructions of the excellent Mr. Thomas Peacock, he was brought under such deep convictions of sin, that for many months he lost his appetite, his sleep, and all peace of mind. In the end, by a continuance in prayer and deep humiliation before God, he found mercy and received comfort. This memorable event was in the thirty-fifth year of his age, when he resolved to enter upon the work of the ministry. Having received comfort from the Lord, he loved much, and was desirous of being employed for much usefulness. On the

---

[q] Commonly called "Golden-mouthed Anderton."

14th of December, 1609, he proceeded B. of D., and was made rector of Broughton in Northamptonshire on the presentation of Sir Augustin Nichols, sergeant-at-law, and left College in December, 1610. Upon his presentation to Broughton Dr. King (Bishop of London) thanked the worthy judge, but observed, that he had deprived the University of one of its brightest ornaments. About the fortieth year of his age he married Anne, youngest daughter of Vincent Boys of Bekesborne in Kent, and thenceforward devoted himself to the duties of his office with unremitting attention. For twenty years successively he preached twice every Lord's day, and catechised in the afternoon; and every day before the Lord's supper, he expounded a chapter, by which means he went through most of the historical part of the Old and New Testament, all which was so well studied and prepared, that it might have served a very learned auditory. In all his ministerial labors he had in view the glory of God and conversion of sinners, which God made abundantly successful to the bringing many unto the righteousness of faith. He was a comely and grave person, commanding in all companies, and ever zealous in the cause of Christ, yet so prudent as to avoid being called in question for those things in which he was unconformable to the ecclesiastical establishment."

The love and veneration he entertained for his persecuted brethren of the Established Church is shown by the following copy of a letter of his to the Rev. Arthur Hildersham, A.M., the pious, learned, and useful vicar of Ashby-de-la Zouch in Leicestershire, whom Echard styles "a great and shining light of the Puritan party"

SR tho I bee not knowne unto you, yet I love and reverence your blessed and worthy partes, and pray that the Lord would stretch out your life to the utmost, and that you may long continue to doe Him glorious service in your ministry I take the boldness at this time to intreate from you this much. That you would bee pleased to certify in a word or two what is the outward estate of one Mr Slige, who lives at Ash in Derbyshire, some sixe miles from Derby. It is reported you were intimately acquainted with his Father, and therefore it seems you can tell what both the outwarde and spirituall state of the young man is. What you know therein I am desired by a speciall frend to know from you I desire to bee so farre troublesome unto you.   Our good God crowne still your godly paines with a blessed success.

Yours, most truly in our Lord Jesus,

Robert Bolton

April 10, 1628.

To my reverend and worthy friend Mr. Haldersham.[r]

"In his last sickness, which was a quartan ague, Mr. Bolton, finding that his complaint increased, revised his will, and retired from the noise of the world, employing the remnant of his time in sweet meditation on the joys of heaven. Though his sickness was tedious and painful, he bore it with admirable patience, and endured it as seeing Him that is invisible.

"About a week before his departure, he desired his wife not to be troubled at his dissolution, but to bear it with Christian fortitude, assuring her they should meet again in heaven. Turning towards his children, he observed, that they must not now expect him to say any thing to them, for his strength was gone; and he had told them enough in time past, which he hoped they would remember after he was dead; and he said, 'he verily believed that none of them durst think of meeting him before the tribunal of God in an unconverted state.' A little before his departure, and expecting every moment to be his last, being told that some of his best friends were about to take their last farewell, he caused himself to be raised up, and bowing himself upon his bed's head, after struggling for breath, he spoke as follows: 'I am now drawing on apace to my dissolution. Hold out, faith and patience, your work will soon be ended.' Then, shaking them all by the hand, he said : 'Make sure of Heaven, and keep in mind what I have formerly delivered to you. The doctrine which I have preached to you for the space of twenty years, is the truth of God, as I shall answer at the tribunal of Christ, before whom I must soon appear.' This he spoke when the very pangs of death were upon him. A dear friend, taking him by the hand, asked him whether he felt much pain. 'Truly no,' said he, 'the greatest pain I feel is your cold hand,' and pres-

---

[r] Copied from the original letter in the British Museum. Catalogue by Ascough. 2728. No. 4221.

ently expired   He died in the afternoon of Saturday, about
five o'clock, the seventeenth day of December, 1631, in the
sixtieth year of his age, and was buried two days after in the
chancel of St Andrew's church, Broughton."ˢ

Mr. Nicholas Estwick, who preached Mr. Bolton's funeral
discourse, gives him the following character : "How in-
dustrious a student he was, and how well furnished with
learning, is well known.   The Lord enriched him with a great
measure of grace, and his life was unreprovable.   All his
days he was a hard student, and laborious in his ministry, yet
was never ambitious of worldly greatness.   He sought his
own sanctification and the sanctification of others, and was
the means of plucking many out of the snares of Satan.
While his preaching was searching, it was happily calculated
to quicken and strengthen languished souls ; for which many
had cause to bless God."ᵗ   The Oxford historian denominates
him "a most religious and learned Puritan, a painful and constant preacher, a person of great zeal for God, charitable and
bountiful ; and so famous for relieving afflicted consciences,
that many foreigners resorted to him, as well as persons at
home, who found relief.   He was so expert in the Greek language, that he could write it, and dispute in it with equal
ease as in English or Latin."ᵘ   Fuller says : "He was one of a
thousand for piety, wisdom, and steadfastness ; and his ene-
mies who endeavored to injure him in his ministry, were never
able, by all their plottings, to do him any more harm than
only to show their teeth."ᵛ   Echard styles him "a great and
shining light of the Puritan party," and says, "he was justly
celebrated for his singular learning and piety."ʷ

His eloquent and valuable writings will commend his memory to the latest posterity.   Most of them were published
after his death by his worthy friend, Mr. Edward Bagshaw,
who wrote and published his life.ˣ

"It is observed of this holy and reverend divine, that he was
so highly esteemed in Northamptonshire, that his people who
beheld his white locks of hair, could point at him and say,

ˢ Life of Mr Bolton   ᵗ Funeral Sermon for Mr. Bolton
ᵘ *Athenæ Oxonienses*, vol i pp 479–80   ᵛ Fuller's *Abel Redivivus*, p 591
ʷ *Hist of Eng.* vol ii p 98   ˣ Doddridge's Works, vol. v p 429.   Edit 1804

'When that snow shall be dissolved, there will be a grea
flood:' and so it proved; for there never was a minister in
that county who lived more beloved, or died more lamented.
Floods of tears were shed over his grave."ʸ

In the chancel of Broughton church there is a half-length
figure of him, with his hands erected in the attitude of prayer,
resting on a book lying open before him; and underneath is
the following monumental inscription upon black marble:

ROBERTUS JACET HIC BOLTONUS,

CÆTERA NOVIT

**OCCUBITUS DEFLENS ANGLIA TOTA
DIEM.**

**PRIMUS ET OPTIMUS HUJUS EC-
CLESIÆ PRÆCO.**

**DOCTISSIME PIUS QUI, 17 DIE
DECEMB**

ANNO DNI. 1631 PLACIDE OBDOR-

MIVIT IN DOMINO.

Of which the following is a translation:

HERE LIES,

PEACEABLY SLEEPING IN THE LORD,

THE BODY OF

ROBERT BOLTON,

WHO DIED DECEMBER THE SEVENTEENTH

IN THE YEAR 1631.

He was one of the first and most learned of our Church
His other excellencies all England knoweth,
lamenting the day of his death.

ʸ Bolton on Usury Prep　Edit 1637

Rev. ROBERT BOLTON'S MONUMENT in St. Andrew's Church, Broughton.

There is an old portrait of Mr. Bolton in panel at the Hohne near Burnley, Lancashire, in the possession of the grandson of Dr. T. D. Whitaker, the historian. Also a good engraving of him, executed by John Payne, in 1632, accompanying the first volume of his works, by Edward Bagshaw. Underneath the portrait is the following Latin verse:

"Aspicis effigiem tantum: par nulla figura
BOLTONI Genio, qui super astra manet.
Doctior an melior fuit, haud scio Dicere fas est.
Secula vix referent, quem tulit una dies.
                                        E. B.

thus englished—

Behold an Image onely : There is none
That BOLTON's ghost can paint: To Heav'n it's gone.
More learn'd or good, I know not: This is true,
Whom one day lost scarce can an age renew.
                                        E. B."

His will bears date, Broughton, November 12th, 1631, and was proved in the Prerogative Court of Canterbury on the 3d of June, 1632:

THE WILL OF THE REV ROBERT BOLTON, RECTOR OF BROUGHTON, NORTHAMPTON, CLERK

LET MY HELPE COME FROM THE LORD, the Maker of Heaven and Earth, in his blessed name   I, ROBERT BOLTON, considering the certaintye of o^r death, the uncertainty of the tyme thereof, have thought yt my dutie (that I may the more readily accompany the Bridegiome with my lampe light at whatsoever houre of the night he shall come) to dispose of those things wherwth God hath blessed me by this my last Will and Testament.   Fiist, therefoie, I comend my soule into his hands, beseeching him most humbly that as hee hath created, redeemed, and sanctified yt of his gracious favour and unspeakable goodness, soe he will vouchsafe to receive yt into joy and everlasting gloiy in the inheiitance of his Kingdome; then my body, I wish that whether at Broughton, if I dye there, or wheisoever God shall take mee out of this life, yt be christianly interred, in hope of having yt raised againe out of the dust and re-united to my soule to be p'taker therwith of endlesse joy and blisse by the power of my Saviour at his Glorious appcarance at the last day.   And for and concerning all my Messuages, Lands, Tenements, and hereditaments in Broughton, in the County of Northampton, and all my goods and chattells whatsoever, I devise, will and bequeath them in manner and forme followinge; and first, my will is, that Anne Bolton, my wife, shall have & enjoy my messuage and five yard Land and an halfe, and all other my Lands, tenements, and hereditaments in Broughton aforesaid, with the appurtenances; for soe long tyme as she shall continue a Widdowe and unmarryed , towards her maintenance and good education of my children, and in case she shall marry, then my will ys that she shall resort to her Dower and thirds of my said Messuage, Lands, Tenements, and hereditaments, according to the Lawe and Custome of England.   Item, I will and devise to Hannah Bolton, my eldest daughter, two hundred and fiftye pounds to be paid to her at the day of her Marriage or within one month after the death or Marriage of the said Anne, her Mother, wch shall fiist happen. Item, I will and devise unto my daughter Mary Bolton one yard Land in Broughton, aforesaid, with the appui tenances parcell of the three yard Land wch I purchased of Sr Augustine Nicholls, one of his Maties Justices of the Comon Pleas deceased, to be severed out for her *my* metes and bounds—To have and to hold the said one yard Land to the said Mary, her heires and assignes forever   Item, I will and devise unto my Daughter, Elizabeth Bolton, one other yard Land in Broughton aforesaid, wth the appertenances parcell of the three yard Land aforesaid, to be severed out for her by metes and bounds—To have and to hold the sayd one yaid Land to the said Elizabeth, her heires and assignes forever. Item, I will and devise to my Daughter Sara Bolton, one other yard Land in Broughton aforesaid wth the appertenances parcell of the three yard Land aforesayd to be severed out for her by metes and bounds—To have and to hold the sayd one yard Land to the Sarah, her heires and assignes for ever   And for the increase of my youngest Daughter's portion, I will and devise one halfe yard Land wth the appertenances in Broughton aforesaid, parcell and residue of that one yard Land and a halfe wch I purchased of Thomas Hackney, to the said Mary Elizabeth and Sara, their heires and assignes forever, equally to be devided amongst them, and also forty pounds in money to be devyded amongst them, if that they shall please their Mother.   And my will ys, that all other my Messuages, Houses, Closes, Tenements, and hereditaments whatsoever in Broughton aforesaid, and not hereby form'ly devised or bequeathed, shall descend and goe to Samuel Bolton, my sonne and heire, and to his heires and assignes forever.   Item, my will is, that my said Sonne Samuel Bolton have all my Bookes, and that my wife Anne Bolton shall have the use and occupacon of all my plate and houshold stuffe whiles she lives, but after her decease, my will is, that it be devyded equally amongst my foure daughters, Hannah Bolton, Mary Bolton, Elizabeth Bolton, and Sarah Bolton   Item, I give three pounds to the poore of Broughton, to be distributed by mine Executor in this manner   twenty shillings upon the fifth day of November next ensuing after my death, the second twentie shillings that day twelvemonth; the third twentie shillinges a twelvemonth after that upon the said fifth day of November   Item, if anie of my children dye before Mariage, my will is that herein is bequeathed to them be given to and devyded amongst the rest of my children then living   Of this my last Will and Testament, I make Anne Bolton, my dearest Wife, my sole Executor, to whom I give the rest of my goods unbequeathed   And I make my worthy Freinds Mr. Francis Nicholls of Faxton, Mr. Edward Boys of Bekanger, Mr Downes of Pitchley, Mr John Sawyer of Kettering, Mr Bagshawe of Broughton, Mr. Richard Andrews of Thorpe Underwood, Overseers of this my Will   In witnesse of this my last Will and Testament I have put to my hand and seale, November 12th, Anno Dni 1631.   ROBERT BOLTON   O Lord, into thy hands I comend my Spiritt!   Thou hast redeemed yt!   O Lord, God of Truth, Lord Jesu, receive my Spiritt

Witnesses, JOHN SAWYER, GEORGE CORAN, ROBERT WOODFORD.

> The Original Will was proved in common form of Law in the Prerogative Court of Canterbury, on the third day of May, 1632, and a copy thereof in the Consistory Court of Peterborough, on the fifth day of June, 1632 [z]

HIS WORKS—1 *A Discourse about the State of True Happiness*, delivered in certain sermons in Oxon, and at St. Paul's Cross; on Psalm i verse 1, and 2, 1611.[a] 2. *Directions for*

---

[z] Copied from the original in H M Court of Probate, Northampton Registry

[a] These sermons, from their excellence of matter and style, went through six editions

Walking with God, 1625. 3   *Meditations of the Life to Come*, 1628. 4. *Instructions for the Right Comforting Afflicted Consciences*, 1631. 5. *Helps to Humiliation*, 1631. 6. *The Four Last Things—Death, Judgment, Hell, and Heaven*, 1632.[b] 7. *Assize Sermons and other Sermons*, 1632, *etc*. 8. *Funeral Notes on his Patron, Sir Augustin Nichols*, 1633. 9. *Carnal Professor; or, the Woful Slavery of Man guided by the Flesh*, 1634   10. *The Saints Sure and Perpetual Guide*, 1634. 11. *The Saints Self-Enriching Examination; or, a Treatise concerning the Sacrament of the Lord's Supper*, 1634. 12. *The Saints Soul-Exalting Humiliation; or, Soul-fatting Fasting*, 1634. 13. *A Short and Private Discourse between him and M. S. concerning Usury*, 1637. 14. *Devout Prayers on Solemn Occasions*, 1638. 15. *A Cordial for Christians in the Time of Affliction*, 1640. 16 *The Last Visitation, Conflict, and Death of Mr. Thomas Peacock, B.D., and Fellow of Brazen-Nose College, Oxford*, 1646.

ROBERT BOLTON[14] married Anne, daughter of Vincent Boys[c] of Bekesborne, Kent, A.D. 1612. In his *Life and Death of Mr. Bolton*, Edward Bagshawe says: "About the fortieth year of his age, for the better setling of himselfe in house-keeping upon his Parsonage, hee resolved upon marriage, and took to wife Mrs. Anne Boyse, a gentlewoman of an ancient house and worshipfull family in *Kent* to whose care hee committed the ordering of his outward estate, hee himselfe onely minding the studies and weighty affaires of his heavenly calling." By his wife Anne, Robert Bolton had five children,

I. SAMUEL BOLTON[15], born, says Wood, at his father's rectory,

---

b Bagshaw, in his "Epistle Dedicatory" to this volume, addressed to the "Rt worshipful Francis Nicolls, Esq ," says "Sir, it was the desire of this Reverend Author, when that furious messenger of Death (a quartan ague) seized upon his spirits, giving him no more intermission than what would serve for some feeble preparations against a *New Encounter*, that I would, in case he died, (which afterwards lamentably fell out,) frame an epistle to this worke, which hee had then made ready for the presse, and dedicate it (in his name) to yourself, as a pledge of his avowed thankefulnesse for these many favours he received from that religious and renowned Judge, his noble patron, and from your selfe, his immediate heir and successour "

c Arms of Boys, (Kent,) or, a griffin, segreant, sa within a bordure, gu

at Broughton, Northamptonshire, 1613.   He was baptized in
St. Andrew's church, Broughton.   "He was educated at Lincoln College, Oxford, where he took his degree of B.A., Oct.
19th, 1637, and afterwards became an eminent preacher in
London, and much followed by the priests' party.   After the
restoration of King Charles II, he was made Prebendary of
Westminster, and actually created D D. at Oxford.   This is
all I know of him, only that he, dying on the seventh of September, 1668, was buried in the Abbey church of St Peter,
at Westminster, on the south side of the choir, near to the
stairs leading up to the pulpit."[d]

"1661, June 12th, Samuel Bolton of Lincoln College, now
one of the King's chaplains, was created D.D at Oxon, by
virtue of the Chancellor's letters, which say, 'that he is a man
of extraordinary abilities and great integrity, and one who,
by his preaching in the city of London, is very serviceable to
the interests of the King and Church, etc.'   On the 15th of
January, 1661, he and Dr. Bruno Rogers preached before the
House of Commons at St. Margaret in Westminster, and were
by them desired to print their sermons."[e]

The Oxford historian, in his account of Lincoln College,
thus describes him :

"Robertus Bolton, Pastor ille celeberrimus, Broughtonæ
in agro Northamtoniensi (de quo plura vide in Collegio
Æncinasi) filium habuit, cui nomen Samuel Bolton, qui in
hoc Collegio educatus est, S. Theologiæ Professor creatus an.
CIDDCLXI Regiæ Majestati Caroli II. à sacris & Westononas
terriensis Præbendarius.

"Publicavit ille quidem Theologica quædem ; verum cum
difficile fit illa ab alterius cujusdam ejusdem cum illo nominis
(qui tamen Cantabrigiensis erat) scriptis distinguere, hoc ipsum
obiter notasse in præsentiarum sufficiat.   Ob. xi. Feb. (sty.
angl.)   An CIDDCLXVIII. & in Ecclesia S. Petri Westmon-

---

d Wood's *Athenæ Oxonienses*

e MSS British Museum ; also, "Sam Bolton, S T P , admissus ad eccl S. Leon-
ardi, Foster lane, London, die 26 Januar, 1668, vac per conservitatem Joh
Nalton." "Sam Bolton, S.T.P , admissus ad eccl. S Petri le Poor, London, 22
Dec 1662, ad coll. deca et capit Paul KENNET"

ast. ad australe latus non longe à suggesti gradibus, sepultus est."[f]

The following extracts are taken from the registers preserved in Westminster Abbey :

"Samuel Bolton, S T P , chaplain in ordinary to King Charles II , installed Prebendary 23d of April, 1662, obiit 11 February, 1668 "

"1668, Dr. Bolton, Prebendary of Westminster, buried February 13th."[g]

In the South transept of Westminster Abbey, on a grave-stone, is the following plain inscription :

" Here lieth the body of SAMUEL BOLTON, Doctor in Divinity, Chaplain in Ordinary to his Majesty Charles II., and Prebendary of this Cathedral Church ; deceased the 11th of February, 1668 "[h]

The will of Samuel Bolton, D.D , bears date the 27th day of December, 1668, and was proved the 22d day of February the year following.

WILL OF THE REV. SAMUEL BOLTON, D D., PREBENDARY OF WESTMINSTER.[i]

IN THE NAME OF GOD   AMEN   I, Samuel Bolton, Doctor in Divinity, and one of the Chaplains in Ordinary to the Most Excellent Majestie of Charles the Second, by the Grace of God, of Great Brittaine, &c , King ; being sound in memory, doe make and ordain this my last Will and Testament in manner and forme followinge . First, I give thanks to God my heavenly Father, That hee was pleased to ordaine mee to be borne of Christian parents whereby I was almost as soone made a member of his Catholic Church by my new birth as of mankind by my naturall birth, especially that hee was pleased so to place mee as to be bred up in a church the most pure and primitive, if after my little search I cann judge anythinge of any at this day professing christianity.   For my soule, I resign it into the hands of God as of a faithful Creator, trusting and beseeching him that through the satisfaction of his sonne my deare Lord and Saviour Jesus Christ, I may obtaine remission of all my sinns, and by the meritts of the same Lord and Saviour a crowne of immortall glory   For my body, my will is that it bee Christian like and decently buried according to the forme and order of the Church of England, at the discretion of my Executor in the place where I shall happen to die , Except I should die within tenn miles or thereabouts

---

[f] Wood's *Historia Universorum Oxonienses*, lib ii p. 165
[g] Extract from Register of Burials at Westminster.
[h] Neale's *Hist of Westminster Abbey*, vol ii p 269
[i] Extracted from the principal Registry of Her Majesty's Court of Probate

of London. Then my will and desire is that I may bee buried in the Collegiat Church of St Peters, Westminster, not farr from the pulpitt stayres towards the Royal monuments, the Deane's leave being obtained. And for that outward estate which it hath pleased God to bless me with, I thus dispose of it: First I give and bequeath to my yongest sister, Mrs. Sarah Simpkin, as a token of my kindness to her, the sume of twenty pounds, I likewise give unto the Library of the Collegiat Church of Saint Peter, Westminster, Kircher his Oedipus Ægiptiamo in two volumes in folio, his Prodromus Coptuo, his Onamastian Coptum. I lastly give unto the poore of Westminster five pounds to be distributed at the discretion of my Executor All the rest of my estate not before disposed of, all my just debts and funerall expences being paid, I will to come to and be possessed and disposed of by my dear wife, Mrs Mary Bolton, whome I make and ordain sole Executive of this my last Will and Testament, desiring and appointing my good friend Thomas More, Doctor of Physicke and one of the Fellowes of the College of Physicians in London, to be overseer of this my last Will and Testament. In witness whereof I have put my hand and seale, and published this my last Will, &c., SAMUEL BOLTON.

Sealed, subscribed and publisht on St John's Day, the 27th day of December, 1668, in the pr'sence of CHARLES GIBBSI, D D, Prebendary of Westminster—DAVID EVANS.

Probatum fuit hujus modi Testamentum apud cedeo Examen in le Strand in Com. Midd. coram venerabili viro Leolino Jenkins Legum Doctore curia prerogative Cantuariensio Magro Custode sive Comissario Legitime Constituto Vicesimo secoundo die mensio Februarii Anno Dni (Stilo Anglie) Millesimo Sexcentesimo Sexagesimo Octano Juramento Mariæ Bolton Pelitœ Dicti Defuncti et Executricio in hujusmodi Testamento nominat Cin Comissa fuit Administraco omnium et singulorum bonorum jurium et Creditorum Dicti Defuncti de bene et fideliter Administrand ead Ad Sancta dei Evangelia Jurat [j]

II. HANNAH BOLTON.

III. MARY BOLTON.

IV. ELIZABLTH, who was married to Mr. John Wyatt of Bugbrook, Northamptonshire. In St. Michael's church, Bugbrook, upon a brass plate, on the north side of the chancel, is the following inscription:

M. S.

"Here resteth the body of JOHN WYATT, gentleman, who tooke to wife ELIZABETH, daughter of ROBERT BOLTON, Batchelor in Divinity, and Rector of Broughton in this County, by whom he had five sons and four daughters; whose piety towards God, prudence in his affairs, faithfulness to his friends, christian courtesy to all, ELIZABETH, his sorrowful wife, hath cause at this stone to tell the

---

[j] Her Majesty's Court of Probate, Doctors' Commons, London

passenger, Thou mayest read and imitate—he here expects a joyful resurrection—the memorial of the just shall be blessed. He
departed this life October 4th, 1658, in the forty-seventh year of
his age."[k]

V. SARAH BOLTON married —— Simpkin, a legatee under
the will of her brother, in February, 1669.

COPY OF SEAL (enlarged) on Will of the Rev. SAMUEL BOLTON, D.D., in 1669.

---

[k] Bridge's *Hist. of Northamptonshire.*

SECTION IV.

JOHN BOLTON[16], Esq., of Wales, in the West Riding of Yorkshire, the only son and heir of John Bolton[15] of Brookhouse, gentleman, was baptized in St. Mary's church, Blackburn, Saturday, March 6th, 1658. He was a religious and godly man, and much esteemed by a large circle of friends, many of whom held high posts of honor connected with the government. It appears that his father, who died in 1688, was the last tenant at will of the Brookhouse estate, (which had been handed down in the name from father to son for over two hundred years,) by the name of Bolton. Some time prior to this event he had removed to Wales, in Yorkshire, from a desire to be near his relations residing in and about Laughton in that county, and Chesterfield, in Derbyshire. From the happy and serene pleasures of a domestic life, this good man was prematurely taken in 1693-4, to the great grief of a beloved wife, for his two children were too young to know their loss. He left, however, "a pretty estate, which gave his family a sufficiency and a promise of small fortunes when the children came of age." His wife Ann, we are informed, "was a woman of exemplary piety and prudence." Her greatest fondness was lavished upon her only son, whom she ever partially loved, and to her he was every way deserving of it, he behaving always in the most filial manner until her death, which probably occurred in 1714. The children of John[1] and Ann Bolton were,

I. ROBERT BOLTON[17], of whom in Part III., Section I.

II. ANN BOLTON, born in the parish of Wales, circ. 1690, and baptized there. One who was personally acquainted

---

[1] In the Inventory of the goods, etc, of Robert Bolton, (only son of John Bolton of Wales,) of Philadelphia, Penn, deceased in 1742, is the following item "John Bolton's Picture." This is supposed to have been his father's portrait

with her, says: " Her whole person was exceedingly beautiful,
which, added to an accomplished education, made her beloved
and admired by every noble and generous breast that could
behold her without envy. She was of a sharp wit and pierc-
ing judgment, devout to her religion, affable and obliging in
conversation, yet satirical and sharp to those she thought deserved it. She married young, to her mother's satisfaction,
Mr Thomas Richmond, a worthy gentleman, by whom she
had one daughter, a mirror of beauty. She enjoyed her happiness in a married state not many years before he died ; however, she was invested in his estate about one hundred pounds
per annum, a sufficiency for one of her piety, prudence, and
frugality."[m] She died young, but when and where buried is
not known.

> " Only the Actions of the Just
> Smell sweet, and blossom in the Dust "

---

[m] Extract from Mrs Ann Bolton's MSS This lady, the wife of Robert Bolton
of Philadelphia, left in her own handwriting a diary of many pages, commencing
with the year 1739, and continued with few intervals to her death, in 1747. All
the extracts are given from these MSS

PART III.

SECTION I.

ROBERT BOLTON[17], Esq., merchant of Philadelphia, Pennsylvania, only son of John[16] and Ann Bolton, was born in the parish of St. John's, Wales,[n] in the Wapentake of Strafforth and Tickhill, West Riding of Yorkshire, on Thursday, 26th of July, 1688,[o] and baptized at St. John's church, in Wales, July 3d, 1692.[p] He was honored as being the offspring of a long line of pious ancestry, and a child of the covenant promises of God. His wife, in her journal, records the following notice of her husband's birth and parentage:

"Robert Bolton was born in the same year that my husband, Mr. Robert Clay, was, (that is, in 1688,) in Yorkshire, of religious and godly parents, both by his father's and mother's side. His father, dying young, left his son Robert and only one daughter, named Ann, to the care of his wife, who

---

[n] St. John's, Wales, is a parish in Union of Worksop, partly within the liberty of St Peter's, West Riding, but chiefly within the South Division of the Wapentake of Strafforth and Tickhill, West Riding. In Domesday book, entitled "Walise," it is a perpetual curacy, and belongs to the peculiar of Anston, Handsworth, etc, under the jurisdiction of the Chancellor of the Cathedral church of St Peter York, where the wills and other registers are kept

[o] "A year memorable for the Revolution which gave England the Democratic bill of rights which has been justly styled 'her second Magna Charta'" "General James Ogelthorpe, the founder of Georgia, was born on the 21st of December 1688" (Stevens' *Hist of Georgia*)

[p] The following entry occurs in the Parochial Registers: "Robert Bolton, son of John and Mary, his wife, baptized July 3d, 1692." "In many of the Registers there is a marked falling off in the baptisms about, or previous to, 1688, caused, probably, from those troublesome times" "At that time, too, the baptisms were not all entered," "and the names of the mothers were very rarely given, if at all" This may account for the non-appearance of his sister's baptism, and the discrepancy that exists between the two names of his mother, namely, *Ann* and *Mary*. It may have been *Mary Ann* See Appendix for Registers of Wales and Tickhill.

5

was a woman of exemplary piety and prudence; so she carefully educated her two children in all manner of ingenious
and skilful learning and knowledge; but much more careful
she was in teaching and having them taught and brought up
in the nurture and admonition of the Lord. His father left
him a pretty estate, which gave them a sufficiency and a promise of small fortunes when they came of age. Many great
persons of his father's acquaintance constantly assured his
mother of their care and protection of her son and of advancing him to some considerable posts of honor and profit when
he should be of age and capable to act up to them All this
kept his mother from apprenticing him, according to his desire, to a near relation of hers, a merchant at New-Castle-upon-
Tyne, who was very rich and also very desirous to take him.
Though his mother had hopes of a higher station in life for
her son, yet after consideration she consented, and he staid a
long time with her kinsman, delighted much in the business,
and became very useful to him. At this time he was taken
ill with a lingering consumption and confined to his bed. At
the age of eighteen he returned to his mother, where he found
all hopes of preferment fled by the death of one great man
and the fall (through change of government) of others. This
increased his indisposition, until his physicians concluded he
was beyond recovery. At the age of twenty-one, he lay at
the point of death to all appearance, and continued so nearly
a whole year; he was then advised to go to Ireland, when,
after a few months, some signs of recovery appeared. He
had a rich uncle by his mother's side, who sent him supplies
of money. The city of Dublin was his place of residence,
where he met with many friends of well-known worth and
integrity, as well as large fortunes, who, by their kindness,
were instrumental in his recovery, which was effected by the
blessing of God, and the skill of his physician and careful
nurse a year after his coming thither. Mr. Bolton was now
in the prime of life, with a tolerable state of health, but nothing
more to depend upon but a genteel education; this would
have proved a blessing in easy circumstances, but his long illness had drained both his and his mother's purse, and his rich
uncle, like many others, was unwilling to relinquish any thing

until his death. This was likely to have driven Mr. Bolton into a melancholy, which was perceived by a grave old gentleman, a dancing-master, who offered to teach him the art of dancing. Mr. Bolton being in a strait, and having nothing in view, accepted it. Besides this, he learned the art of embroidery in gold and silver, for which he was beholden to his own sister, in which he, being sickly, assisted her.

"Mr. Bolton has told me that he was born on the Romish St. Ann's day, that his mother's name was Ann; a young lady he should have married, Ann, his sister, and his wife, Ann. Also my husbands both Roberts, both born in one year, and so near in one shire, that nothing but a small run parted their native places."

Alluding to the strict piety and virtue of Mr. Bolton's sister, she says: "For of such a stock indeed my dear Mr. Bolton and his sister came, as appears by a treatise written by their *great uncle," Robert Bolton,* "called a 'General Direction for a Comfortable Walk with God.'" (Here the MS is much defaced.—Author.) "This lies on the table[q] on which I write this present letter to you. Sir, God grant the contents of this book and of his other works for good of this pious writer and most godly minister of the Church of England, as were *some others of the family and relations, of his father's side,* as I have heard him say frequently. I think it ——— having mentioned it in ———, to which I refer you. All I shall now say is, that I value and venerate my dear Mr. Bolton for having been a branch of that godly family: had he been allyed by blood and worldly pomp and riches to kings and princes, but been vicious! had he imitated them in all their impiety!"[r]

Mr. Bolton, desirous of becoming more independent, and in hopes of still further improving his health, by a change of climate, at length determined to leave his native country, and remove to the American Colonies, which he accordingly did, some time in 1718, and settled himself in the city of Philadelphia, Pa.

---

[q] This volume is now in possession of the author. See Appendix for letter of Rev. A. Poe.

[r] Copied from the original MS in possession of her great-grandson, James C. Booth, Esq., of Philadelphia.

On Sunday, the 19th of February, 1721, he was married, in Christ church, Philadelphia, by the Rev John Vicary, the rector, to Ann Clay, widow of Robert Clay, (formerly of Chesterfield, Derbyshire,) a merchant of that city. For some years after his marriage, he appears to have met with good success in business, as a merchant, until an unhappy fate drew him to open a store in Trenton, New-Jersey, much against the wishes of his best friends. He was now obliged to divide his time between Philadelphia and the former place, so that he was in a constant hurry of business, and became much embarrassed. In 1726 he was elected junior, and the following year senior warden, of Christ church, Philadelphia. He was also one of the petitioners to the venerable Propagation Society the preceding year, in behalf of the Rev. John Talbot, of Burlington, New-Jersey, one of their missionaries, as appears from the following document:

Extract from a Memorial to the Society from Churches in Pennsylvania and New Jersey

SHEWETH

"That the melancholy circumstances of the Church of England in these Colonies is a subject, we hope, worthy, not only your compassion but tender regard, having not above one Minister to seven or eight Churches or Congregations, and we bemoan our case, when we behold so many churches, lately built, lie as desolate around us, convincing arguments of our affection for the Church, and of our great misfortune in being destitute of pastors. When at the same time we daily see Dissenters of all denominations, continually supplied, and increase, through this, our misfortune, and upbraid us with this defect. It is, therefore, with the utmost concern, we express our unhappiness, when we view our circumstances rather decline than flourish. In particular, that Mr Talbot, who for nigh thirty years past has behaved himself with indefatigable pains, and good success in his ministry, among us, under your Honours' care, has by some late conduct (nowise privy to us) rendered himself disagreeable to his superiors and departed from us We cannot, without violence to the principles of our Religion, approve of any acts, or give in to any measures inconsistent with our duty and loyalty to his Majesty, whom God long preserve; yet in gratitude to this unhappy gentleman, we humbly beg leave to say, that by his exemplary life and ministry, he has been the greatest advocate for the Church of England, by Law Established, that ever appeared on this shore. This unhappy accident, together with the death and removal of some other clergymen from us, has very much increased the cause of our complaint, and we have no other recourse but to your Honours for relief. Having well-grounded hopes, that the same good spirit which prompted you to undertake the glorious work of propagating the Gospel in foreign parts will continue your pious regards to these Colonies, and the rather, since so many stately monuments are erected for God's service, testifying our sincere willingness to embrace your charitable assistance, and to answer the glorious ends you have in view

"Therefore, your petitioners most humbly beg your Honourable Society will please to extend your wonted charity and necessary supply to the several Churches and Congregations, of which particular accounts are hereto annexed.   And your Petitioners, as in duty bound,

"Shall ever pray," etc.

"*Christ Church, Philadelphia.*

"SAMUEL HASELL, }
"ROBERT BOLTON, } *Churchwardens* "

He was also actively engaged as a vestryman of Christ church, as appears by the following extracts from the vestry minutes: "21st of June, 1725, Robert Bolton and Thomas Leech were requested to collect the remaining part of the subscriptions yet to be-paid for the purchase of a lot for the new burial-ground." "Jan. 13th, 1726, the Rev. Dr. Walton being called home to England, the wardens were requested to collect pew-rents in advance, to help the Doctor, and that Mr. Bolton and Mr. Chase assist them to collect the same with all possible dispatch." "April 25th, 1729, it was resolved that a Committee give Mr. Bolton notice in writing that he lay before them the accounts of subscriptions for purchase of lot." His name occurs for the last time on the vestry minutes, May 3d, 1731.

Robt Bolton

"After the severe losses he met with at Trenton, he appears to have labored hard and successfully to repair them, and would probably have been a rich man in a few years, had he not continued trading too largely. He was concerned, at this time, in country stores, owning parts of vessels, and all manner of foreign merchandise. In 1731, by the persuasions of Maryland traders, and some others, he was prevailed upon to open a store in Somerset county, where he remained until a train of misfortunes opened his eyes; for what with losses by sea, and bad debts on land, the trading in his store declined, so that where he used to take a pound, he scarcely took a penny. In the course of three years he saw himself plunged in difficulties, without the power of extricating himself, but as a melancholy spectator viewed his misery. His trade in Somerset county only involved him in debts; besides tobacco shipped to England, cast away, also the same commodity sent to Philadelphia to pay the merchants was lost on the coast; and to add to his misfortunes, at this distressing time, he was compelled to return home ill with fever and ague, a disease which he never had before going to Maryland. On his recovery, he was solicited by some friends to open a boarding-school at Chestertown, Maryland, where he remained nearly a year, much admired and beloved. But various circumstances compelled him to return to Philadelphia in 1738 Some time in November, 1739, he was visited by the worthy and Reverend George Whitefield, and the good Mr. William Seward, who, unsolicited, at once took a great interest in his welfare, and in June, 1740, established him in a school, placed his family in a genteel house, and relieved them from all fears and terrors; and not only so, but that faithful minister of God added his prayers to Heaven in their behalf. They also continued to relieve Mr. Bolton and his family by considerable sums of money at divers times; and Mr Seward, in 1739, settled an annuity upon Mrs. Bolton of thirty pounds a year, at the same time, Mr. Whitefield took their two daughters, Mary and Rebecca, under his special care, and with their parents' consent, sent them to his Orphan House in Georgia.[s] Thus, by God's kind providence, the clouds and darkness passed away, and the sun arose brightly once more upon this aged and patient Christian. He was now able to live free from earthly cares, retired from the pomp and extravagance of the world. His little school, and the bounty bestowed on his wife by Mr. Seward, gave them a good competence, so that they needed no more. It was indeed a great struggle to come to

---

[s] "An account of the orphans and children that have been maintained and educated at, and are now in, the Orphan House at Georgia, from a pamphlet printed in the year 1746, etc, by George Whitefield, A.B, late of Pembroke College, Oxon · Nos 77, 78, Mary Bolton, Rebecca Bolton   Daughters of Robert and Ann Bolton, of Philadelphia, said Robert since dead. Ages, 16, 10. Taken in February, 1739-40   Mary Bolton, 26th December, 1740, married to Jas Habersham   Rebecca Bolton, February, 1745, sent to Philadelphia, to assist her aged mother "

this content, but they now enjoyed that peace which the gay world could neither give nor take away."

During the temporary absence of Mr. Whitefield from Savannah, Mr Habersham thus addressed his father-in-law:

"BETHESDA, September 3d, 1741

"HONOUR'D FATHER: I thank you for your kind letter of June 1st. I hope that God the Father of our Lord Jesus Christ will hear your prayers for us. My wife has her health exceedingly well—I suppose she never enjoyed a greater share of it—and Becky, likewise, has much reason to be thankful on that account. I think I love you and all your family for her sake

"I expect Mr. Whitfield will call at Philadelphia before he comes here By this occasion I have wrote a letter to be left at Mr Read's, to be sent or given to him upon the first notice of his arrival in any part of North America. We have not heard from him since he first landed in England, and we have reason to fear his letters and probably supplies have been interrupted by ye Spaniards, who have done much mischief on our coast. Blessed be God, he supplies us, notwithstanding this and many other disappointments we have met with, and glory and praise to him for ever.

"If dear Mr. Whitfield puts in to your city, you may then talk to him about dear Becky I should be very glad to have your son John with me, but at present my business is here. Nothing but want of health and incapacity to do my duty, I trust, will move me to desert the good work I am engaged in, both which I want However, if Mr. Whitfield will bring Johnny, and you will let him come, I will endeavor to instruct him in everything I can. My wife speaks so respectfully of his kind and affable temper that I am fond of having him with me, particularly if dear Becky leaves us, who is, I could almost say, dearer to me than any of my own sisters. The Lord direct you. When dear Mr Whitfield comes amongst us, I shall see clearer I wish it may ever be in my power to manifest my love to you and your family, however, I hope you will accept of my will though the Lord may never put it in my power actually to show it. I have much business before me, and can only recommend you to God, who is able to do abundantly more for you than I can wish or think. That ye Lord may guide you in time, and glorify you in eternity, is the hearty prayer of your affectionate and obedient son and servant,

"JAMES HABERSHAM.[1]

"To my Honoured Father, ROBT. BOLTON, in Phila."

During Mr. Whitefield's stay in Philadelphia, Mr. Bolton appears to have been a regular attendant on his preaching. The former, speaking of the little interest some felt in his efforts to do good, thus alludes to the latter: "The least con-

---

[1] Copied from the Habersham MS.

cern, I think, was one afternoon when I was carried out to talk against reasoning unbelievers. One of them, a little after, meeting Mr. B——n, said: 'What! Mr. Whitefield could not make the people cry this afternoon.' 'A good reason for it,' says Mr. B——n, 'he was preaching against Deists, and you know they are a hardened generation.' 'Lord, take from them a heart of stone and give them a heart of flesh. Abba Father, all things are possible with thee.' "[u]

Mr. Bolton survived the happy change in his circumstances only two years, dying on Wednesday, June 23d, 1742, at the age of fifty-four, greatly admired, beloved, and lamented. His end was peace. His remains were interred on Friday, 25th of June, 1742, beside those of his four children, in what was then styled the New Building Burying-Ground, (now Arch street,) Philadelphia. There is no monument erected to his memory, or to those of any of his deceased relations at that place.

His sorrowful widow, who survived him nearly five years, records the following of him in her diary: "Mr. Bolton, though not handsome, was of an aspect most agreeable and good, that at once commanded the respect and esteem of all; his deportment, both in public and in private, possessed so much of the gentleman and of the Christian, that even now I am writing about him, I am fired with love to his beloved self, soul and body adorned with such peculiar graces, as are seldom to be found in one man; indeed, to declare the truth, I know not another so well educated in every respect. So refined and seraphic far above my praise, nor am I able to express the height of his deserts. What have I not gained by his humility, unparalleled meekness and patience, even in his greatest adversities?" "In his deportment to all persons and in all places engaging, he was grave, yet cheerful in conversation, very religious, and a constant attender at the church and all its sacred solemnities" "He was tall and well shaped, his skin fine, but inclining to pale through many years' sickness when he was but a youth In his dress he was neat and

---

[u] The two first parts of his Life with his Journals, by George Whitefield, A D 1756, p 430

exceedingly genteel, in which he rather affected gravity than gaiety, had not his employment led him aside from his actual humour."

His will bears date seventeenth January, 1734, and was proved fifth July, 1742.

LAST WILL AND TESTAMENT OF ROBERT BOLTON OF PHILADELPHIA, MERCHANT.

In the Name of God: Amen. I, Robert Bolton, of the City of Philadelphia, in the Province of Pennsylvania, Merchant, being weak in health of Body, and of sound, Perfect, and disposing mind, memory, and understanding, do make and ordain this my last will and testament in manner and form following, (that is to say,) first, my will and mind is that my Just debts and funeral expences be duly paid and discharged by my executrix hereinafter named. Item, I give and bequeath unto my sons in law, Slater Clay and Thomas Clay, Five pounds a piece, to be paid them at their respective ages of Twenty-one years. Item, I give and bequeath unto my sons, Robert Bolton and John Bolton, Five pounds a piece, to be paid to them at their respective ages of Twenty-one Years. Item, I give and Bequeath unto my daughters, Ann Bolton, Mary Bolton, and Rebecca Bolton, Five pounds a piece, to be paid them at their respective ages of eighteen years. Item, all the Rest and Residue of my estate—Real and Personal—Lands, Tenements, Hereditaments, Goods, and Chattels, whatsoever and wheresoever, I give, devise, and bequeath unto my dear and loving wife, Ann Bolton, her heirs, executors, administrators, and assigns for ever; and I do hereby revoke and make void all former Wills and Testaments by me Heretofore made. In witness whereof, I, the said Robert Bolton, have to this, my last Will and Testament, set my hand and seal, this seventeenth day of January, in the year of our Lord one thousand seven hundred and thirty Four.

Signed, sealed, published, and declared by the Testator, as and for his last Will and Testament, in the presence of us, whose names are subscribed as witnesses,   Thos. Byles,
                                   Fras. Richardson, appd. 3 July, 1742.

Philadelphia, July 3d, 1742. Item, personally appeared Thomas Byles and Francis Richardson, the witnesses to the within written Codicil, and the said Francis Richardson on his solemn affirmation, according to law, the said Thomas Byles on his oath, did declare they saw and heard Robert Bolton, the testator therein named, sign, seal, publish, and declare the same codicil to be his last Will and Testament, and that at the doing thereof he was of sound mind, memory, and understanding to the best of their knowledge   Coram.

PET EVANS,
Register General [v]

Know all men by these presents that we, Ann Bolton of Philadelphia, Widow and relict of Robert Bolton, merch[t], Dece[d], Thomas Clay, merch[t], and Jn[o] Doe of Philad[a], are held and firmly bound unto Peter Evans, Reg[r] Gen[l] for the Probate of Wills and granting Letters of Administration in and for the province of Pennsylv[a], &c., in the sum of One Hundred Pounds Lawfull money of the s[d] province to be p[d] to the s[d] Reg[r] Gen[l], his ceartain Attorney Exec[s], Admin[s], or assigns, to the which pay m[t] well and truly to be made and done we bind ourselves, our Heirs, Exec[rs], and Adm[rs], jointly and severally for and in the whole firmly by these presents. Sealed with our seals.   Dated the fifth day of July Anno 1742

The *Condicon* of this obligacon is such that if the bounden Ann Bolton, administratrix of all and singular the Goods, Chattels, rights, and Credit which were of Robert Bolton, deceased, with a codicil annexed, do make or cause to be made a true and perfect Inventory of all and singular the Goods, Chattels, Rights, and Credits which were of the said deceased, which have or shall come to the hands, possession, or knowledge of the said Ann Bolton, or into the hands or possession of any other person or persons for her, and the same so made do exhibit or cause to be exhibited into the Reg[r] Gen[l] Office at Philad[a], at or before the fifth day of August next, and the same goods and chattels, which were of the said dec[d] at the time of his death or which at any time after shall come to the hands, possession, or knowledge of the said Ann Bolton or into the hands or possession of any other person or persons for her, do well and truly administer, according to law, and further do make or cause to be made a true and just account, calculacon, or reckoning of the s[d] adm'ton when required, and all the rest and residue of the s[d] goods, Chattels, Rights, and Credits, which shall be found remains upon the s[d] adm[s] acc't, the same being first ex[d] and allowed of by the Orphans' Court of the County of Phil[a], shall deliver and pay to such person or persons respectively as the said Court by its decree or sentence shall limit or appoint ; then this obligacon to be void or else to be and remain in full force and virtue.

Ann Bolton

THOMAS CLAY,
JOHN DOE

Sealed and delivered in the }
presence of us   }

LIT HODGSON.

---

[v] Register General's Office of Wills, Philadelphia

AN INVENTORY OF ALL AND SINGULAR OF THE GOODS
AND CHATTELS OF ROBERT BOLTON, LATE OF PHILAD^,
DECEASED. (Apraised at the Desire of the Execut^r, ANN BOLTON.)

In The Back Garrett, viz. :

A Bedstead and bottom	12	0	
1 Feather bed bolster & 2 pellows	4	0	0
1 Callico Quilt & 2 Blanketts	1	5	0
1 Red Ceader Chest of Drawers	1	0	0
1 Walnut Chamber Table		10	0
3 Arm'd Cane Chairs & 9 without arms	2	8	0
1 Old Velvet Man's Saddle		8	0
1 Old Demy Peak Do.	1	0	0
1 Pilion Cloth		3	0
4 Old green Window Curtains		5	0
1 Bed Tick & Bolster	1	0	0
2 Setts bed Curtains, one being for a Pallet Bed	1	10	0
2 Setts of Callicco Window Curtains		12	0
2 pair Fire Shovell & Tonges		5	0
2 Stone Juggs		5	0
12 Pewter & 12 tin Candle Molds		12	0
3 Glass Globes		1	6
Some Brass Wire on Quills		5	0
6 knives & 6 forks Silvered		15	0
6 Do & 6 forks Ivory handles		7	6
5 Picturs & 2 Smaller Do Glass'd		10	0
2 Broken glass Saucers		1	6
1 Glass Lanthorns		6	0
1 Gold Bootes		5	0
In and Old Chest & Trunk, some lumber		5	0

The Front Garrett :

2 Bedsteads & Bottoms & Iron rods	2	0	0
Some old Books of Divinity		10	0
1 Feather Bed Bolster & 2 Pillows	1	10	0
2 Bolsters & 2 Small Pillows		5	0
1 Quilt & 2 Blanketts	1	0	0
9 Tin hanging Candlesticks		4	6
2 Lines for Drying Cloaths		3	0
1 pair Stylyards		2	6
His Wearing Apparrel, Woollen & Linnen	6	0	0
1 Old Trunk & Chest		5	0
11 Old Table Cloaths	2	4	0
7 pair Old Bed Sheets	4	0	0

Carried over £36 15 6

Brought over	£36	15	6
17 Pillow Cases.		17	0
7 Towells		7	0
33 Napkins	1	13	0
7 Blew & White Window Curtains & Valens		15	0
1 Sett Curtains & Teaster for a Pallet bed		12	0
1 White Cotton Counter Pain		12	0
1 White Linnin Quilt	1	0	0

In the room up one pair Stairs, viz. ·

Mr. Whitefields Picture—a Present to Mrs Bolton .   .

One Bedstead, bed & Bolster, Pillows, Quilt, and 1 Blanket			
Worked Curtrings & Cushings	7	0	0
1 Easey Chair		10	0
1 Mahogany Chest of Drawers & Table	3	0	0
1 Old Corner Cupboard		2	6
John Bolton's Picture[w]		10	0
21 Glass'd Pictures	1	1	0
A Tea Table & Tea Chest		15	0
1 Swinging Looking Glass		15	0
1 Ditto Broke		2	6
3 Small Trunks		10	0
1 Small Walnut Table		8	0
1 Coffey Mill		3	0
1 Fire Screen		2	0
1 pair Fire Tonges, Shovel, and andirons		12	0
Old China and Earthen		10	0
2 Small Chamber Bells		4	0
Sword & Broken Cane		12	0

	Oz.	Pwt
One Silver Tankerd w .	20	10
1 Cann Ditto	12	0
1 Small Ditto	7	5
2 Pottingers Ditto	15	1
1 Server Ditto	9	18
2 Salts Ditto	3	7
3 Glassers Ditto	17	0
4 Table Spoons & 1 Child's . .	7	17
9 Tea Spoons & Tonges . . .	3	10

96 8 at 7s. 6d. per oz. .	36	3	0
1 pair small gold buttons, Silver Shoe buckles & stock. buck. .	1	5	0

---

[w] This must have been the portrait of John Bolton[16], Esq., of Wales, Yorkshire

In the Lower Room :

1 Pine Desk, 2 forms, 4 benches & Chest	12	0
7 Walnut Chairs wth Leather Bottoms	1 8	0
1 Walnut Table	1 0	0
1 Clock and Case	5 0	0
1 pair Fire Doggs	7	0
1 Skillet	5	0
2 Copper Coffey Potts	5	0
1 Pestel & Morter	5	0

Carried over	£105 18	6
Brought over	£105 18	6
7 Old-Fash^d Brass Candlesticks & Snuffers	15	0
1 Chafing Dish Ditto	2	6
3 pair Flatt Smoothing Irons	9	0
Some Silver & Gold Thread	15	0
About a ¼ pound of Damag^d Sewing Silk	3	0
1 Dz. of Children's & Wom^s Gloves	6	0
1 Pudding Pann	2	6
13 Old Pewter Dishes	1 15	0
35 Old Pewter Plates	1 5	0
1 Stool Pan & Small Funnel	3	0
1 Old Cold Still of Lead & Pewter	10	0
2 y^{ds} ¾ of Pertian	10	0
5 y^{ds} of fustian	10	0
7 y^{ds} serge	10	6

In the Cellar or Kitchen, VIZ. :

1 Old Brass Kettle	1 5	0
1 Small d^o	2	6
2 Small Iron Potts	7	6
Tonges, Gridiron & Old Iron	5	0
1 frying Pan & Spit	3	0
1 Warmping Pan	5	0
1 Iron Dripping Pann	2	6
1 Iron Fire Back	1 0	0
3 Washing Tubbs & some lumber	5	0
1 Tea kettle	5	0
One old two wheel Chaise	5 0	0
One Mullatto Girle about 4 years old . . .	5 0	0
One Negro Man about 28 years old, named York. Is the property of Robert Bolton's Estate	35 0	0

	£127 15	6

PHILAD^A, July 3, 1742. Appraised by us, as Witness our hands,

STEPH ARMITT,
JOHN NELSONE.^x

ROBERT BOLTON[17] married Ann, widow of Robert Clay, merchant, the only daughter of Winlock Curtis and Ann Bowers, (fourth daughter of Banuel Bowers[y] and Elizabeth Dunster[z] of Boston;) she was born in Kent County, Delaware, on the 15th of November, 1690.   Her grandfather, John Curtis,[a] Esq, (descended from an ancient family, resident at Appledore, in the county of Kent, England, " as far back as can be traced,") was a wealthy, landed proprietor in the county of Kent upon Delaware, in the Province of Pennsylvania.   Her only brother was the Hon. John Curtis, upon whose tombstone, near the porch of Immanuel Church at New-Castle Delaware, is the following epitaph by Franklin :

IN MEMORY OF

JOHN CURTIS, ESQ,

LATE SPEAKER OF THE ASSEMBLY,

A JUDGE OF THE SUPREME COURT,

TREASURER AND TRUSTEE OF THE LOAN OFFICE,

WHO DEPARTED THIS LIFE NOV 18TH, 1753,

AGED 61 YEARS.

If to be prudent in council,
Upright in Judgment,
Faithful in Trust,
Give value to the public man,

---

[y] Banuel Bowers, son of —— Bowers, of England, married Elizabeth Dunster of Lancashire, a niece of Henry Dunster, the *first President of Harvard College*

[z] " Henry Dunster was educated at Magdalen College, Oxford, where he took his A B degree, in 1630, and proceeded A.M in 1634   He retired to New-England in 1640   He is denominated 'one of the greatest masters of oriental learning that New-England had ever known'"   "He was inducted President of Harvard College 17th August, 1640, resigned 24th October, 1651, died at Scituate 27th February, 1659, and was buried at Cambridge "   "His wife, Elizabeth, died 23d (6·,) 1643 His sons were David, Henry, and Jonathan "   See Brooks's *Lives of Puritans,* Farmer's *Register,* etc

[a] The arms of Curtis of Kent   Arg a chev sa between three bulls' heads, cabossed gules —Crest, a unicorn passant, or, between four trees, ppr

If to be sincere in friendship,
Affectionate to relations,
And kind to all around him,
Make the private man amiable;

Thy death, O Curtis,
As a general loss,
Long shall be lamented

Her father dying young, she was left to the care of a maiden aunt, named Bathsheba Bowers, who resided on Society Hill, Philadelphia. Under the cruel treatment of this woman she was brought, about the age of twelve, almost to death's door. At the age of thirteen she returned to her mother, and proved of great assistance to her in the care of household and business affairs. She was early distinguished by considerable natural abilities and an extraordinary thirst of knowledge. Though brought up a member of the Society of Friends, reading and reflection had induced her to join the communion of the Church of England; and she thenceforward devoted all her time and energies in its cause. While many of her dissenting brethren were embroiled in endless disputes, she remained constant, and trod the Christian road with love, and peace, and joy in the Holy Ghost, daily striving to abound in the work of the Lord. On the 16th of December, 1710, she married Robert Clay of Philadelphia, eldest son of Robert Clay. Esq., of Sheffield, Yorkshire, by whom she had several children. Mr. Clay, to whom she was greatly attached, was lost at sea in 1716, while on a trading voyage from Philadelphia to Liverpool. In 1714 she visited England, spending much of her time with her husband's relations at Sheffield She sailed from Liverpool in 1719, and arrived in Philadelphia April 15th, 1720. On the 19th of February, 1721, in Christ church, Philadelphia, she was married to Robert Bolton, Esq, who was born the same year (1688) with her former husband, "and so near in one shire, that nothing but a small run parted their native places." Some time in November, 1739, she commenced writing her autobiography, which she completed in the spring of 1747. On the 12th of November, 1739, she became acquainted with the celebrated Mr. White-

field, then just arrived from England.   She thus describes the
event in her journal :

"The coming of the worthy and Rev. Mr. Whitfield and
the good Mr. William Seward opened a year of jubilee to me.
They at once took a great interest in our welfare.   In June,
1740, they set up my husband in a school, placed us in a genteel house of small rent, and released me from all my fears
and terrors.   I now no longer dreaded poverty nor feared
want, that faithful minister's prayers reached Heaven in my
behalf.   My dear husband and family were relieved by considerable sums of money at divers times from them ; and Mr.
Seward, Esq., in 1739, settled an annuity upon me of thirty
pounds a year, at the same time Mr. Whitfield took my two
daughters, with their father's and my consent, to the Orphan
House in Georgia."

To a friend in Maryland she writes :

"SIR · In my last I gave you an account of the prodigious and surprising
changes brought about by those worthies, Messrs. Whitfield and Seward.
I well remember six days before their coming hither : I endured a night of
the deepest affliction, far from the least thought that deliverance was so
nigh—on the contrary, poverty stared me in the face in such frightful form
as really drove me distracted.   'Twas a night never to be forgotten—
November 6th, 1739.   My dear husband, aged and weak as he was, could
scarcely lie down to sleep two nights in the week before two or three o'clock
in the morning, and so exhausted with the fatigues and anxieties of the day
that a burning fever was his nightly companion   But clouds and darkness
passed away, and the sun arose once more brightly upon us   Thus, Doctor, you now see such a change wrought in me as nothing less than the
power of God could work , therefore to God be all the glory !   O God !
while thy hand supports me I am safe, and I trust thou wilt never leave nor
forsake me !   With thee, the spring of life remaining, thy presence is eternal day !   I have now, my dear friend, learned the Apostle's lesson, to be
careful for nothing, but in every thing to make my requests known unto
God.   Surely, if there be Heaven upon Earth, it is here with our contentment.   However, the parting with my two daughters for Georgia, is a
struggle to nature ; but I am resigned to it, hoping in three years to receive
them again.   My dear Becky was that same little maid Mr. W——d mentioned in his Philadelphia Journal, Nov. 10, page 123, who requested Mr
Whitfield to take her to Georgia ; and I myself am that person, whom he
mentions, page 125,[b] who had received no such peace of mind and comfort

_____

[b] Mr Whitfield writes "Sunday, November 10th   Read prayers in the morning and dined with the Collector   Preached in the afternoon to a very thronged

for twelve years as God had been pleased to communicate at that time—for which I adore the Divine Goodness, he adds 'The Gospel has taken root in many hearts.' O sir! I wish that I could be the means of bringing you acquainted with this wonderful person: he is, I think, if there can be one upon earth—'an Israelite, indeed, in whom there is no guile.'

"My dear Mr. Bolton having the good fortune to teach a lad the art of reading well, who scarcely knew how to speak before, his father made me a present of Mr Whitfield's portrait, framed in gilt, with many grateful acknowledgments in favor of my husband, beside the usual quarterly payment for his son. This pleased me exceedingly; indeed, I almost idolized the picture. Indeed, all the bounties of Mr. Whitfield and Mr. Seward came unasked, for I abhorred begging or exposing any wants."

Again she writes to the same friend:

"PHILADELPHIA, June 16th, 1740

"DEAR SIR: I must now acquaint you in what an easy, delightful manner Mr. Bolton and I spend our days—in sweet contentment, free from anxious cares and restless nights, which so long disturbed us.

"Our home resembles a neat little chapel, our voices are raised in chanting hymns of praise to the Creator at the dawn of every day and the close of every eve, bespeaking the gladness of our hearts and our joy in our Redeemer and Preserver. Mr. Bolton and I often say to each other that if the rich and great knew our happiness, they would so envy us as to be glad to change conditions, but never would I consent to return to the gay world with all its diversions, cares, fears, and pleasures. Indeed, Doctor, I now live the life I have so long desired."—"Mr. Bolton is engaged almost all day in his school and a part of the evening, so that I am alone great part of the time, however, I often repeat these lines, I learned when very young, of a clergyman—

"'He's still himself when company is gone,
    Too well employed, ever to be alone'

This day fortnight I received news of the death of our worthy friend and benefactor, Mr. Seward, and a melancholy news it was for us."

"March 26th, 1741

"DEAR SIR: This day I received a charming letter from Mr. Whitfield from the Orphan House in Georgia, in which he mentions that he had mar-

congregation. Visited one sick person, and administered the Holy Sacrament to another, who has received no such peace and inward comfort for these twelve years, as God has been pleased to communicate to her soul at this time. Not unto me, O Lord, not unto me, but unto thy name be all the glory. For ever adored be the Divine Goodness, the Gospel has taken root in many hearts." The continuance of the Rev Mr Whitfield's Journal, etc, vol. ii Philadelphia. Printed and sold by B Franklin, in Market street, 1740.

ried my daughter Polly to the worthy James Habersham, Esq. In this marriage I have greatly rejoiced."

"Blessed be God! I am furnished with books of the best and most profound authors, besides my Bible, which I have usually made my daily study, so that I am seldom alone and at a loss for company, as I used to be in Maryland. I now solace myself in converse with the dead, and reap great benefit and delight from their great minds outliving the body. To converse with the spirits of just men made perfect makes me indeed long for that conversation in full fruition, but above all for the sight and blissful enjoyment of the Holy Jesus, who disdained not when upon earth to style us his friends, if we only did the thing he commanded us! Indeed the being separated from all my children is attended with much feeling and concern, but then again I consider these lovely creatures as lent, and I ought not to consider them as my own, so that I can but receive them when time shall be no more in that world of joy and bliss, where, if we only safely arrive, nothing can separate us more! My whole soul desires their temporal and spiritual profit, but as the soul is above the body, so my longing for their eternal welfare is above that of their temporal.

"How this letter may suit your taste I know not, but when I write in spiritual matters, it is as the Spirit gives me utterance; therefore to that Divine Spirit I commend you, beseeching him to have you under his protection, so guiding you in all truth here, that you may not fail of eternal happiness hereafter."

Mr. Whitefield appears to have maintained a correspondence with her until her death. On his return to England, he addresses her as a widow:

' LONDON, Dec. 18th, 1743

"DEAR MRS. BOLTON. Accept a few hasty, though loving lines. I thank you for your last letter, and rejoice to hear our Saviour is so good to you. His name, His nature, is love I prove it to be so, and daily say, 'Grace, grace' I hope yet to see you this side Eternity—when, can not be determined I desire to tarry the Lord's leisure. I heard lately from Georgia; all are well. I hope offenses abroad will cease My dear son lived about four months, and died a fortnight ago. The Lord enabled me and my dear wife to give him up freely. The first-born is a present meet to be made to Jesus! Our all is too little for the Lord Dear Mrs Bolton, I must bid you adieu, since I expect this letter to be called for every moment, and hasten to subscribe myself,

"Your truly affectionate friend,

"brother, and servant in Jesus,

"G. WHITEFIELD

"My dear wife would salute you were she here, but she is in Wales I salute you and yours for her."

The following are a few extracts from Mrs. Bolton's Journal :

"PHILADELPHIA, Sept. 1744.

"Yesterday I received two letters from good Mr Whitfield, both showing his singular esteem and love for myself, which can not but be of infinite satisfaction and comfort to me. But what rejoices me most, is his treading down Satan under his feet, and building up and establishing the kingdom of Christ wherever he goes. In his letter, dated Dec. 12th, 1743, he says : 'There are many fresh openings in England for preaching the everlasting Gospel, and our Lord is pleased to bless me more and more I long to see dear Mr. Habersham and the rest of my family at Savannah. I had letters from them ; all were then well, and blessed beyond expectation I find more and more, dear Mrs. Bolton, that God is a Father of the fatherless, and delights to plead the cause of the widow He never can, he never will, forsake you. I thank him for raising up such friends, above all, I thank him for giving you a contented mind, amidst all your trials at the dear Redeemer's feet. Here, and here only, is my refuge and constant resort ; and that you may always have free access here, is the earnest prayer of your most affectionate friend and servant in Jesus,

"'G. WHITEFIELD.'"

Addressing a friend, she says :

"PHILADELPHIA, Nov 15th, 1744.

"SIR : I am this day fifty-four years old, in the thoughts of which I bow before the Almighty God, saying . 'Few and evil have been the days of the years of my pilgrimage.' How many more await me, I know not, but to reach the age of my much honor'd grandmother, by my mother's side, I shall live to the age of sixty. This month five years ago I was first visited by the Rev Mr. Whitfield in a wonderful manner, and now I have received a letter from him even this day, dated from Mr Smith's, a merchant and a worthy gentleman and Christian in Boston. I can not but admire and wonder at the lovingkindness of the Lord in sending that worthy messenger once more among us. You see, Doctor, I am true as steel. I can not profess a friendship without going through with it, nor drop it upon any occasion, much less a light one, as the manner of the world is, but as constancy, truth, and integrity are gifts from above, so thither I trust my praises will ascend till time shall end with me in a happy eternity I shall no more at present of this godly minister and faithful messenger, but give you the remainder in his own words, which are as follows

"'YORK, Nov. 5th, 1744.

"'DEAR MRS. BOLTON : Tho' I have been absent from you so long, yet I still retain that cordial respect for you which I had given me when God, by his all wise providence, bro't me to Phil^a. first ; this has been still increasing ever since you have been so nearly related to my very dear Mr. Habersham. Pray have you heard from him lately ? I long to hear from him and see him. God willing, the time will now shortly come. I purpose going by land to Georgia, and to call at Phil^a. in the way, where I hope to see you joying in God and rejoicing in God your Saviour. My dear wife will, by divine permission, accompany me. We both salute you most heartily, and all dear friends, praying that you may be filled with all the fulness of God I subscribe myself, dear Mrs. Bolton,

"'Your most affect. friend and serv't,

"'G. WHITEFIELD

"'Pray direct for me to Mr. Smith's, merchant, in Boston.'"

The arrival of her daughter and son-in-law, after five years' absence, is thus noticed :

"I have trusted in the Lord, and been helped. My ever worthy son, Mr Habersham, and my dear Becky arrived safe, and were brought to my chamber, where, for a whole year, I had been confined with illness. Mrs Franklin conducted and introduced them to me in a most tender and civil manner. After apologizing for her long absence from me, and promising to be more attentive in future, she went out and brought in those two long-longed-for-much-loved ones, at which sight my eyes were full. I embraced and kissed the one and then the other. Never had I a greater struggle for life through excess of joy. But what are mortal things? Why are they thus beloved? Don't they each moment fly from us to the grave, where we must follow also, and where there is no remembrance of either joy or grief? But oh! the hope of a future immortality wings the soul, and fills us with life and transport in the assurance of meeting them with our gracious and glorious Redeemer who hath made us more than conquerors through the blood of the everlasting Covenant, to whom be glory for ever. Amen."

While living in this blissful retirement, she writes to her friend :

"PHIL^A., Dec. 15th, 1744.

"To-morrow will be four weeks since I was seized in a most violent manner with death, I should have thought, had I not frequent alarms of this sort, to warn me of my approaching dissolution. I have also been informed of our friend, the good Mr. Whitfield's illness, by which he was in jeopardy of his life, at the same time of my late grievous illness. I am but recovered, as it were, to-day, for which I praise the Lord and hope that I shall ever continue to praise his name, and say by experience with the Psalmist (new version)—

'He that has God his guardian made,
Shall under the Almighty's shade,
Secure and undisturbed abide:
Therefore it is to Him I'll say,
Thou art my fortress and my stay,
My God, in whom I will confide'

"My situation in being placed between the church and Quaker burying-place and in the midst of the new building burying-ground, (so called,) beside the sight of my dear husband's grave and four of my young children lying beside him in my view, I say, all these afford a melancholy prospect, beside the almost daily funerals of acquaintances or strangers, makes this world appear but a theatre of misery! O Heaven! grant that I may be duly prepared to enter eternity, from whence there is no returning; the same that I beg for myself, I beg also for you, and am your unalterable friend,   ANN BOLTON."

June 24th, 1746. "O Jesus! when time shall be swallowed up in eternity, then this corruptible shall be clothed with incorruption, and this mortal shall be covered with immortality. This is what I wait for. Come quickly, dearest Lord! Oh! quickly come, my Saviour!"

The following paragraph closes her journal of eight years:

"God be praised everlastingly for his inestimable riches in Christ! My soul does often mount up above this earth and converse with the holy Jesus, with prophets and apostles, with Philpot, Latimer, Cranmer, Ridley, and all that glorious company of martyrs. Dear Lambert, Hooper, and Bradford, oh! my soul longs to flee away and be at rest with you and all pious and holy souls who have been made perfect through sufferings! Oh! fit me for thy kingdom, dearest Lord, then take me to thyself. Amen."

Her happy spirit took its flight "towards those regions of bliss where there will be no more sighing or sorrow, but all tears shall be wiped from our eyes," Tuesday, May 5th, 1747. Her remains were interred beside those of her beloved husband, in the Arch street cemetery, May 7th.

The following entry, in the Christ Church Register, closes the last account we have of this poor but humble Christian:

"For breaking ground and use of pall—Widow Bolton, 1747—4s. 6d."

ARMS OF JOHN CURTIS, ESQ., OF KENT COUNTY, DELAWARE.

The children of Robert[17] and Ann Bolton:

I. ROBERT BOLTON[18], of whom in Part III., Section II

II. ANN BOLTON, eldest daughter of Robert, born in Market street, Philadelphia, February, 1723, baptized 27th. Married first, in 1739–40, Mr. Wood; secondly, John Mercer, Esq., of Sassafras Neck, Cecil county, Maryland, by whom she had one son, John Mercer, of Chestertown. She was buried on Sassafras Neck. The time of her death is unknown.

III. MARY BOLTON, second daughter of Robert, born in Philadelphia, May 5th, and baptized May 8th, 1724. "She received an excellent education in her native city, and when quite young, was highly complimented for her fine dancing, agreeable manners, and great accomplishments She had been much caressed by the great and gay, but grace contrived a way to awaken her to a sense of her danger; for, reading one day the fifty-seventh Psalm, she found comfort and consolation. In 1739 she accompanied Mr. Whitefield to Savannah, and entered the Orphan House, June, 1740. On the 26th of December, 1740, she was married at Bethesda to James Habersham, Esq., by the Rev. George Whitefield, A.B., Rector of Christ church, Savannah. Mr. Habersham, who was born at Beverley, in the West Riding of York, A.D. 1712, was the first President of the Orphan House, and also President of his Majesty's Council in Georgia from 2d July, 1771, to 11th February, 1772, and in 1744, together with Charles Harris, established the first commercial house in Georgia. The following notice of Mrs. Habersham's death was penned by her bereaved husband:

"Mary, the most beloved wife of James Habersham, dyed fourth day of January, 1763, and, as she was esteemed and honored when living, for her eminent and exemplary virtues, her death was universally regretted, but how much lamented by her bereaved and sorrowful husband and children, words can not express. She was a loving, faithful, and dutiful wife, a tender mother, a kind mistress, a sincere friend, rejoiced in the happiness of all her fellow-mortals, and truly sympathized with the distressed, and is now enjoying the glorious reward reserved for her by her heavenly Father, through 'the all-atoning blood of her dear and precious Redeemer.'"[c]

Her remains were interred in the Habersham vault at Savannah. By her, Mr. Habersham had ten children, three of whom, sons, survived him, and were zealous in the cause of American liberty. Mr. Habersham departed this life at New-Brunswick, New-Jersey, on 28th of August, 1775.

IV. JOHN BOLTON[18], second son of Robert, born in Philadelphia, 20th of March, 1725, baptized 28th of March, and died 21st of May, 1726.

V. JOHN BOLTON[18], third son of Robert, of whom in Part III, Section III.

VI. JOSEPH BOLTON[18], eldest of twin, fourth son of Robert, born in Philadelphia, 20th of June, 1727, baptized 22d, and died 10th October, 1727.

VII. HANNAH BOLTON, third daughter of Robert, and youngest of twin, born 20th of June, baptized June 22d, 1727. Buried at Philadelphia, 28th of April, 1729.

VIII. JOSEPH BOLTON[18], fifth son of Robert, born in Philadelphia, 25th of August, 1728, baptized 2d of September, and died 10th of June, 1729.

IX. REBECCA BOLTON, fourth and youngest daughter of Robert, born at Philadelphia, December 20th, 1729, and baptized the 24th. "As an infant, she exceeded in beauty all her brothers and sisters, (as all who saw her allowed,) and as she was lovely in her infancy, so she continued in her childhood and maturer years. Her fine singing, dancing, sparkling wit, and easy manners, made her the admiration and envy of many, nor was she wanting in beauty, as we have seen; all these charms made her greatly praised in public and in private. Many were the snares surrounding her, but grace got the victory over nature in a most extraordinary manner. She was that same little maid the Rev. George Whitefield mentions in his Philadelphia Journal, November 10th, page 123, who requested him to take her to Georgia."[d] "Rebecca entered

[c] Copied from original in Habersham family Bible

[d] "Soon after, says Mr. Whitefield, (November 10th, 1734,) came a little maid about seven years of age, telling me she heard I took little children to Georgia, and desired me to take her."—*Whitefield's Journal*, 1756, p. 271.

the Orphan House, near Savannah, with her sister Mary, where she remained until February, 1745, when she returned to Philadelphia to assist her aged mother.   On this occasion she was accompanied by her brother-in-law, Mr. Habersham, and upon their arrival in Philadelphia, May 27th, 1745, were conducted to Mrs. Bolton's residence by Mrs. Benjamin Franklin, who introduced them to her in a most tender and civil manner.   After her beloved mother's death, in 1747, she resided in the family of Capt. Grant of Philadelphia, where she was very much esteemed   She survived her mother hardly a year, dying in the bloom of her youth, some time in February, 1748, and was buried in Mr. Grant's family vault on the 7th of March, 1748. So little change did death produce in this lovely girl of nineteen, that her remains were preserved eleven days prior to interment.

SECTION II.

ROBERT BOLTON[18], Esq., eldest son of Robert[17] and Ann Bolton, was born in Market street, Philadelphia, Province of Pennsylvania, Monday, January 1st, 1722, and baptized the 22d of the same month.

He acquired an excellent education in his native city, and at an early age went to Trenton, New-Jersey, where, not succeeding in business to his wishes, he returned to Philadelphia. Though possessed of an amiable temper and good intellectual endowments, he was, for several years, a stranger to religion, being very gay and thoughtless. But it pleased God who separated him from his mother's womb, and called him by his grace, to reveal his Son in him. His pious mother, in her Journal thus records the wonderful change:

"I was under great concern of mind regarding this child Robert; he seemed to be wild, thoughtless, and negligent in the matter of the one thing needful, till the age of about nineteen it pleased God to awaken and instruct him by his Spirit through the preaching of the Rev. George Whitfield. His sermon was upon the prodigal son, delivered upon Society Hill, Philadelphia.[e]

Like his father, he was of a slender and delicate constitution, and early threatened with a pulmonary disease, in consequence of which he travelled to Savannah, Georgia, when about twenty-two years of age, and finding great benefit from the climate, he was induced to become a permanent resident.[f]

----

[e] MSS of Mrs Ann Bolton

[f] Testimony of Miss Anna M McClean, half-sister of Mrs Robert Bolton   Mr. Bolton must have been residing in Philadelphia in 1741, for in the Habersham MSS is a letter from his brother-in-law, Mr. Habersham, addressed to "My Dear brother Rob't Bolton in Philadelphia, 31st August, 1741"

His two younger sisters, Mary and Rebecca, had preceded
him in 1739, having been placed, with their father's and mother's consent, by the Rev George Whitefield, in the Orphan
House or Bethesda College, near Savannah.[g] The affairs of
this institution were now in the care of Mr. James Habersham, who had married the eldest sister Mary in 1740. For
his encouragement the Court of President and Assistants in
Georgia made him the following allotments of land, namely,
in 1748, on the 16th of March, a town lot in Savannah, and
on the 8th of December, 1752, ninety acres of land. In 1755
he purchased a town lot in Hardwicke on the Great Ogeeche
River The following year a lot in the city of Savannah was
granted by the Provincial Government to Robert Bolton and
others in trust for a meeting-house to be erected thereon for
the use of such persons as were professors of the doctrines of
the Church of Scotland, etc. Upon the 4th of July, 1758,
his Majesty King George II. granted to Robert Bolton a lot
in the town of Hardwicke, on the Great Ogechee River, at
the quit-rent of a pepper-corn, in the following manner :

GRANT OF A TOWN LOT IN HARDWICKE

"GEORGE THE SECOND, by the Grace of God, of Great-Britain, France,
and Ireland, King, Defender of the Faith, and so forth, To all to whom these
Presents shall come, greeting . Know ye that we of our special grace, certain knowledge, and mere Motion, have given and granted, and by these
presents, for us, our heirs and successors do give and grant unto Robert
Bolton, his heirs and assigns, all that town lot in the town of Hardwicke in
our Province of Georgia, known by the number eighty-one, bounded as in
and by the certificate hereunto annexed, under the hands of our Surveyors-
General of lands in our said Province may more fully appear, and contains
seventy-six feet and a half in width and one hundred and thirteen feet and a
half in depth To HAVE AND TO HOLD the said town lot hereby granted,
with the appurtenances, together with all timber and trees thereon growing

---

[g] His grandson, Robert Bolton, in giving an account of the family, says " When
Mr Whitefield visited Philadelphia, he became acquainted with my great grandmother, and took a kind interest in them   There are several of his letters to her,
which she has copied into her memoir   Her eldest son, Robert, heard Mr Whitefield preach on Society Hill on the parable of the prodigal, and it was the means
of a total change of his character   Mr Whitefield persuaded the family to give
up to his care my grandfather Robert, then about twenty, and his sister Mary, and
he took them with him to Georgia, where they became part of his family."

or being, ways, waters, paths, passages, privileges, and appurtenances whatsoever, to the lot belonging or in any wise appertaining, unto the said Robert Bolton, his heirs and assigns for ever, in free and common soccage, he
the said Robert Bolton, his heirs or assigns *yielding and paying* for the said
town lot unto us, our heirs and successors, yearly and every year, *One
Pepper-Corn*, if demanded. PROVIDED ALWAYS, and this present grant is
upon condition, nevertheless, that the said Robert Bolton, his heirs or assigns, shall, within three years next after the date of these presents, erect
and build upon the said lot hereby granted one good and sufficient tenant-
able house, with one brick chimney at least, of the dimensions of twenty
feet in length in front and sixteen feet in breadth or depth at least; and if it
shall happen that the said Robert Bolton, his heirs or assigns, shall neglect
to build a house of the dimensions aforesaid, on the lot hereby granted, then
and in that case, the said Robert Bolton, his heirs and assigns, shall forfeit
and pay unto us, our heirs and successors, the sum of *One Pound* sterling
money, yearly and every year, for not building upon the said lot as aforesaid, until such house shall be compleatly finished. And also if the said
Robert Bolton, his heirs or assigns, shall not, within the space of *ten* years
from the date hereof, erect and build an house upon the said lot according to
the dimensions aforesaid, that then the said lot hereby granted (not being
built upon as aforesaid) shall revert to us, our heirs and successors, as fully
and absolutely, to all intents and purposes, as if the same had never been
granted. PROVIDED ALSO, if this Grant shall not be duly registered in the
Register's Office of said Province, within *six* months from the date hereof,
and docquet thereof also entered into the Auditor's Office of the same, (in
case such Establishment shall hereafter take place,) that then this grant
shall be void, anything therein contained to the contrary notwithstanding Given *under the Great Seal of our Province of Georgia* Witness
our Trusty and well beloved Henry Ellis, Esquire, our Lieutenant Governor
and Commander-in-Chief of our said Province, the fourth day of July in the
year of our Lord 1758, and in the thirty-second year of our reign [h]
"Signed by his Honour the Governour in Council
"HENRY ELLIS.
"CHAS. WATSON, D C C "

"The following lotts of land were laid out unto Robert
Bolton, and allowed upon his claim before his Excellency the
Governor in Council the 28th day of July, 1775:" "A town
lott in Savannah, No. 3, in the third Tything Anson Ward,
containing sixty feet in width and ninety feet in length; and

[h] Registered in the Register's Office, 24th July, 1758, Book A, p 666 This
property was bequeathed by Robt Bolton, Sen, in 1786, to Robt Bolton, Jr, and
his heirs. Taxes were paid for it in 1823 as the property of Robert Bolton of
Savannah

also a garden lott, containing five acres, No. 147, situate east of the Town, with the farm lott thereunto belonging, containing forty-five acres," &c., "situate in the third tything Anson Ward, and known by the number 8."¹

Upon the 3d of November, 1761, his Majesty King George the Third granted to Robert Bolton and his heirs "lot number 4 in Savannah, in the parish of Christ church, in the third tything Anson Ward, in consideration of eighteen pounds sterling money of Georgia."ᴶ

In 1764 he applied for the office of Post-Master of the Province of Georgia. The following is a copy of the letter written by his brother-in-law, the Hon. James Habersham, Secretary of the Province, to Benjamin Franklin of Philadelphia in this behalf:

"To Benjamin Franklin, Esq., in Philadelphia.

"Savannah in Georgia, 14 July, 1764.

"Sir: Last fall I made my two sons a visit at New-Jersey College, and at the same time embraced the opportunity of paying my respects to my friends in Philadelphia, among whom I waited on Mrs. Franklin, but was deprived the pleasure of seeing you, as they informed me you were on your way from Boston and met with an unlucky accident, which I hope you have entirely recovered from. My brother-in-law, Mr. Robert Bolton, is the bearer of this. He goes to visit his native place and his relations, after being settled here near twenty years. He has some thoughts of setting up a post between this and Charlestown, which, if he can meet with success, must be of public utility. To this end he tells me he has been advised by our worthy Governor to get an appointment from the Post-Master General, and as I suppose it may be in your power to constitute him Post-Master of this Province, your doing so would lay me and him under great obligations. I am sensible, I have no pretentions, to ask this favour from the slender acquaintance I have with you, but I will venture to say, from many years' experience, that if you should be pleased to confer any trust on Mr. Bolton, you will find him an honest, prudent, and punctual man. He has lately buried an excellent wife, and is left with seven fine children, whom he has hitherto supported and brought up reputably,

---

¹ Henry Yong, Surveyor Genl's certificate, dated 13th January, 1757. This property was bequeathed by Robt Bolton, Sen., in 1786, to his son Robert Bolton, Jr., and his heirs.

ᴶ Memorial Regᵈ in Auditor's Office, Book A, fol 258. This property was first bequeathed by Robt. Bolton, Sen., in 1786, to his son Robert, who, by will, conveyed it to his daughter Ann in 1802.

and as his trade has lately declined, any additional means of getting him money, must greatly assist him.

"I need say nothing in regard to his family connexions in Pennsylvania, as they must be better known to you than to me. You will please to excuse the freedom I have taken, and if in my power, I shall be pleased with an opportunity of showing that I am, with great truth, dear sir,

"Your most obed , h'ble servant,

"JAMES HABERSHAM

"Please make my respects acceptable to Mrs. Franklin."[k]

The same year "Robert Bolton, Esq., was appointed first Post-Master of Savannah, by Benjamin Barron, Esq., Post-Master General of the Southern District of America."[l]

Mr. Bolton, greatly promoted the cause of Christ in Savannah, and had the Gaius-like spirit of loving to entertain good men, remembering the wise man's injunction : "Thine own friend, and thy father's friend, forsake not." (Prov. 27 : 10) He treated the Rev. George Whitefield with great hospitality, and, together with his brother-in-law, Mr. Habersham, encouraged him in his missionary work.[m] The history of Mr. Whitefield's settlement in Georgia was this: " Urged by the letters of Wesley, (says Bishop Stevens,) the Rev. George Whitefield resolved to answer his call for help, and go over to his assistance in Georgia. This young gentleman, born in an inn, of humble yet worthy parents, was early left fatherless, and thrown upon resources so slender as scarcely to give him support. At school his talents for oratory were very nearly turned towards the drama; but, at the age of fourteen, he persuaded his mother to take him from school, and putting on his 'blue apron, washed mops and cleaned gowns ' in his mother's tavern. Learning, accidentally, from a Pembroke servitor, that, by aid of such a menial office, he could go through College with small means, and having already made himself a good scholar in the classics, he hastened, when eigh-

---

[k] MSS. of Habersham family.

[l] Census of the city of Savannah, etc , by Joseph Bancroft, 1848

[m] A niece of Mr. Bolton's informed the author "that Mr. Whitefield generally made his home at Mr Habersham's, but sometimes at Mr Bolton's, and that he was remarkably cheerful and agreeable in company, always having appropriate anecdotes at command."

teen years of age, to Oxford, and by the aid of £10, borrowed from a friend to defray the expense of entering, he was admitted as a servitor in Pembroke College.

"Soon drawn towards the religious club, of which the Wesleys were leaders, he found in their society just what his earnest and seeking heart desired, and he cast in his lot among them. preferring to endure their worldly reproach if he might partake of their heavenly joy.

"Recommended to the notice and benefactions of Sir John Philips, Bart., one of the Trustees for Georgia, and winning by his general character the favour of the good Doctor Benson, Bishop of Gloncester, he was by that prelate ordained, 20th of June, 1736, at the age of twenty-one, to the office of Deacon in the Church of England.

"A profitable curacy in London, with the great preferment which his talents opened before him, he refused; and offering himself to the Trustees as a missionary to Georgia, was, on December 21st, 1737, when he had just completed his twenty-second year, accepted.

"He left London December 28th, 1737, after administering the Sacrament at St. Dunstan, where 'the tears of the communicants mingled with the cup,' and in the strength of God as a poor pilgrim, went on board the *Whittaker*, to embark for Georgia He had with him, however, one friend, Mr. James Habersham, whom he affectionately styles his 'dear fellow-traveller,' who, relinquishing the kind offers of friends in England, and in opposition to the views of his uncle and guardian, resolved to cast in his lot among the people where Whitefield was to labor.

"The passage to Gibraltar, whither they were bound, to take in two companies, which had been detailed as part of General Oglethorpe's regiment, to Georgia, was one of peril; but the kindness they received at that military stronghold made ample amends for the roughness of the voyage. He here wrote to the Trustees, inquiring of them if they desired any change in his plans, since Wesley had returned to England; for it so happened that Whitefield had only sailed from the Downs to Georgia, in the *Whittaker*, the day before Wesley arrived there from Georgia in the *Samuel*. They, in reply, commissioned him to 'perform all religious offices as deacon of the Church of England, in Savannah and Frederica.' Having taken in their complement of men, the *Whittaker* sailed in March for Georgia.

"The two friends landed in Savannah on the evening of Sunday, 7th of May, and were warmly welcomed by Mr. Delamotte, the catechist, and the authorities of the town. His induction to Georgia was a severe illness, and when he recovered, the desolate condition of the colony forced itself upon him 'However,' he remarked, 'that rendered what I had brought over from my friends (he had collected £300 for the poor in Georgia) more acceptable to the poor inhabitants, and gave me an ocular demonstration, which was what I wanted when the hint was given of the great necessity and promising utility of a future Orphan House, which I now determined, by the Divine assistance, to get about in earnest.' That no time might be lost in carrying into effect this scheme, originally suggested by Charles Wesley and General Oglethorpe, after the pattern adopted by the venerable Professor Francke at Halle, and resolved upon before he left England, it was determined by Whitefield and Habersham, that the latter should at once open a school for children eligible to such an institution, and bring them under a regular course of tuition and discipline, while the former proceeded on a tour for the collection of funds to carry out the plan.

"He remained in Georgia until August, visiting the various settlements, laboring in his clerical duties with great diligence, and endearing himself to his parishioners by his piety, generosity, and zeal.

"'What I have most at heart,' he writes, 'is the building an Orphan House, which, I trust, will be effected at my return to England.'

"He reached England, after a most uncomfortable passage, in the beginning of December, having been absent nearly one year. As yet, he was only in Deacons' orders; and to obtain priest's ordination was one of the motives of his return. This he received from Dr. Benson, Bishop of Gloucester, January 12th, 1739; the Trustees having previously, in anticipation of his admission to the priesthood, appointed him missionary of

Christ church in Savannah. They also gave him five hundred acres of land on which to erect his Orphan House. In appointing him to Savannah, they had annexed to the office the salary of £50, but he acquainted the Common Council in person that he declined the acceptance of any salary as a minister at Savannah or for the management of the Orphan House in Georgia. In his multifarious labors in England, he did not forget the Orphan House, but generally took up collections for it, so that by August, 1739, having obtained over £1000 for that purpose, he embarked for Georgia via Philadelphia."[n] It was during his stay in Philadelphia that he first became acquainted with Mr. Bolton's parents, (Robert and Ann Bolton,) and their two daughters, Mary and Rebecca. The two latter he forwarded to the Orphan House in the sloop *Savannah*, which sailed immediately after his leaving Philadelphia.[o] "Travelling" from Philadelphia "overland," Mr. Whitefield "reached Savannah on the 11th of January, 1740,[p] and found that his faithful coadjutor, Habersham, had selected the five hundred acres grant, about nine miles from town, being the best place he had seen for the Orphan House, and had begun to collect materials, and erected a dwelling. On the 25th of March, 1740, he laid the first brick of the central building, and named the institution 'Bethesda,' praying that it might ever prove to the orphans what its name imported, 'A House of Mercy.' "[q] It was in behalf of this institution that he began circuit preaching, both in America and England ; and it was not until churches were refused him that he preached out of doors. "The journeys and voyages of this indefatigable minister amount to a number almost incredible. He has stated in his memorandum book, that 'from the time of his ordination to a period embracing thirty-four years, he preached upwards of eighteen thousand sermons, crossed the Atlantic seven times, travelled thousands of miles both in Britain and

[n] Stevens' *Hist of Georgia*, vol. i pp. 343–50.

[o] In his Journal, Mr. Whitefield observes: "Sloop *Savannah*, bought by Mr Seward, in which I left orders for my family to set sail immediately after my leaving Philadelphia, Nov. 29th, Thursday "

[p] In his Journal he says he arrived in Savannah, Jan'y 9th, 1739–40

[q] Stevens' *Hist of Georgia*, vol. i. p. 351

America,' and when his strength was failing, he put himself on what he termed 'short allowance,' namely, preaching only once in every day of the week, and three times on the Sabbath! The death of this eminent and most useful servant of God was sudden, having been produced by a cold caught while preaching at Portsmouth, in New-Hampshire, and followed by a severe attack of asthma, which put a period to the life and labors of one of the most devoted and successful ministers of Christ since the days of the Apostles."[r] He expired at Newburyport, Massachusetts, on the thirtieth of September, 1770, aged fifty-six.

Mr. Bolton was also a zealous friend of the excellent Cornelius Winter, who had come out to Georgia in Whitefield's train as a catechist to the negroes of the Rev. Bartholomew Zouberbuhler, the former rector of Savannah, lately deceased, who, though a clergyman and a good man, had thought it nothing strange to possess slaves.[s] By his will, however, he had provided for their religious instruction. This was the post Mr. Winter had come out to occupy; but he was little aware of the opposition he was to encounter in this philanthropic enterprise. In Mr. Winter's difficulty Mr. Bolton not only received him under his roof, but encouraged him in his efforts to do good. He says in one of his letters to Mr. Jay "We arrived at Charlestown on the 30th of November, where we stayed ten days. On our way from that place we stopped at a plantation called Port Royal, where we were most truly respected and entertained, and safely arrived at Savannah on the evening of December 14th."[t] "Continually under the Divine protection, we may enjoy perfect peace; and being devoted to the will of God, he will take possession of the mind and keep it. What is now the matter of observation, was the

---

[r] Appleton's *Cyclopedia of Biography*

[s] "Mr Whitefield, as early as 1741, gave that body (the Trustees) a most practical lesson on his views, by planting a portion of his land in Carolina, which he called 'Providence,' with negro labor, bought and paid for as his own slaves, with the design of thereby supporting his Orphan House at Bethesda in Georgia" (Stevens' *Hist of Georgia*, vol i. p. 309.)

[t] *Autobiography of Rev Wm. Jay*, vol. i. p 105 Published by Carter & Brothers, New-York 1855

matter of experience, when sitting for a little while alone in
the canoe, where I was desired to remain, at the bottom of
Savannah-bluff the guardian of our property, while Messrs.
Whitfield, Wright, and Smith ascended to the town. It was
dark before I was disengaged and escorted to Mr. Habersham's
house, where Mr. Whitfield had preceded me. Mr. Habersham met me at the door, embraced me in his arms, saying:
'I will be your friend if nobody else will.' It being his first
salute, I supposed it was in consequence of something previously said by the company, and by the tenor of the conversation which went forward, I understood that I was but an
unexpected guest. Mr. Habersham, slapping me upon the
knee, repeated: 'I will be your friend if nobody else will; I
will stand by you; you shall instruct my negroes, whoever
else refuses you.' This brought to my recollection instantly
what Mr. Whitfield said on board ship, namely: 'That I
might be thankful if I had as many to preach to as his bed-
cabin would hold, and must not wonder if, for attempting to
instruct the negroes, I were whipped off the plantation.'
However, most of Mr. Zuberbuhler's executors, the gentlemen into whose service I was entering, saw me, and all except
two behaved to me in a very respectful manner. The first
night I lodged in Mr. Habersham's house; the next day I was
fixed at a Mr. Bolton's. The room appointed for me had no
fire-place in it, and the weather becoming very cold, I was
put to much inconvenience, but was determined I would not
make my company cheap, whatever I might suffer; and that
whatever reserve might be in my conduct, it should be entirely with a view to the glory of God. It was well in the
end I adopted and maintained this resolution. Previous to
my settlement, I spent some days with Mr. Whitfield at the
Orphan House, and by the time I returned to Savannah, the
report of my design in coming into the Province, was noised
abroad. Some of the more sensible negroes facetiously said
they were too wicked to be made good now. A few had their
expectations raised by my coming, and seemed pleased with
my errand. The white people in general conceived that
I came there because I could not live in England, and I
scarcely ventured out without hearing one and another

say, with the accent of contempt: 'There goes the negro parson.'

"Perceiving that Mr. Bolton, at whose house my residence was fixed, was a serious man, I told him I longed to begin my mission in some way. I offered to be his chaplain, and asked him if he would allow me to open a public exposition in his house. He generously consented; and notice being given of my design, numbers both of white and black came, and I opened with Romans 1 : 15 : 'I am ready to preach the Gospel to you.' The word was well received by the serious part of the audience, and perhaps would have been by the others, if I had not particularly discovered myself attached to the more sensible negroes, and given them to understand they were the subjects of my ministry. I continued to preach in Mr. Bolton's house to white and black all the time, I stayed in Savannah, once or twice a week, as it was most convenient to me, and on the Sabbath day evenings. This gave great offense, and the Rev. Mr. Zubly, the Presbyterian minister, did not a little oppose it. I applied for the use of the old Lutheran church, which stood unoccupied, and offered any moderate rent the proprietors should require for the use of it, but it was refused merely because I preached to and aimed at instructing the negroes. All were up in arms against me, many threatened me if I presumed to come into their plantation. A motion was made in the council to consider me as a nuisance to the province, and as such to silence me, but they could not carry the motion. However, time and circumspection retrieved my reputation in some degree. The house I lodged in abounded with company, particularly at the sitting of the Assembly. I generally endeavored to be affable but not forward, conversant but not loquacious; short in my sittings after meals and constantly in my study. I was generally indulged with much liberty in family prayer, mornings and evenings, and frequently dropped a short pertinent hint from one or two verses out of the portion I read. This gained attention, and by degrees I acquired credit, being mostly reproached by persons who knew the least of me." " I was not long before I was introduced to my immediate charge, that is, the negroes upon the late Rev. Mr. Zuberbuhler's plantation, among whom I was to reside as soon as the house was put in proper condition for my residence." "The following Lord's day I went up for the first time to introduce divine worship among them; but it is impossible to describe the scene, nor can any person or stranger to it conceive it. Mr. Bolton, my host, bore me company to give me countenance and to assist me to sing. Two or three overseers from the neighboring plantations, with the person in the same capacity on the spot, men of a similar cast with the Smithfield drovers, were all the white people I had present. Some negroes from the neighboring plantations came, and I opened with as plain an exhortation as I possibly could, but felt it was like shooting darts against a stone wall. I prayed, read the lessons for the day, and used a very small part of the liturgy, namely, the Confession, the Lord's prayer, and the Creed; but the greatest part of my poor congregation were either asleep or making some of them figures on the wainscoat, or playing with their fingers, or eating potatoes, or talking with each other. This was very discouraging, but I thought I must get through it as well as I could. My intended plan was, if I had settled with them, to have attempted to make them rational in order to make them capable of understanding my addresses, and to have begun with them as children, teaching them the alphabet, etc. But knowing I must come home for ordination, and my house not being ready for me, I could only design the plan without putting it forward till after my return.

"I visited the Orphan House as often as possible, and was in perfect love and harmony with the family. Death made a sad inroad among them in a very little time; but the affliction was completed by the death of Mr. Whitfield. He left Georgia to go on his northern tour the latter end of April, and while his return was anticipated and supposed to be near, his removal was announced. It was opened to me by Mr. Habersham, who was much affected with it. It may be supposed I could not be insensible; as soon as I heard it I retreated to pray and pour out my soul to God. I continued in one steady tract, desirous to be fully qualified for my office and vigorously enter upon it in its full extent, which I could not without episcopal ordination.[u] I indulged the idea of a speedy return to England, and consulted Mr. Habersham upon the expediency of it. He, and all with whom he consulted upon the subject, saw it in the same light. For what end I was permitted to go to America, and why prevented from settling there, is among the secrets of the Almighty. He directs our steps. It is not for us to demand the reason of his conduct, but to submit to his will," etc.[v]

Upon his return to England, and after the refusal of the Bishop of London to ordain him, he thus writes to his friend :

"To ROBERT BOLTON, ESQ., SAVANNAH

"DEAR SIR : Yours of June the 30th gave me inexpressible pleasure, and I am infinitely obliged to you for the candidness of your judgment and the sincerity of your friendship, which, though it does not divest me of an affectionate concern for the poor people of my late charge, considerably relieves me of an uneasiness, lest my not returning should be misconstrued to be occasioned by an unsettled mind, and thereby the glorious Gospel should be eclipsed in the eyes of any who before had formed a favorable opinion of it. It is true, dear sir, the bounds of our habitation are fixed, and therefore every disappointment our schemes meet with should be resolved into the will of God. I had laid a large plan, and was in hopes bond and free would have received an advantage it was designed to afford, and had I been favored by Divine Providence to make trial of, or succeeded in it, the very sufficient emolument the worthy trust conferred upon me would have been no more to *me* than I now enjoy in a station which makes me an entire dependent upon Providence, without the least obligation by any kind of contract from any man. I only mention this to assure you, you are right in your persuasion. *Indeed I had no loaves and fishes in view ;* though the Bishop of London was so ungenerous as to reflect on me for receiving so large a salary. Let the good gentlemen you mention rejoice without a rival. I will not say I wish them an increase of it, because it is only like the joy of the drunkard, the materials of which it is made will serve to make the reflection more exquisite in the day when God shall prove himself no respecter of persons. Had I returned to you, I should certainly have set my face like a flint, and by the grace of God persevered till the issue of

---

[u] The Rev. Bartholomew Zouberbuhler, minister and rector of Christ church parish for twenty-one years, departed this life the 11th of December A D 1766, aged forty-six years, having bequeathed the greater part of his estate to the purpose of promoting Christianity in the Province of Georgia. In his will he provided for the support of a minister to instruct his negroes, but enjoining that the person employed should be a clergyman

[v] *Memoir of Rev Cornelius Winter   Works of Rev Wm Jay,* Letter x. p 69. G A Bartlett   London   1843

my endeavors had given conviction to my greatest opponents The inhabitants of the woods are certainly to be pitied on account of their ignorant and benighted state; but I don't see how it may be remedied at present Good Lady H—— told me the Bishop of London would ordain two of her students upon condition they should be confined to the Orphan House, which no thinking man who knows anything of the state of affairs in Georgia would submit to; and as the way seems to be hedged up for ministers in the Establishment, I pray the Lord to raise up people of some other denomination to espouse his injured cause, and carry on his despised work.

"At present, the conduct of our dignitaries is dreadful and affecting; and *what they think*—if they do think at all—must be left for some future day to determine I have not seen Dr Franklin since I last wrote to you, and have reason to think the whole affair is entirely at an end. I can not omit my repeated thanks for every personal token of your friendship, which, considering myself a mere stranger, and the out-of-the-way and unacceptable sphere I have been and am now engaged in, is great indeed; and though I should never see you any more, has so deeply impressed your eternal interest on my heart, that I shall consider myself under an indissoluble obligation to remember you in my nearest accesses to the throne of grace. There, dear sir, may you, midst all the hurry of business and the many avocations of a mercantile life, constantly resort in quest of the Gospel pearl of great price; and when the mammon of unrighteousness shall fail to afford any longer support, may its unsearchable riches give you a kind reception into the everlasting habitations I am very glad to hear all your little ones are well Oh! that, as they grow up, they may be made acquainted with the best things! In hopes the kind Colonel is living, I have dropped him a line I am, my dear sir, yours, &c.

"LONDON, ——, ——"[w]

After Mr. Winter's return to England, Mr. Bolton thus writes to him:

"SAVANNAH IN GEORGIA, Feb'y 16th, 1771

"DEAR MR WINTER. The favorable opportunity of Capt. Watts of Witby seems to awake my sluggish pen to its performance of promise to write you a few lines, by whom goes passenger Jamey, that lived with Mrs. Stirk

"Our dear friend, Mr. William Gibbons, departed in seeming much peace on Sunday last, after ten days' illness. There are now three numerous families in your intended neighborhood bereaved of their heads, which is very affecting—may the Lord comfort and support them My wife was assisting William as long as he lived with her good nursing. We purpose visiting the family this evening. They all seem to long for your coming again, as also does many of your poor negroes. Mr and Mrs Mauve are well, as also my

---

[w] *Mem of Rev. Cornelius Winter*, by Rev. William Jay, p. 421. G A. Bartlett, London 1843.

sons and daughters and their respective families, and Mr. Bryans and Foxes and all your Ogechee friends, who have bought the former Tavern there for a meeting house for forty pound, generous Mr. Bourguin having given the other thirty pound for that good purpose. Mr. Zubly is one of the bond-men, but you have a majority of friends to open the doors of said house. He is also executor to Wm. Gibbons' estate—pitty Our Bethesda friends are all well, except Mr Robt. Wright, still poorly. Reverend Mr Allington gone to settle at Pond Pond in Carolina." "I hope ere now God hath suc-ceeded your endeavors for Holy Orders, and hath laid his hand upon you and blessed you. May you go on and prosper, and may He also bless you in a suitable companion and help mate, and return you to us laden with the Gospel of Peace. Mr. Langworthy is returned to his charge at Bethesda, and has already six scholars and boarders. May God continue to bless that institution. There is now great want of two schoolmasters here, as Mr. Seymour, I am told, is going home for orders, and has sold his house.

"My wife and children join in sincere love to you and yours—pray for us. Wee often think, pray for, and talk of you.

"I intend directing this for you to the care of my dear nephew, Joseph Habersham, whom I wish a line from. Please tender our kind love to him, as also the worthy Mr. Knox, Mr. and Mrs. Dixon, if she is not gone to Heaven, and accept all our joynt love and thanks for all favors.

"From the pen of,

"Reverend Sir,

"Your friend and h'ble servant,

"ROBT BOLTON "ˣ

But, though impatiently expected at Savannah, Mr. Winter was destined never to return. "This happiness, (he states in a letter to a friend,) I am obliged to say, the Bishop of Lon-don most unkindly and most ungenerously deprived me of, though I sought it at the hazard of my life."ʸ

The following letter, from Mr. Bolton, shows the unabated interest Mr. Winter still felt in the preaching of the Gospel at Savannah and the work at Bethesda:

"SAVANNAH, Feb'y 11th, 1773

"MY DEAR FRIEND:

"I received your kind favor by Mr. Cosson at the President's house, at which time I gave them a plain hearty welcome to Georgia, and gave them also a general invitation to my house.

"Three other young gentlemen arrived here via Charlestown two days past, and yesterday I sent them to Bethesda I know not whether they are

---

ˣ Copy of original letter in the author's possession.

ʸ Rev. William Jay's *Life of Winter*, p 216.

any of them ministers or not. There is a few days past a young English minister, via the northward, preaches every evening at our meeting. Some say a Wesley man, but he is zealous in a good cause, and gives a general satisfaction, and is the cause of a crowded meeting-house, and I readily comply with your desire of encouraging Gospel Preachers except they be dumb orators. I heartily wish with you Bethesda may arise out of the ashes and shake off her dust, arise and shine   I rejoice to hear of your welfare and well doing, may God continue to bless your chearfull labors with success. This is the second letter I have received from you, accept my poor single return but hearty thanks   My wife and family are favored with recovery from their late disorder, and desire kindly to be remembered to you   Mr. and Mrs. Mauve are well. Our Governor is just arrived, which obliges me hastily to conclude myself,

"Dear sir,

"Your friend and h'ble servant,

"ROBERT BOLTON."[z]

The following notice of Mr. Winter's death appeared in the *Evangelical Magazine* for February, 1808 · " We have to announce the death of another distinguished servant of God. Sunday evening, January tenth, gently expired the Rev. *Cornelius Winter*. He has been long known and highly honored in the religious world, as a man of the most unblemished reputation and exemplary piety, innocence, benevolence, and kindness."

It was a singular circumstance that Mr. Winter afterwards educated the Rev. William Jay of Bath, England, for the ministry, whose son-in-law was himself the grandson of Robert Bolton of Savannah.

At a meeting of the freeholders and inhabitants of the Parish of Christ church, held at Savannah, on the 20th of April, 1772, Robert Bolton was appointed one of the five Commissioners of the Work-house. On the 6th of October of that year, King George III. granted to Robert Bolton a town lot in Brunswick, and upon the 27th of August, 1774, the Governor in Council granted him a tract consisting of five hundred and fifty acres of land in St. Paul's Parish.

Mr. Bolton does not appear to have taken a very prominent part at the first commencement of the difficulties between Great Britain and her colonies, but no sooner were active

---

[z] Copied from the original letter in the author's possession

measures begun, than, fearing an open rebellion against the parent state, and consequently among themselves, we find both his brother-in-law (Mr. Habersham) and himself with many others, entering their public dissent against certain resolutions passed at what was called " a general meeting of the inhabitants of Georgia, to consider the state of the Colonies, assembled at Savannah on the 10th of August, 1774 "[a] But notwithstanding he was favorably disposed to the mother state, he was by no means insensible to the rights of the Colonies, for he lamented to see that by the imposition of internal taxes the colonists were deprived of privileges which they believed to be their indubitable right. As soon, therefore, as hostilities actually commenced, he at once espoused the cause of the latter. He used to relate that, on one occasion, during a sharp skirmish near Savannah, just as he was about to present his musket to fire, a ball shot by the enemy was driven directly into the barrel, and with such force as to completely disable him from discharging it. When Count D'Estaing and General Lincoln attempted to recover Savannah from the British under Major-General Prevost, in October, 1779, his house in Anson Square suffered some damage from the cannonade and bombardment, and being in feeble health at the time, his family were compelled to remove him to the cellar for safety.

His name does not appear in the disqualifying act passed by the Royal Government on the 6th of July, 1780 But on his refusing to appear as a grand-juror at the Court of Sessions, the same year, the following order was issued:

" GEORGIA. By His Majesty's Court of Sessions of Oyer and Terminer and General Gaol Delivery, holden at Savannah the 13th, 14th, 15th, 16th, and 17th days of June, 1780,

" *Whereas* Jacob Behler of St. Matthew's parish, &c, and Robert Bolton of Savannah, saddler, were severally drawn by ballot and summoned to appear as Grand Jurors at this Court, (as it is said,) but they, Jacob Behler," &c, "and Robert Bolton did respectively neglect to appear at this Court, it is therefore ordered, that they shall be severally fined in a sum not exceeding £8 sterling, and that a capias do issue out against each of them, &c.

" Dated in Court the 17th June in the year of our Lord 1780. By the Court,   JOHN SIMPSON, P. & C.C.[b]
" Crown Office, 5th July, 1780."

---

[a] *Hist Coll of Geo* By Rev. Geo. White, M.A , pp 45, 48, 49.
[b] Copied from original file of newspapers in possession of Georgia Hist. Society.

On the 11th of July, 1783, Savannah was formally given up by the British to the Americans. Soon after this event Mr. Bolton retired to White Bluff, Vernonburgh, about four miles from Savannah, where he was universally esteemed, and gained much honor by his upright conduct as a Justice of the Peace. He was familiarly called "the peace-maker" by his neighbors; and one who knew him intimately, has left us this testimony: "That a better man never lived." On the 3d of May, 1787, he was chosen, with others, to receive the returns of all taxable property for White Bluff. The following entry occurs in the parochial records of Christ church, Savannah:

"25th of July, 1787. Dr. Cash to Robert Bolton, ditto rent of half a pew No. 13, £2.14. Contra, Cr. 25 July. By cash paid do., per order on Mr. Bolton."

He survived the founder of Georgia, (General Oglethorpe,) four years, dying at White Bluff, on Monday, May fourth, 1789, in the sixty-seventh year of his age. His remains were brought to Savannah, and interred in the Habersham family vault in the general burying-ground, but there is no memorial of him. The following notice of his death appeared in the *Georgia Gazette* for Thursday, May 7th, 1789:

"Savannah, May 7th. On Monday last died at White Bluff, Robert Bolton, Esq., aged sixty-seven years, more than forty of which he had resided in this country. It may be truly said that he died, as he had lived, the cheerful Christian, meeting death with a fortitude and resignation that a virtuous life and a well-grounded hope of happiness hereafter naturally inspire."

His niece, the late Mrs. Ann Booth of Philadelphia, who had a perfect recollection of him, says, that he was of middling stature, fair complexion, and resembled her brother, the late Curtis Bolton, of New-York, in a remarkable degree.

His Last Will and Testament bears date, Savannah, 24th of July, 1786, and was proved the 22d of May, 1789.

THE LAST WILL AND TESTAMENT OF ROBERT BOLTON, Sen , OF SAVANNAH.

This is the last Will and Testament of me, Robert Bolton, Sen⁣ʳ , Esqʳ , in Savannah, State of Georgia, made this Twenty-fourth day of July, in the year of our Lord One Thousand Seven Hundred and Eighty-six. Being weak of body, but of sound and disposing memory and understanding.

First, I commit my Spirit to God who gave it, and my body to the Dust to be decently interred; and my Funeral charges I desire may not exceed Seven Pounds Sterling, and the Estate with which it hath pleased God to bless me, I give, devise, bequeath, and dispose of as follows:

First, I will that all my just debts be paid and discharged as soon after my decease as possible

Then I give and devise unto my dutiful and affectionate Son, Robert Bolton, Jun , all that my Town Lott in Savannah, Number four, in the third Tything Anson's Ward, with all the Improvements on Said Lott to him, my said Son Robert, his heirs and assigns forever. And I also bequeath unto my said Son Robert all that forty-five acre Lott with the improvements thereon, situated in Hamsted, four miles from Savannah, and between the High gate & White Bluff roads, to him my said Son Robert, his heirs & assigns forever. I also bequeath to my said Son Robert and his Heirs and assigns forever, all that Tract of Land containing Five Hundred & fifty acres of Land in the Parish of St. Paul, agreeable to the grant now in possession of my said Son. I also bequeath to my said Son a Town Lott in Brunswick, Number One hundred and Seventy-Two. Also one Town Lott in Hardwick, Number Eighty One. I also bequeath to my Son Robert my Negro man named Quash, the whole of the said bequeath I give to him my said Son Robert and his Heirs and assigns forever. I Bequeath to my dutiful and affectionate Daughter Rebecca Newell, all my Town Lott in Savannah, known by the Number Three with the improvements thereon. Also my Negro Man named Peter, which I devise to her & for her use forever. I Bequeath to my Grandson, Thomas Newell, Junʳ, One Town Lott in Sunbury, known by the Number Two Hundred & fifty Seven, to him & his Heirs forever. I bequeath to my Grandson, Robert Newell, Junʳ, and his heirs forever One Town Lott in Sunbury, known by the number Two hundred and fifty eight

I bequeath to my dutiful and affectionate daughter Ann Adams my Negro woman Precilla with her daughter Affee, with their increase for her and her heirs forever.

I bequeath to my dear and affectionate wife, for her remarkable good to my children and myself, My Negro woman Bella, with all her children, namely, Hannah, Eve, & Luesa Also all my stock of Cattle except Two Cows called old and young Blakeley, which I devise to my Son Robert, and one Cow & Calf to Rebecca Teaveaux. I also devise to my dear wife, all my Household Furniture & my Horse & Riding chair, the whole of which I bequeath to my dear wife, is for her use during her natural life, and at her death the whole to be divided amongst my children equally.

I desire that my adopted orphan child Rebecca Teaveaux shall be maintained by my dear wife as long as my wife shall think proper to keep her, and then it's my desire that my dear Daughter Rebecca Newell do take charge of her and have her educated to read and write plain, and keep her in the character of a Handmaid untill she arrives at the age of sixteen years. I devise to my Grandson Nathaniel Adams, Junr, my Silver watch. I devise to my afflicted Neighbour John Warnock such of my old wearing apparel as my executors shall think proper to give, and that my executors shall pay to John Warnock Twenty Shillings per annum during his natural Life, to be paid out of my Estate not before bequeathed. I devise to my neighbour Jacob Ties one of my best Suit of Clothes.

Lastly, I desire that the residue of my Estate not before disposed of shall be sold by my Executors to the best advantage, and after paying my just debts, demands, & Legacies, then the remainder to be equally divided among my children.

Finally, I nominate, constitute, and appoint my well beloved Son Robert Bolton, Junr, Merchant in Savannah, and my kind & affectionate Son-in-law Nathaniel Adams of White Bluff, Planter, my Lawful Executors, and my dear wife to be my Executrix of this my last Will & Testament. And in Testimony whereof I have hereunto set my hand and seal, and published the same as such the Day & Year First above written.

Robt Bolton Senr

Signed, sealed, published, and declared by the said Testator to be and contain his last Will and Testament, in the presence of us and attested by us in his presence.   JOHN HAMILTON,
            JOHN RICHARDS,
            JOHN HEWELL.

GEORGIA :

Before me, James Whitefield, Register of Probate for the County Chatham, in the state aforesaid, Personally appeared John Hamilton, one of the Subscribing Witnesses to the within Last Will & Testament of Robert Bolton, Senior, Deceased, who, being sworn on the Holy Evangelist of Almighty God, maketh oath that he was present and did see the said Testator sign, seal, publish, pronounce, and declare the same to be and contain his Last Will and Testament, and that he was of sound and disposing mind, memory, & understanding to the best of this Deponent's knowledge at the execution thereof, and that he, the Deponent, together with John Richards and John Hewell, since deceased, subscribed their names as witnesses thereto at the request and in the presence of the said Testator, and in each other's presence.   (Copy.)   JOHN HAMILTON.[c]

Sworn this 22d May, 1789.

    J. WHITEFIELD, R. P. C. C.

---

[c] Registry Office of Wills, Savannah.

SCHEDULE OF APPRAISEMENT OF THE PERSONAL PROPERTY BELONGING TO THE ESTATE OF ROBERT BOLTON, SENR, DECD, JULY 29TH, 1789.

	£	s	d
Negro man Peter	50	0	0
" " Quashy	50	0	0
" " Will	40	0	0
" Woman Hannah £50 0s. 0d. do do Bella £40. 0s. 0d. . .	90	0	0
" " Pricella "30 0 0. Affee & child £50 0 0 . .	80	0	0
" Girls Eve & Tilla	30	0	0
One Riding Chair £12 0s. 0d Two Horses £10 0s. 0d. . . .	22	0	0
One Cart £3 0s 0d 1 Desk 1 Chest Drawers & 1 Press £12 0 0	15	0	0
One Corn Mill £0 10s 0d 1 Dining Table & Stand £2 0 0. .	2	10	0
One Bedstead £2 0 0 Five Chairs £1 5s 0d.	3	5	0
One pr. Dogs. Shovel & Tongues £0 15s. 0d. 6 Pictures & Ink Stand £0 10s 0d.	1	5	00
Three Beds & Linen &c	15	0	0
One small do Cott & Blankets	2	0	0
One Chest. 1 case & bbl. Bottles £0 10s. 0d. Pewter & Earthen Plates &c £0 19s. 4d.	1	9	4
Sundry articles in Store Room	3	0	0
Lot books £1 0s. 0d. Sundry articles in closett £0 15s. 0d. .	1	15	0
Kitchen Furniture £1 10s. 0d. Two Canoes £5 10s. 0d . . .	7	0	0
One cross cut Saw		9	4
One Silver Ladle 1 pepper Box & 6 Spoons	3	10	0
One Silver Watch £2 0s 0d. 25 head of cattle £30 0s. 0d . .	32	0	0
Twenty-five head of Hogs	6	5	0
Two Sheep	1	0	0
(Copy.)	£457	8	8

The above Schedule was taken and the property appraised by us the subscribers—the day and date first above written.

(Copy.)

DAVID JOHNSTON,   [L S]
EDMUND ADAMS,   [L S]
MATTHEW SALFNER, [L.S.]

ROBERT BOLTON[18] married twice; first in 1747, Susannah,[d] daughter of Matthew[e] and Jane Mauve,[f] the former a native

---

[d] The necklace and bracelets of this lady are in the possession of James C. Booth, Esq, of Philadelphia

[e] The will of Matthew Mauve of Savannah bears date June, 1775, and was proved 7th of August, 1777

[f] Her grandson, Wm Matthew Evans, says. "She was a native of Switzerland, and her parents were French, who left France in consequence of persecution on account of their religion Mr and Mrs. Mauve were exemplary characters, and

of Berne, the latter of Vevay, Switzerland. This excellent and pious lady, who was also born in Switzerland, A.D. 1729, and died at Savannah in the spring of 1764, is said, by one who knew her intimately, to have been, "if not the best, yet among the very best of women." After her death, he married in 1770 ——, widow of Samuel Stirk, a native of Germany. This lady, who was a most devoted wife and mother-in-law, died at Savannah on Thursday, the 30th of January, 1794. The following notice of her death appeared in the *Georgia Gazette:* "January 30th, 1794, died Mrs. Bolton, widow of Robert Bolton."

By his second wife, Robert Bolton[18] had no child, but by the first several.

Children of Robert and Susannah Bolton :

I. SUSANNAH BOLTON, born A.D. 1748, eldest daughter of Robert Bolton; married William Moore of Savannah. She died in 1810, and was buried in the family vault at Savannah. Their son, John Moore, married, on the 17th of December, 1791, his cousin, Ann Bolton, eldest daughter of John Bolton of Chestertown, Maryland. There is a fine miniature of Mrs. Moore in the possession of James C. Booth, Esq., of Philadelphia.

II. SARAH BOLTON, born July 23d, 1750, O. S., married William Evans, 23d of August, 1769, and died at Savannah on the 17th of February, 1817.

William Evans, (eldest son of Middleton and Hannah Evans and grandson of William Evans and Miss Middleton,) was born on the Island of St. Helina in S. C., 13 April, 1747, O. S., and died at Vernonburgh, 21 June, 1781. His children were :

1. SARAH JANE EVANS, nat. 26 November, 1770; married William Lamb.

2. WILLIAM BOLTON EVANS, nat. Savannah, 30th August, 1772; ob. 20th December, 1773.

3. WILLIAM MATTHEW EVANS, nat. Savannah, 4th Septem-

were very wealthy, etc." "Jane Mauve," says Mrs. Ann Booth, "was from Vevay, a sensible, accomplished, and elegant woman, as I have often heard from others beside the family." The arms of Mauvy en Bretagne are: Papelonné de gueules et d'hermine's au canton sinistre de sable, chargé d'une demi-fleur-de-lis d'argent ber, 1774; ob. 18th November, 1837; buried in the family vault, Pelham.

4. HANNAH EVANS, nat. Savannah, 20th November, 1776; ob. 1st July, 1777.

5. ROBERT EVANS, nat. Vernonburgh, Georgia, 1st January, 1779; ob. 4th November, 1780.

III. JANE BOLTON, born in 1751, married Charles Young, and died without issue.

IV. ANNE BOLTON, born May 2d, 1752, married Nathaniel Adams of Savannah, by whom she had several children, and died 27th April, 1818. Her remains were interred in the family vault, Savannah.

V. MARY BOLTON, born in 1754, died unmarried.

VI. REBECCA BOLTON, born in 1756, married to Thomas Newell of Savannah, by whom she had, beside others, Thomas and Robert, devisees of their grandfather, Robert Bolton, Sen. To Rebecca, her father bequeathed his town lot in Savannah, known as Number 3. She was one of the first managers of the Female Asylum of Savannah; died in 1833, and was buried by the remains of her beloved brother, Robert Bolton, in the family vault at Savannah. There is an excellent portrait of this lady in the possession of her grand-niece, Miss Henrietta Bolton of Baltimore.

VII. ROBERT BOLTON[19], only son and heir of Robert[18], vide his life in Part III., Section IV.

ARMS OF MATTHEW MAUVÉ, ESQ., OF SAVANNAH.

SECTION III.

John Bolton,[18] Esq, third son of Robert[17] and Ann Bolton, was born in Market street, Philadelphia, Pennsylvania, on Monday, the twentieth of June, 1726, and baptized the fifth of July following.

He received a liberal education in his native city, and early entered the mercantile profession. His kindness and affability of temper greatly endeared him to his relations, but especially to his half-brother, Thomas Clay, with whom he resided until the death of the latter in 1745.[g] He subsequently removed to Chestertown, Maryland, where he purchased a large estate, a portion of which still goes by the name of *Bolton's Meadows*, and finally settled. On the 29th of December, 1771, he was married, by the Rev. John Hamilton, to Eleanor Dougherty.[h] In 1773 his name occurs in a list of subscribers, for £51, towards the erection of a Presbyterian church at Drawer's Creek, St. George's Township, Newcastle county, Delaware, of which Society the Rev. Thomas Reed, A.M., was pastor. He was very zealous in the cause of American liberty, and was a member of the association of the Sons of Liberty for the Eastern Shore of Maryland, who were leagued together with the avowed determination to resist oppression to the utmost, and represented that body as a delegate in a General Convention of the Sons of Liberty, held in New York, A D. 1774-5. This league constantly corresponded and aided effectually in preparing the way for the Revolution. The following is a copy of his letter to William Bradford, editor of the *Aurora* newspaper, published in Philadelphia:

g His brother-in-law, Mr Habersham, addresses him as " My dear brother Jackey Bolton, in Philadelphia." Habersham MSS

h The arms of Doherty are—arg a stag, couchant, ppr, on a chief vert, a mullet of the field.

"Sir: If you will turn over your book to first entry made of the News Papers directed to me, you will find they were sent at the request and for acco' of Mr. John Wallace, but he had them directed to me for the more ready getting them. Please, therefore, make out your acco' against him for the same to the 20th of August, 1770, at which time he died, since which I am chargeable with them. The acco' ag'st him must be drawn off separate and proven before the Mayor or a Justice of the Peace with a certificate from a Notary Publick or the Clerk of the County, that the Person signing the Deposition was at the time qualified to make the deposition.

"You are much blam'd here for publishing Lord Dunmore's Proclamation, as the negroes and servants in this Province would have been entirely ignorant of it had it not been for your's and Mr. Town's publication.

"I am, s', y' most h'bl servt.,

"Chester Town, S' 21, 1775.

"To Mr. William Bradford, at the Coffe House, Philadelphia."

About this time he received the appointment of Commissary for Kent County, Maryland, for procuring military supplies, and, like many patriots of that period, came out with heavy losses from depreciation of currency and debts which could not be collected. In this office and all other public stations he conducted himself with singular ability, honor, and integrity, which gained him the love and esteem of his compatriots. Nor was Mr. Bolton less distinguished in private life, as a tender and affectionate husband and parent, a sincere friend and a kind master. He was permitted to see the return of peace and prosperity, and his native country declared free and independent. His beloved wife, Eleanor, died of a fatal attack of dysentery on Friday, January 2d, 1784, at half-past ten at night; he caught the infection with his two children, Robert and Mary, and died of the same terrible disorder at half-past nine o'clock at night on Tuesday the 2d of March, 1784, and was buried in the cemetery at Chestertown.

There is an excellent portrait of him by Hesselius, in the possession of his grandson, James C. Booth, Esq., of Philadelphia.

The children of John Bolton[18] and Eleanor Dougherty were,

1. Ann Bolton, born at Chestertown 5th of October, 1772,

8

married first John Moore, Esq., of Savannah, son of William Moore and Susannah Bolton, (eldest daughter of Robert and Susannah Bolton,) 17th December, 1791, and secondly George Booth of New-Castle, Delaware. Mrs. Booth died in Philadelphia on Wednesday, the 28th of March, 1855. The children of George and Ann Booth were,

1. JAMES CURTIS BOOTH, Esq , of Philadelphia, who, 17th of November, 1853, married Margaret Martinez Cardeza, by whom he had issue,

1. JAMES CURTIS BOOTH, born 10th December, 1854, died 10th of August, 1857.

2. ANN BOOTH, born 24th May, 1856.

3. MARGARET CARDEZA BOOTH, born 23d June, 1857.

4. LAURETTE BOOTH, born 10th February, 1861.

Mr. Booth has published, in conjunction with Prof. Campbell Morfit, the *Encyclopedia of Chemistry*, also a *Report on Recent Improvements in the Chemical Arts*, published by the Smithsonian Institution. Besides these, he has edited several chemical works, and written a few essays on chemical subjects for the journals.

II. ANNA BOLTON BOOTH, married in 1829 Conrad William Faber, of Hessia. She died in May, 1830, leaving one son, William Leonard Faber, born April, 1830.

II. JOHN BOLTON[19], Esq , merchant, eldest son of John and Eleanor Bolton, born at Chestertown, Maryland, Wednesday, 31st of August, 1774. At the age of ten he and his younger brothers, Edwin and Curtis, were left orphans under the protection of a guardian, who, perhaps, cared little for them, so that he could retain their property. Their cousin, Robert Bolton, of Savannah, hearing of their cruel treatment, immediately went on to Philadelphia, found means to communicate with them, appointed a place of meeting unknown to the guardian, and brought his young relatives in safety to Georgia. When the guardian claimed the charge and education of his wards, Mr. Bolton, at the age of twelve, appeared in Court, and for two hours pleaded his own cause and that of his orphan brothers so eloquently that a full release was granted them. He was brought up by his cousin as his own son, taken into business, and ultimately became junior partner of the great commercial house of Robert and John Bolton. He subsequently, as we shall see, married his second cousin, and on her father's death, in 1802, was appointed one of the executors of his will. He took a very active part with his father-in-law in draining the low grounds around Savannah. In May, 1816, he was chosen one of the first Vice-Presidents of the American Bible Society for Georgia, an office he continued to hold until his death. He was likewise, for some time, acting President and a Life Director of that noble institution. He afterwards removed to New-York, and was elected Alderman of the ninth ward of that city in 1834. He was one of the first organizers of the Delaware and Hudson Canal Company,[1] elected Treasurer in March, 1825, and January 21st, 1826, was made President, which office he continued to hold until April 13th, 1831, when he resigned. He resided for some time at Rondout, and built the mansion now occupied by Lorenzo A. Sykes, Esq. Mr. Bolton died at Baltimore on Monday, the 15th of October, 1838, and was buried in the family vault, St. Luke's church, New-York. The following notice of his death appeared in the *Baltimore American* and *Commercial Advertiser* for October 19th, 1838 :

" Died in this city on the 15th inst., which he had visited for the benefit of his health, John Bolton, Esq., in the sixty-fifth year of his age, formerly of Savannah, but for many years past of the city of New-York. In both cities stations of high responsibility were conferred upon him, in moneyed institutions, public works, and city government. He has closed a long life of activity and usefulness, honored and beloved, with the Christian's well-grounded hope of a blessed immortality."

He was twice married; first to his second cousin, Anne, daughter of Nathaniel Adams and Anne Bolton, by whom he had no issue; and secondly, in 1804, to his second cousin Sarah, eldest daughter of Robert and Sarah Bolton of Savannah, who died at Baltimore on Monday, 14th of April, 1851,

---

[1] This great undertaking was commenced in 1825, first coal received, in 1829, amounting to 11,950 tons; in 1861 coal received, 600,000 tons. Boats of 25 tons in 1829, and in 1861 of 125 tons. The coal is shipped from Honesdale, Pennsylvania.

aged sixty-nine, and was buried in the family vault, St. Luke's church, New-York. By the latter he had issue,

1. John Bolton[20], died aged eight

II. Sarah Bolton, died unmarried.

III. Robert Bolton[20], died young

IV. James Bolton[20], M.D., a distinguished oculist of Richmond, Virginia, who married Anna Maria, daughter of Philip Harrison, Esq., of Fredericksburgh, Va., by whom he had issue,

1. Cora Bolton.   *Mc Bryde. Va*

2. Harrison Bolton[21], died young.

3 John Bolton[21]

4 Channing Moore Bolton[21].

5. James Bolton[21].

6. Charles McNeil Bolton[21]

7 Jackson Bolton[21]

8 Maria Bolton.

9 Benjamin Meade Bolton[21]

V Ann Bolton, married first, Frederick O. A. Sherrod. Esq., of Georgia, by whom she had issue,

1. John Bolton Sherrod

2. Frances Antoinette Sherrod.

3. Frederick Sherrod.

4 Felix Sherrod

5. Benjamin Sherrod.

Ann Bolton espoused secondly Samuel C. Farar, M.D., of Virginia.

VI Frances Bolton, died unmarried.

VII Henrietta Bolton, now residing in Baltimore.

VIII. Honora Eleanor Bolton, died unmarried

III. Robert Bolton[19], second son of John and Eleanor Bolton of Chestertown, was born Tuesday, October 15th, 1776, and died in 1784.

IV. Edwin Hamilton Bolton[19], third son of John and Eleanor Bolton, born in Chestertown on Wednesday, January 13th, 1779. He was a most ingenious mechanician, well versed in the principles of machines, and spent much of his time at the South in constructing some large ships. One of these was the

Guerriere, built for the firm of Robert and John Bolton, and subsequently lost on the coast of Africa. In his life was truly shown, that "an honest man's the noblest work of God." Possessing under all circumstances a remarkably happy, cheerful disposition; noble, generous, and brave; with ready hand to aid, and heart to feel, he was beloved by all who knew him. Although it was near the close of his life before he deemed himself worthy of approaching the table of the Lord, yet he possessed and practised, to an eminent degree, those virtues which adorn the Christian. He died in New-York on Sunday, 15th of June, 1856, and was buried in Greenwood Cemetery, Long Island. Mr. Bolton married, 1st September, 1808, Mary Douglass of New-London, Connecticut, who died in New-York on Monday, 6th of April, 1857, by whom he had issue,

I. Edwin Douglass Bolton[20], born in Savannah, Georgia, 26th June, 1809, died 13th February, 1811.

II. Richard Richardson Bolton[20], Esq., of Pontotoc, Miss., born in St. Mary's, Georgia, 1st May, 1811; Colonel of the Pontotoc Dragoons, and agent of the New-York and Mississippi Land Company. Married first, 13th February, 1840, Martha Lightfoot, daughter of West Dandridge of Virginia, by this lady, who died at Pontotoc, June 3d, 1850, he had issue,

1. John Curtis Bolton[21].
2. William Hereford Bolton[21].
3. Richard Bolton[21].
4. West Dandridge Bolton[21].
5. Rosalie Dandridge Bolton, died young.
6. Edwin Bolton[21].

He married secondly, in 1854, Frances Warner, of Castleton, Vermont, by whom he has issue,

Clarmer Bolton[22].

III. Edwin Curtis Bolton[20], Esq., of Pontotoc, born in Philadelphia, 15th May, 1817; married first Barbara Ann Caldwell of Penola, Alabama, by whom he had issue,

1. Mary Matilda Bolton, born in Penola; married Jefferson Root, Esq., of Pontotoc, Miss.
2. Ella Jane Bolton, born in Penola, Ala., married ——.
3. Joseph Edwin Bolton[21], died aged two.

4. WILLIAM EVANS BOLTON[21].

He espoused secondly, July, 1850, Margaret Root of Pontotoc, by whom he has issue,

1. WALTER BOLTON[21].

2. A daughter.

IV. MARY ANN BOLTON of Brooklyn, Long Island, eldest daughter of Edwin Hamilton and Mary, born in Springfield, Massachusetts, Monday, 22d February, 1813; married 5th December, 1835, Charles Conrad Post, Esq., of Hersfeld, Germany, and had—

1. EDWIN BOLTON POST.

2. CHARLES WILLIAM POST.

3. MARY POST.

4. HENRIETTA POST.

5. JAMES JULIUS POST.

6. JAMES AUGUSTUS POST.

7. RICHARD HENRY POST.

V. ELEANOR BOLTON of New-York, second daughter of Edwin Hamilton and Mary, born in Philadelphia, Pennsylvania, Sunday, 20th of November, 1814; married November 25th, 1846, Benjamin Salter, Esq., of Portsmouth, New-Hampshire, and has issue,

1. ELLA SALTER, born in New-York, June 5th, 1852.

2. EDWIN EWEN SALTER, born in New-York, March 17th, 1855.

VI. FRANCES BOLTON, third daughter of Edwin Hamilton and Mary, born at Kingsbridge, New-York, 17th of April, 1819, died 16th of June, 1819.

V. MARY BOLTON, second daughter of John and Eleanor Bolton of Chestertown, was born Thursday, 5th October, 1780, and died on Sunday morning, April 25th, 1784

VII. CURTIS BOLTON[19], Esq., merchant, of New-York, fourth son of John and Eleanor Bolton, was born at Chestertown, Maryland, Friday, January 10th, 1783 He was brought up by his cousin, Robert Bolton, of Savannah, subsequently married his second daughter, and was taken into business with his own brother John He afterwards became junior partner of the second commercial concern, at first called "Robert and John Bolton of Savannah," known as "John and Curtis Bolton of New-York." He stood very high in the commercial world for ability and integrity, for fairness and honor, and prior to the death of Francis Depeau, Esq , in 1835, was placed at the head of the house so long known as " Curtis Bolton, Fox, and Livingston," owners of " the Union Line" of packets, running between Havre and New-York. In May. 1825, he was appointed by the United States Government, in company with Blunt and other civil engineers, to survey a canal route through Guatemala, in Central America, " which canal, when completed," " to be free for all nations whether in peace or war." His correspondence on this occasion is very voluminous and valuable. It was a prominent trait in his character that he loved to set forward the interests of the great Christian institutions of the day. He was the first Treasurer of the New-York Institution for the Blind, and continued to hold the office from 1832 to 1835. In 1821 he was elected a member of the Board of Directors for the Institution of the Deaf and Dumb, and held the same for ten years. Dr. Harvey P. Peet, the late President of that institution, thus writes to the author: " Curtis Bolton was elected a member of the Board of Directors in 1821, and held the office for ten years. I knew him well as an active and valued friend of the institution and as a personal friend of mine." He died in New-York on Thursday, the 6th of February, 1851, and was buried on the 8th in the family vault, St. Luke's church, Hudson street. The following notice of his death appeared in the New-York *Journal of Commerce* for February 7th, 1851: " Died on the 6th inst., at the house of his son, Dr. Jackson Bolton, Curtis Bolton, in the seventieth year of his age."

He married Ann, second daughter of Robert[19] and Sarah Bolton of Savannah, who was born in that city in 1785, and died at New-York on Monday. 6th of December, 1847. The following notice of her death is taken from the *Journal of Commerce* for December 7th, 1847: " Died on Monday morning the 6th inst., Mrs. Ann Bolton, wife of Curtis Bolton, aged sixty-two years." Her remains were interred on Wednesday, the 8th of December, in the family vault. Curtis and Ann Bolton had issue,

I. A son[20], died young.

II. CURTIS EDWIN BOLTON[20], Esq., of Alta California, born in 1810, married Eleanor Post, by whom he had issue, one son,

CURTIS BOLTON[21], Esq., of California.

III. JACKSON BOLTON[20], M.D., of New-York, born in Philadelphia, Pennsylvania, Thursday, 31st March, 1814; married October 5th, 1841, Anna Hinman, daughter of Elisha North, M.D., of New-London, Connecticut, born 25th December, 1817, by whom he has issue,

HENRY CARRINGTON BOLTON[21], born in New-York, 28th of January, 1843

IV. ELIZABETH BOLTON, died young.

V. ROBERT COATES BOLTON[20], Esq , of New-York, born in that city 1815, married in 1840, Helena Lucilla, daughter of Basil John Bartow and Elizabeth Ann Honeywell of Westchester, Westchester County, New-York, by whom he has issue,

1. ANN BOOTH BOLTON.

2. BASIL BOLTON[21],
3. ELBERT BARTOW BOLTON[21], } twin.

VI. SARAH BOLTON, born in New-York, 1821, married January, 1851, Barton Stone Alexander, Esq., of Kentucky, Colonel of the United States Corps of Engineers, and has issue,

1. LOUISA FREDERICKA ALEXANDER.

2. BOLTON ALEXANDER

3. ANNA NORTH ALEXANDER.

4. WALTER ALEXANDER.

5. MARION ALEXANDER.

VII. JOHN HABERSHAM BOLTON[20], Esq., merchant, of San Francisco, California, born in New-York City, December 18th, 1826, married in San Francisco, September 8th, 1855, by the Rev. William Speer, Sarah Ann Fowler, who was born at Little Neck, Long Island, February 14th, 1837, and had issue,

1. SARAH BOLTON, born in San Francisco, June 3d, 1856.

2. GEORGE BOLTON[21], born in San Francisco, November 26th, 1858.

3. LAWRENCE BOLTON[21], born in San Francisco, December 9th, 1860; died in San Francisco, October 5th, 1861, aged nine months and twenty-six days.

SECTION IV.

ROBERT BOLTON[19], son and heir of Robert Bolton[18], Esq., and Susannah Mauve, was born in Christ Church parish, Savannah County, (now Chatham,) Georgia, on Thursday, December 1st, 1757, and baptized the same month, at Christ Church in Savannah.

He was the youngest child of his parents and the only son, so that his birth diffused the greatest joy throughout the house, particularly in the heart of his pious father, who accepted him as a gift from the Lord. He received the best education which the infant colony afforded, and was placed out in early life in one of the first commercial houses in Georgia. There he improved his advantages and acquired a thorough knowledge of business, so that by the blessing of God and his own industry, integrity, and economy, he acquired one of the largest estates in Savannah.

Upon the 6th of October, 1772, his majesty King George III. granted unto "Robert Bolton the younger" a lot in the town of Brunswick, in the parish of St. David, to be holden of the King, in free and common soccage, the grantee yielding and paying therefor yearly and every year *One Pepper Corn*, if demanded.[j]

Robert Bolton Junr

His maternal grandfather, Matthew Mauve, bequeathed to him in 1777 " all that lot of land in the town of Hardwick granted him by his majesty King George II. on the 6th of

---

[j] Register of Grants Office. Registered in Book i. fol. 81, 25th November, 1772. A memorial hereof entered in Auditor's Office, Book B, fol. 21. Taxes were paid for this property in 1823 as property of Robert Bolton of Savannah.

December, 1757." His father subsequently left him by his will several grants, to which he added by extensive purchases of improved lands and city lots. His estates, in Georgia only, would now bring in as large a revenue as any land-owner at this time enjoys.

At the very beginning of the difficulties between Great Britain and the Colonies, he espoused the cause of the latter. He served in several expeditions at the North, and was with General Washington when he surprised the Hessians at Trenton, December 25th, 1776. He was also actively engaged at sea and assisted in the capture of a British privateer off Sandy Hook. When the town of Savannah was taken by the British on the 29th of December, 1778, he took part in its defence, and was captured by a party of Highlanders, and because he refused to enlist in the British service, placed on board a prison-ship [k]

Mordecai Sheftall, Deputy Commissary-General of Issues to the Continental Troops for the State of Georgia, thus relates the circumstances connected with his capture and about one hundred and eighty-six officers and privates. Mr. Bolton was one of the party:[l]

"December 29th, 1778. This day the British troops, consisting of about three thousand five hundred men, including two battalions of Hessians, under the command of Lieutenant-Colonel Archibald Campbell, of the 71st Regiment of Highlanders, landed early in the morning at Brewton Hill, two miles below the town of Savannah, where they met with very little opposition before they gained the height. At about three o'clock P.M., they entered and took possession of the town of Savannah, when I endeavored, with my son Sheftall, to make our escape across Musgrove Creek, having first

---

[k] "Many of the inhabitants of Savannah who were not in action were bayoneted in the streets, and those who refused to enlist in the British service were placed on board of prison-ships" (*Hist Coll of Georgia*, by Rev. George White, M.A., p. 339.)

[l] Captain Thomas Newell of Savannah, a nephew of Mr Bolton, says. "That when Savannah was taken by the British, Mr Bolton and Sheftall, (son of Mordecai,) being about the same age, (about twenty,) escaped together from the city, and being pursued, ran up the Augusta road On reaching Pipemaker's Creek, about seven miles, the former plunged in and swam across, leaving Sheftall behind."

premised that an intrenchment had been thrown up there in order to cover a retreat, and upon seeing Colonel Samuel Elbert and Major James Habersham endeavor to make their escape that way; but on our arrival at the creek, after having sustained a very heavy fire of musketry from the light infantry under the command of Sir James Baird, during the time we were crossing the Common, without any injury to either of us, we found it high water, and my son not knowing how to swim, and we, with about one hundred and eighty-six officers and privates being caught, as it were, in a pen, and the Highlanders keeping up a constant fire on us, it was thought advisable to surrender ourselves prisoners, which we accordingly did, and which was no sooner done than the Highlanders plundered every one amongst us, except Major Low, myself, and son, who, being foremost, had an opportunity to surrender ourselves to the British officer, namely, Lieutenant Peter Campbell, who disarmed us as we came into the yard formerly occupied by Mr. Moses Nunes." "This over, we were marched in files, guarded by the Highlanders and York Volunteers, who had come up before we were marched, when we were paraded before Mr. Goffe's door, on the bay, where we saw the greatest part of the army drawn up. From there, after some time, we were all marched through the town to the court-house, which was very much crowded, the greatest part of the officers they had taken being here collected, and indiscriminately put together."[m]

But to return. From the prison-ship, Mr. Bolton, after a few days, was removed to various wretched out-buildings on shore, where he suffered many indignities. He soon, however, managed to escape; his negro guard having recognized him, and like the daughter of Danaus, "nobly false," not only watched a good opportunity to liberate his prisoner, but swam with him across the river on his back. Safe in South-Carolina, Mr. Bolton joined the patriots, and continued, as long as the struggle lasted, to do every thing in his power to advance the cause of liberty. His silver-mounted small sword, which is said to have been the gift of Washington, he subsequently

---

[m] *Hist. Collections of Georgia*, by Rev. George White, A.M., p 340.

bequeathed to his youngest son, James McClean Bolton, with this injunction: "Never to be unsheathed but in a virtuous cause."

Soon after his marriage to Sarah McClean of Chestertown, Maryland, which took place in 1781, Mr. Bolton removed to Philadelphia, but subsequently returned to Savannah; where he soon became a prominent citizen and one of its most successful merchants. He was one of the first to export that fine staple so well known and esteemed in all the cotton markets of the world as "Sea-Island Cotton." The firm was first known by the name of "Newell and Bolton," and subsequently as that of "Robert and John Bolton." The foreign correspondence and importations of the latter firm probably exceeded any other commercial house in Georgia. When the French Directory in 1798–9 authorized depredations upon American commerce, he was a considerable sufferer, losing several vessels with their cargoes. Every effort was made by him at the time to obtain satisfaction from Congress for his claims, as well as those of other American citizens, but nothing was gained. Sixty-four years have now elapsed since they originated, and notwithstanding the manifest injustice that has been done to the owners of these claims, they still remain unsettled by Congress.

The following letter, describing the capture of the brig *Fame* of Savannah, was written by Mr. Bolton to a friend in Paris:

"SAVANNAH, Oct. 28, 1800

"DEAR FRIEND: I have to solicit your friendly aid in a matter that may promote my interest and do no injustice to any person. I have a copper-bottom'd brig, called the *Fame* of Savannah, Thomas Newell, master, which was taken into Algiceras, in Spain, on the 2d day of December last, by a French privateer, called the *Determinada*, commanded by Capt. Francis Laurenzenty, while she was proceeding on a voyage from London to Venice, the cargo being fish; was freighted by my London correspondents, and ship'd (as was said) on acc't of a Venetian merch't; the freight amounted to upwards of eight hundred pounds sterling, but the owner of the privateer, (a Mr Ray at say Cadiz,) would neither give up the vessel nor freight, (as the treaty demands,) but insisted on fifteen dollars contribution, which, being properly refused, the papers were forwarded to the tribunal of prizes at Paris for trial. Mr Montflorence is charged on my part with the care of this business; but my present motive to trouble you, sir, is, as you are acquainted with me, to make these circumstances known to our respectable friend, Mr Galatin, who, no doubt, will favor any just claim, (under the treaty,) by writing to Mr Livingston, our minister at Paris, to give my claim his support. The Capt will be in Paris in about three months to pursue this business. It is a fact well known that there is an infamous banditti residing at Algiceras, who protect themselves under the French flag, and at calm times run out with their row-boats and carry in the unguarded neutrals; then the first steps they take, (being such a distance from the seat of Government,) is to insist on a heavy contribution—this the Americans prefer rather than go to law—but in this instance they are deceiv'd, I am determined to see if justice will not be given by France or claim'd by my country.

"I am fully persuaded that a letter from Mr Galatin, (if even private,) would have a good effect with Mr. Livingston, to whom I am unacquainted, and let the event be what it may, I shall be equally gratified by your friendly endeavors. Mrs Bolton and the whole family join in their most ardent wishes for the health of you and your good family.

"I remain, with respect,

"Y'r friend,

"ROBERT BOLTON.

"It may be proper to observe, that the Capt. shew'd all his papers, and did not conceal the ownership of the cargo, (being enemy,) but I am certainly entitled to my vessel, her freight, and detention, altho' the cargo was the property of an enemy—this our treaty justifies me in expect'g"

Mr. Bolton was not slothful in business, and God blessed the labor of his hands. But as riches increased, it may be truly said of him, that he set not his heart upon them, but received [them as a talent for which he was responsible, and by which he was to do good and to communicate. Nothing was firmer set in his convictions than the familiar proverb: "Business is what it is made to be." He loved all who love our Lord Jesus Christ in sincerity, and was constantly devising liberal things. Under the pious instructions of his honored father, he feared the Lord from his youth, and as he grew up to the age of manhood, he delighted to tread in his footsteps.

In his private life he seems to have been exemplary. He was a pew-holder of Christ Church, Savannah, until the day of his death, and a vestryman of his native parish from 1793 to 1796.[n] His name also occurs in the parochial register, as a

[n] Records of Christ Church, Savannah.

liberal subscriber towards the rebuilding of Christ church in 1799.° Upon the 4th of April, 1787, Robert Bolton, Jr., was appointed, with two others, to receive certain arrearages due the Rev. Mr. Bowen for his services as minister of the Presbyterian church. Like his father, he was a great encourager of Gospel preachers. His son Robert mentions in a letter, "My father was so much engaged with his business, that all the recollections I have of him are his spending his evenings with his family. We had not family worship, but I remember my father taking me into his room and praying with me;" and in proof of his kindness of heart as well as decision of purpose, it is added: "Hearing that some of his young relatives in Maryland had been imposed upon and cruelly treated by their

RESIDENCE OF ROBERT BOLTON, ESQ., OGLETHORPE SQUARE, ANSON WARD, SAVANNAH. (Erected in 1798.)

° Above the entrance of Christ church, Savannah, is placed the following inscription: "I. H. S., Christ Church. Founded A.D. 1743. Chartered, 1789. Destroyed by fire 1796. Rebuilt and enlarged, 1803. Injured by a hurricane, 1804. Constructed anew, 1810. Taken down and this edifice erected, 1838."

guardian, he sent and had them brought away without the guardian's knowledge, who, perhaps, cared little for the children, so that he could retain their property." We have already seen that he brought up these children as his own, two of them subsequently marrying his daughters, and being taken into partnership in business with his own son.

He usually enjoyed a good state of health for one who inherited a weakly frame, but his constitution at last gave way to the severity of the climate. The cultivation of rice being then practised around Savannah, aggravated a severe cold contracted whilst on a journey from his country plantation, called "Bolton's Retreat," Washington, Wilkes County.

From his death-bed he dictated the following letter to his young family :

"MY DEAR CHILDREN. Being about to be called by my heavenly Father to my eternal home, and leaving you in a world full of vice and wickedness, I feel it my particular duty, as your earthly father, to enjoin you to remember your God, while you are young walk in his ordinances *faithfully* Be ye *honest, virtuous, sober-minded, meek and lowly in mind, charitable in every sense of the word, loving your mother and other relations with tenderness, comfort the distressed ;* these graces will make your pillow easy and the burdens of this life light.

"Avoid bad company, nay, even what the world calls good , the drunkard, the lascivious person, and those intoxicated with earthly pleasures, they will endanger your spiritual happiness, therefore I say avoid them.

"Be you contented with enjoying a little good company, such as is calculated to improve you in your religious and moral life.

"Study the Holy Scriptures, read them with attention, and they will furnish you with a fund of wholesome knowledge; other good books you can read to improve your understanding.

"Never suffer the poor and distressed to depart from your doors with a frown; remember you are but stewards, and woe be to those that are unfaithful to the trust reposed in them. Be you kind to your servants, know that they are not your slaves by right, but by custom God made all free ; but man in his depraved state, enslaves man; therefore it is your duty to make their servitude more a pleasure than a burden. I trust we shall meet in a happier world than this , so I, for the present, bid—adieu.

"ROBERT BOLTON."

He died at his residence in Anson Square, Savannah, on Saturday, December 4th. 1802, aged forty-five years, and was buried by the Rev. Mr. Holcombe, in a brick vault, which he had caused to be built in the public cemetery. Over his remains is a neat marble monument, surmounted by an urn, under which is the following inscription:

Departed

THIS LIFE ON THE FOURTH DAY OF DECEMBER, A.D. 1802,

ROBERT BOLTON,

OF SAVANNAH, MERCHANT,

Aged 45 Years and 3 Days.

MONUMENT OF ROBERT BOLTON, ESQ., IN THE CITY CEMETERY, SAVANNAH.

The following notice of his death appeared in the *Columbian Museum and Savannah Advertiser*: "Tuesday, December 7th, 1802, died—In this, on Saturday, first inst., Robert Bolton, Esq., of the house of Robert and John Bolton. In him the community have sustained a real and heavy loss as a merchant and a man."

Mr. Bolton was rather tall in person and of fine figure. He wore the cocked hat to the last, which gave him an old appearance. There are portraits of himself and wife, painted by Waldo of New-York, in the possession of his grand-children.

His will bears date, Savannah, 19th of November, 1802, and was proved in the Honorable Court of Ordinary for the County of Chatham, 7th February, 1803.

THE WILL OF ROBERT BOLTON OF SAVANNAH, MERCHANT.

In the Name of God: Amen   I, Robert Bolton, of the City of Savannah in the State of Georgia, merchant, being of sound and disposing mind and memory, and knowing the uncertainty of life, do make the following arrangement and disposition of my worldly estate, with which Divine Providence hath been bountifully pleased to bless me. To Wit.—First and principally I commit my soul to Almighty God, in full assurance of a happy immortality.

I desire my executors to have a brick vault erected for the deposit of my body, with that of my family and friends

My debts I wish paid, (if any,) altho' to my knowledge, I do not owe one dollar except the debts which may be contracted by the concern of Robert and John Bolton.

To my dearly beloved wife, who has aided me by her frugality when poor, and consoled in tribulation when rich, I would freely give all my property at her disposal, but believing it would prove burthensome to her,

(Signed) ROBERT BOLTON [p]

I make the following arrangement, to wit: To my dear wife I give during her natural life, the house we at present occupy, in Anson Ward, and all the buildings on lots Nos. 2 and 3, and as much of lot No. 1, as is now occupied by the buildings appertaining to said house, together with all the household furniture, horses, carriages, and as many of the negroes as she may wish to keep about her, also whatever money she may want out of the annual income of my estate, submitting the disposal (by her will) of any of the furniture, horses, or carriages, to such of my children as she may choose.

I give to my daughter Sally, at the death of her mother, the two lots Nos two and No. three, and so much of lot No. one as is occupied by the buildings

---

[p] The signatures of Robert Bolton, occurring repeatedly, indicate that he signed each page of the original.

which we at present occupy, and which is intended for her mother during her natural life, which said lots I give to her my s^d daughter Sally during her natural life, and in case of issue,

(Signed)   ROBERT BOLTON.

then to such issue for ever—for want of issue, then to my next eldest daughter, also the following negroes, to wit: Sam, a Blacksmith, and Harlow, his wife, with their children Jenny and Sam, with the future increase, during her natural life, and after her death to her children, but in case of her having no children, then the negroes to go to such of my daughters as they may choose at the time—also the sum of Ten thousand dollars to be paid her as follows. two thousand dollars when she arrives at the age of twenty-two, and two thousand dollars each succeeding year until she receives the whole sum; but in case of her death before that period, say the age of twenty-two, then the sum above stated to be divided among her surviving sisters and the issue of such as may be dead, per Stirpes and not per Capita; also all the Furniture belonging to the house, that may not be otherwise disposed of by her mother, shall be hers at the death of her mother.

(Signed)   ROBERT BOLTON.

To my daughter Nancy I give the lot No. 4, (with the improvements,) in Anson Ward Tything, adjoining the Lot No three, given to my daughter Sally, which said Lot No. three I give to my daughter Nancy during her natural life, and in case of issue, to such issue for ever, for want of issue, then to my next youngest, say next younger daughter who may survive her, also the following negroes: George, a Blacksmith, and Hannah, and all her chilren; also the sum of Ten Thousand Dollars, to be paid her as follows two Thousand Dollars when she arrives at the age of twenty-two, and two thousand Dollars each succeeding year, until she receives the whole sum; but in case of her death without issue before that time, say the age of twenty-two, then the sum above stated to be divided among her surviving sisters and the issue of such as may be dead, per Stirpes and not per Capita.

(Signed)   ROBERT BOLTON.

To my daughter Frances Lewis Bolton I give the north Half part of lot No. one with the improvements, (which said half part joins eastward on lot No two, given to my daughter Sally,) which I give to my daughter Frances during her natural life, and in case of issue, to such issue for ever, for want of issue, then to her youngest surviving sister and her heirs for ever. Also to my daughter Frances I give the following negroes: Jack, a Blacksmith, Cudjoe, a boy, Ben, and George, a painter. Also ten thousand Dollars, to be paid her as follows: two thousand dollars when she arrives at the age of twenty-two years, and two thousand Dollars each succeeding year, until the whole ten thousand shall be paid. But in case of her death without issue before that time, say the age of twenty-two, then the sum above stated to be divided among her surviving sisters and the issue of such as may be dead, per Stirpes and not per Capita It is my wish and desire that if my wife dies before my daughter Frances arrives at the age of twenty-two, then that she should receive the interest of her legacy from the death of her mother until she receives the first instalment, which will maintain and educate her.

To my daughter Rebecca Newell Bolton I give the south half part of lot No. one, with the improvements, for and during her natural life, and in case of issue, to such issue for ever; for want of issue, then to her youngest surviving sister and her heirs forever; also give to my daughter Rebecca the following negroes. Joe, Tom, John, Coxe, and Boatswain; also ten Thousand dollars, to be paid her as follows· Two thousand dollars when she arrives at the age of twenty-two, and two thousand dollars each succeeding year, until the whole ten thousand

(Signed)   ROBERT BOLTON

dollars shall be paid her; but in case of death, without issue, before that time, the sum before stated be divided among her surviving sisters and the issue of such as may be dead, per Stirpes and not per Capita. It is my desire that if my wife dies before my daughter Rebecca arrives at the age of twenty-two, she shall receive interest on her legacy from the death of her mother until she receives the first instalment, which will maintain and educate her.

To my son Robert I give my wharf Lott, No. West of Bull street, (bought of Mr Samuel Stiles, by Newell & Bolton, and afterwards bot wholly by myself,) together with all the improvements thereon, to him or his male heirs; but should he die without male heir, this wharf and improvements I devise to my son James McLean Bolton. he paying to the widow or female children of my said son Robert, if any there be, two thousand dollars to each, that is to say,

(Signed)   ROBERT BOLTON.

to the widow of my son Robert in three months after his decease and to each of his daughters, two thousand dollars, as they may arrive at the age of twenty-two, with interest, which interest is to be applied for their maintenance and education   I also give my son Robert my half the rope-walk in Baltimore, (held in joint copartnership with my worthy friend James Piper,) to him and his heirs forever; also my negroes Cudjoe, a cooper, and Eve, his daughter.

I give to my son James McLean Bolton my half wharf lot No. West of Bull Street and adjoining to the west of the wharf given to my son Robert, and bounded east by a half wharf lot owned by Joseph Clay, Sen , Esquire, bot. at Marshal's Sales, being the property of the estate of John Summerville, deceased, with all the improvements thereon, to him and his male heirs; but

(Signed)   ROBERT BOLTON.

should he die without male heir, this half wharf and improvements I devise to my son Robert and his heirs forever, he to pay to the widow and female children, if any, of my sd son James, two thousand dollars each; that is to say, to the widow of my son James two thousand Dollars, to be paid her in three months after his decease, and to each of his daughters two thousand dollars as they may arrive at the age of Twenty two, with interest, which interest is to be applied to their education and maintenance.

I strictly enjoin it on my sons Robert and James, as they respect my memory, to enjoy the possession of their wharves in a brotherly manner, giving each other every accommodation in their power, but should they unfortunately be unfriendly and attempt to interrupt the communication with each other's property, to which it

(Signed)   Robert Bolton.

is liable from its present situation, I desire the offender's property to be liable for the payment of any sum not exceeding five Thousand Dollars to the party injured, to be adjudged of and determined by my executors hereinafter named.

I give my son James my two thirds of the Yamacraw wharf, from the top of the Bluff to low water mark, to him and his heirs forever.

I give to my beloved wife, during her natural life, my plantation in Burke County, with all the negroes thereon, and with all the improvements and stock, and at her death, I give the same to my son James and his heirs forever, on condition that he pays to each of his Brothers and Sisters their equal share of the value of said property when he arrives at the age of

(Signed)   Robert Bolton.

twenty-two years, the property to be valued by my executors, or men appointed by them, and at said valuation my son James is to hold said property and pay his surviving Brothers and Sisters, and to be considered as withholding one share for himself.

I give to my son-in-law, John Jackson, One thousand dollars.

I give to my nephew, Thomas Newell, a Lot in the village of St. Gall, No 15, to him and his heirs forever, and one Thousand Dollars.

I give to my nephew, Robert Newell, a Lot in the village of St. Gall, No. 16, to him and his heirs forever, and one thousand Dollars.

I give to my sister-in-law, Ann Gibson, five hundred dollars.

I give to my nephew, William Gibson, five hundred dollars.

I give to my cousin, Curtis Bolton, one third of a wharf lot at the Trustees Gardens, bought of Mrs Flyming, to him and his heirs forever, and I give to my cousin, Edwin Bolton, the other third of said wharf lot at the Trustees Gardens, to him and his heirs forever.

I give to Gamaliel Newell of Woodstock, in trust for his son Bolton, named after me, one hundred Dollars.

I confirm a deed I made to John Bolton, in trust for my affectionate sister Rebecca Newell, during her life and after to her sons Thomas and Robert Newell, all of the lot letter T, bought at Marshal's Sales, as the property of Thomas Newell, the elder, with all the improvements thereon, and I also give to my said sister a negro boy named Pompey, and at her death to my nephew Thomas Newell.

I desire that two hundred dollars may be distributed among the indigent widows in this city, who are of good character, to be pointed out or approved by my wife.

I desire that two hundred dollars may be paid to the Commissioners of the Academy as soon as the first story of the building is erected, provided the same is built within one mile of this city.

I strictly forbid a Public sale of any of my negroes, either for the purpose of Division or for any other cause, if they must be sold, they shall choose their own masters.

I desire that titles be given to the heirs of Henry Addington for a forty-five acre lot at Hampstead, which I sold said Addington in his lifetime, should I have more children, either male or female, after the date of this will, I desire that they, or each of them, should have ten thousand dollars out of the residue of my estate, either in real or personal property not before bequeathed, which is to be allotted to them or either by my executors; but if the residue is insufficient, then the difference shall be made up out of the other children's property, in proportion to their respective estates.

All the residue of my real and personal property I may die possessed of, I wish held in a general stock; that is to say, let the real property be rented out, and the rents vested in six or eight per cent stock of the United States or other good security upon bond and mortgage of real property, and the personal property remain as a stock in trade, conducted under the same firm as now exists, say Robert and John Bolton, and under the superintendence and direction of my copartner, John Bolton, the drawing —— of the profits, until his brother Curtis Bolton arrives at the age of twenty-one years, when it is my wish and desire that he be taken in as a copartner, and entitled as such to draw —— of the profits, and it is my desire, that when my son Robert attains the age of twenty-one years, he also be admitted as a partner, and entitled as such to draw —— of the profits, and that my said son Robert be immediately after my decease taken into the store and counting-room of Robert and John Bolton, and be brought up and instructed in the business of a merchant; but it is my desire and express direction, that neither my cousin Curtis Bolton nor my son Robert be admitted into the co-partnership unless their conduct until they arrive at age should from their prudence and discretion entitle them to such confidence, the propriety of which measure I leave to be judged of by my executors, and that the business be continued by my present partner under the present firm and names, whether they or either of them be admitted into the partnership or not, until my youngest child attains the age of twenty-one years, then the whole of my surplus Estate not before bequeathed to be divided in the most equitable manner, (without any public sale,) at the discretion of my executors amongst all my children which may be alive at that time or the heirs of their body, per Stirpes and not per Capita.

I should wish that my son James be educated at the northward or in this State, so as to qualify him for the study of Divinity or Physic, (not Law,) but if his mother should not consent to his going away, my executors are requested to decline it—he must be consulted at a proper age as to the business he may wish to follow

I desire that my funeral be plain—there must not be allowed any thing superfluous among those who attend—my friends will not desire it.

I give to my son Robert my gold watch, that he may know how time passes, and to teach him how to improve it, also my largest Bible, which he must have bound in six volumes.

I give to my son James my silver-mounted small sword, never to be unsheathed but in a virtuous cause, also my Bible in two volumes.

To whichever of my sons that may be most inclined to much company and drinking, I give my portrait, strictly enjoining the unfortunate youth to give it the most conspicuous place in his dining-room, that when he views it he may recollect that it represents a father who never was intoxicated and whose detestation of that vice should restrain his sons from the practice of it, but if neither of my sons require this injunction, (which may God grant,) let my portrait remain with that of my wife and sister in the possession of my daughters, who, I doubt not, will respect the charge.

As I have directed that my share, say two thirds of the stock in trade with John Bolton, also the balance that may be due me in private account with the concern of Robert and John Bolton, should remain under the direction of the said John Bolton, as before mentioned, I therefore direct that my other executors claim from him only an account of my private account with the concern, unless John Bolton die, then they are to have the whole property under their direction, and to comply with the requisites contained in this will.

Having bequeathed to my son James the two thirds of the Yamacraw wharf, I desire that the same may continue an undivided property in conjunction with my cousin John Bolton, who owns the other third, and that if my son James should wish to dispose of his part, the whole shall be valued by three respectable and disinterested freeholders, and my cousin John Bolton shall have a preference at the valuation.

There is real property belonging to the concern of R and J. Bolton not before devised, which I desire may be allotted to my children, giving each as near as the case will admit, at the discretion of my executors, share and share alike, as they arrive at age to be entitled to it, but as this is an undivided property and can not be sold in separate parcels, let those who wish to sell dispose of his, or her, or their part, to those who own the other part, or draw lots with my cousin John Bolton, who owns one third, and my heirs owning two thirds, but it is my express desire that none of said real property be sold out of my family connection. I have bequeathed to some of my children several of the negroes belonging to Robert and John Bolton, of which I own two thirds

Now I desire that if my cousin John Bolton should wish to hold any of those negroes, that my other executors should draw lots for the same, and have the negroes valued, and if John Bolton draws them, he will pay two thirds the value with interest to the child they were intended for, or if they are drawn by my heirs, then they shall pay him his one third of their value.

My reason for giving all my Household furniture to my Daughter Sally at the death of her mother, (unless she wills it otherwise,) is, that there is but one complete set for a House she is to occupy, and it would excite an unnecessary confusion to divide it. I have no partiality for any one of my children in particular.

It is also my wish and desire that in case my son James, at his attaining the age of twenty-one years, should feel a disposition to become a partner in the House, that he may be admitted and entitled to the same profits as my son Robert, and on the same conditions, being at present unable to determine what proportion of profits arising from the copartnership shall be drawn by each or either of the copartners, I have left the same blank, and in case the same should not be filled up before my Death, I leave the same to be ascertained and fixed by my Executors hereafter named.

Being desirous of having as large a stock in trade as possible, I hereby direct that the rents, issues, and profits of the real property bequeathed to my children, shall go into the general stock in trade, until each of said children arrive at the age at which they shall be entitled to receive their several portions hereby devised and bequeathed to them and each of them, and whereas I have provided for the education and maintenance of my children during the life of my Wife, in case of my Death before her, I hereby empower their guardians to draw upon my estate from time to time such sum or sums of money as may be judged necessary for their support and education until they severally attain the ages necessary to entitle them to their property, provided my Wife should die previously thereto.

Should it so happen that any of my children should die without heirs of their body, in which event the real property hereby bequeathed to them and directed to their surviving Brothers or Sisters, it is further directed that in case of either of the said survivors dying without issue, the property of the Brother or Sister so Dying without issue, shall descend to and be vested in my surviving children and their heirs, share and share alike as tenants in common and not as joint tenants.

It is my will and desire that the legacies to my daughters shall be paid out of personal estate not herein and hereby otherwise disposed of, but should it so happen, by misfortunes in trade or otherwise, that this fund should prove inadequate to the payment, then it is my desire that the same should become a charge on my estate, both real and personal.

The legacies left to my friends and relations, (the time for payment of my children's legacies being fixed,) shall be paid within twelve months after my decease without interest, unless my executors should prefer paying them sooner.

The plantation and improvements in the County of Burke, which, in the preceding part of this will, I bequeathed to my Wife during life, and then to my son James on certain conditions, I hereby direct to be sold by my executors to the best advantage at private sale, or otherwise, if judged necessary.

Should it so happen that my present partner, John Bolton, dies before my youngest child attains the age of twenty-one, and after the admission of Curtis Bolton or either of my sons into the copartnership, I am willing that the business should be carried on as before directed, provided that my executors are of opinion that the surviving partner or partners can conduct it to advantage, any preceding clause to the contrary notwithstanding.

In witness whereof I have, this nineteenth day of November in the year of our Lord eighteen hundred and two, to this my last will and testament, contained in twenty-one pages of paper, set my hand and seal in manner following; that is to say, to the first ten sheets and to each page thereof I have set my hand, subscribing the same with my name, and to the last sheet thereof I have signed and subscribed my name and set my seal.

       (Signed)   ROBERT BOLTON.

Signed, sealed, published, and declared by the before-mentioned Robert Bolton, as and for his last will and testament, in the presence of three persons, whose names do hereunder appear to be by them subscribed as Witnesses to the signing, sealing, and publishing the same, which several persons did so subscribe their names in the presence of the said testator, and in the presence of each other.

N.B.—The following words : "Say the age of twenty-two," in page three, line sixteenth, and in page four, line seventeenth, the words "without issue," and in eighteenth line, "Say the age of twenty-two," and in page fifth, line second, the word "half," and in line seventeenth, "Say the age of twenty-two," and in page sixth, line fourth, the words "from the death of her mother," and in page seventh, line eighth, the words "from the death of her Mother," and in page ninth, line eighteenth, the word "Should," being first inserted.

                              NATHL ADAMS, SENR.,
                              BENJN BROOKS,
                              JNO. HABERSHAM.

Having, by mistake, omitted to name the executors to this my last will and testament, I do hereby nominate and appoint my beloved wife, Sarah Bolton, executrix, and my worthy friends John Bolton, William Wallace, and George Woodruff, and my sons Robert and James, as they severally attain the age of twenty-one years, Executors of this my last will and testament. Witness my hand and seal, this nineteenth day of November, in the year of our Lord 1802, and I also appoint Col. Joseph Habersham one of my executors.

       (Signed)   ROBERT BOLTON.

Witness, NATHL ADAMS, SENR,
          BENJN BROOKS,
          JNO. HABERSHAM.

GEORGIA :

Before the honorable the Court of Ordinary for the County of Chatham, in the State aforesaid, personally appeared John Habersham, one of the subscribing witnesses to the foregoing last will and testament of Robert Bolton, late of the City of Savannah, Merchant, deceased, who, being duly sworn, saith that he was present and did see the said Testator sign, seal, publish, and declare the same to be and contain his last will and testament, and that he was of sound mind at the time, to the best of this deponent's belief, and that Nathaniel Adams and Benjamin Brooks, together with the deponent, subscribed their names as witnesses, at the request and in the presence of the testator and of each other.   Jno. Habersham.

Sworn in open Court,
    7 Feb'y, 1803
             Ed. White, Clerk
             Court Ordinary.

March 24, 1803. Then John Bolton appeared and was qualified [q]

Mr. Bolton married Sarah, fifth child of James McClean, Esq., and Frances Lewis, of Chestertown, Md. This lady was born at Stirling Castle on the Grove farm, on the 23d of December, 1757. Her grandfather, James McClean, (a descendant of the clan McClean, whose progenitor was the famous Highland warrior, Macgillian,[r]) about the year 1729 emigrated from the north of Ireland to this country. His motive for so doing was to live without that oppression both of his civil and religious rights which he met with in his own country. He was a member and particularly attached to the Protestant Episcopal Church. Landing at Chestertown, and being accustomed to an agricultural life, about two miles from the town he purchased a farm known by the name of the Grove, which has remained in the family till within a few years. His father, James, was a warm patriot, but labored under too much bodily weakness to take an active part during the Revolutionary struggle; a true, genuine Whig, he was not wanting in exertions; his counsel and his pen were ever ready. The soldiers he clothed were known by the superior texture of their garments, manufactured

---

[q] Registry Office of Wills, Savannah.

[r] The surname of this family was originally Macgillian, whose progenitor was a Highland warrior, Gillion, who was denominated Gillian-ni-Tuoidh from his weapon, a battle-axe, (in Gaelic, tuoidh) His descendants wear for a crest from him a battle-axe, between two branches of laurel and cypress. Arms, quarterly; first, ar. a rock, gu ; second, ar. a dexter arm in fesse gules, holding a cross crosslet, fitchée, ar ; third, or, a lymphad, sa. fess, gu.; fourth, ar two griffins' heads, erased, affronté, in chief, gu and in base a salmon, naiant ppr. Motto—Virtue mine honour.

in his family.   He was a man of studious habits, of a reflecting turn of mind.   When he took a stand, not easily moved, though mild and pacific in his temper, unerring in his judgment.   In the disputes in his neighborhood he was called upon as arbitrator.   His benevolent influence was felt not only in his family, but throughout his neighborhood.   In his strict sense of honor and probity consisted his chief excellence.   He died at Chestertown, on Monday, 17th of February, 1783.

Mrs. Bolton married twice.   Her first husband was Dr. Jackson, by whom she had one son, John Jackson, born 6th of September, 1777, the father of the present John J. Jackson, Esq., of Savannah.   Dr. Jackson died soon after the birth of his son.   She married secondly in 1781, Mr. Bolton, who, it is said, felt a great prepossession in her favor before her first marriage ; but was too young, too prudent, and too honorable to address any lady, not being established in business.   This lovely woman did not long survive the death of her second husband, in 1802, for it lay so heavy upon her mind as soon occasioned her death.   "December 29th, 1805, she was seized, at her daughter-in-law's, with paralysis, and immediately appeared to lose all sensibility.   She was brought home, and lay without any returning consciousness till Friday, January 3d, 1806, when her happy spirit departed, to be forever with the Lord."

The following obituary notice appeared in the Georgia *Gazette:* "Sarah Bolton, 1806, aged forty-nine years, widow, died January 3d, buried January 4th.   Was buried from her house in Anson Square.   Has left a numerous family and considerable property."   Her character is thus given by one who knew her intimately: "Her known loveliness, worth, and female excellencies need not be recorded, they are best felt and appreciated in the hearts of her children ; but as a child she was obedient, and towards a step mother had a sweetness of temper which showed a bosom that no unfounded prejudice could enter."

Sarah Bolton.

The issue of Robert Bolton[19] by Sarah McClean,

I. SARAH BOLTON, eldest child of Robert and Sarah Bolton, was born in Philadelphia, Pennsylvania, ——, 1782. She was married in 1802 to her second cousin, John Bolton, of the firm of Robert and John Bolton of Savannah, and died at Baltimore, Maryland, April 14th, 1851 Her remains were interred in the family vault, St. Luke's church, New-York. See Part III., Section III , for the family of John and Sarah Bolton.

II. ANN BOLTON, second daughter of Robert and Sarah Bolton, was born in Savannah, Georgia, 1785, and married her second cousin, Curtis Bolton, of the firm of John and Curtis Bolton, New-York. She died in New-York, December 6th, 1847. The following notice of her death appeared in the New-York *Journal of Commerce* for December 7th, 1847: "Died on Monday morning the 6th inst., Mrs. Ann Bolton, wife of Curtis Bolton, aged sixty-two years." She was buried in the family vault, St. Luke's church, New-York, Wednesday, 8th of December, 1847. See Part III., Section III., for the family of Curtis and Ann Bolton.

III. ROBERT BOLTON[20], son of Robert and Sarah Bolton, died an infant.

IV. JAMES McCLEAN BOLTON[20], son of Robert and Sarah Bolton, died an infant.

V. ROBERT BOLTON[20], of whom in Part III., Section V., as eldest son of Robert and Sarah Bolton.

VI. JAMES McCLEAN BOLTON[20], son of Robert and Sarah Bolton, of whom in Part III., Section VI.

VII. FRANCES LEWIS BOLTON, third daughter of Robert and Sarah Bolton, so named from her maternal grandmother, Frances Lewis ; was born at her father's house in Oglethorpe Square, Savannah, in 1794 ; married, 10th December, 1811, Richard Richardson, Esq., of New-Orleans, (son of Robert Richardson, of Bermuda,) born in Bermuda, W. I., 5th November, 1785, and died at sea, 3d of October, 1833, while on his passage from Havre to New-Orleans. She died at Savannah, June 16, 1822, and was buried in the family vault in the grave-yard of that city, and had issue,

1. FRANCES BOLTON RICHARDSON, born in Walnut street, Philadelphia, Wednesday morning, 16th September, 1812;

married at Henley-upon-Thames, Oxon, 23d January, 1834, Henry Ransford, Esq., of Huron Lodge, Bolton's, Brompton, Middlesex, England, and had issue six sons and four daughters,

1. HENRY BENWELL RANSFORD, born in Canada West, near Lake Huron, lost at sea, April 1st, ——.

2. RICHARD RANSFORD, born in Canada.

3. ROBERT BOLTON RANSFORD, born in Canada.

4. GIFFORD RANSFORD, born in Canada.

5. JOHN RANSFORD, born in Chelsea, London, Middlesex.

6. WILLIAM HENRY RANSFORD, born in Chelsea, London, Middlesex.

7. CAROLINE RANSFORD, born on Lake Huron, Canada.

8. FRANCES BOLTON RANSFORD, born on Lake Huron, Canada.

9. MARIA GIFFORD RANSFORD, born on Lake Huron, Canada.

10. EUGENIE MARION RANSFORD, born on Lake Huron, Canada.

All the above were baptized by the Rev. Robert Bolton of Pelham Priory, Westchester County, New-York, except William Henry, who was baptized at St. Mary's church, Brompton.

2. RICHARD RICHARDSON, Esq., merchant, of New-Orleans, born in Savannah, Georgia, 30th October, 1814, lot 27 Oglethorpe, Yamacraw, died in New-Orleans of fever.

3. JOHN BOLTON RICHARDSON, born in Savannah, December 8th, 1816, died whilst on a summer's tour at Major Haviston's, Germantown, Stokes County, North-Carolina, at sunset, Thursday, 13th August, 1819; buried in the family vault, Savannah.

4. ROBERT RICHARDSON, Esq., merchant, of New-Orleans, born in Savannah, at his great-grandfather's house in Oglethorpe Square, Sunday morning nine o'clock, 31st May, 1818; died in New-Orleans of apoplexy about 1848; married Miss Lesseps of New-Orleans, by whom he had issue three or four children.

5. REBECCA RICHARDSON, born in Savannah in her father's house, Trust lot, letter X; died in New-Orleans, October, 1822, and buried in the family vault, Savannah.

6. JAMES RICHARDSON, of New-Orleans, born in Savannah in his father's house, 2d March, 1822 ; died at Mrs. Priestley's, forty miles above New-Orleans, of yellow fever, 29th September, 1837.

VIII. REBECCA NEWELL BOLTON, fourth daughter of Robert and Sarah Bolton, born in Oglethorpe Square, Savannah, in 1796, and died February, 1825 ; buried in the family vault, Savannah.

ARMS OF JAMES McCLEAN, ESQ., OF STIRLING CASTLE, CHESTERTOWN, MARYLAND.

SECTION V.

ROBERT BOLTON[20], eldest son of Robert[19] and Sarah Bolton, was born at his father's residence in Oglethorpe Square, Anson Ward, Savannah, in the parish of Christ church, Chatham County, Georgia, on Wednesday the 10th of September, 1788, and was baptized by his grandfather, Robert Bolton. "He took his first step in Stirling Castle, Maryland, whither his mother had taken him on a visit to her relatives." "There," writes a connection of the family, "Robert learned to walk. Perhaps I saw the first step he ever took alone. The strongest recollection I have of his mother, was in stooping to catch him delighted in her arms, with that maternal fondness which, from her gentleness of disposition, she was formed to feel."

Among his own earliest recollections, Mr. Bolton notes in a paper he has left behind: "The church in Savannah in which Mr. Whitefield had preached, and the school-house near the church, where I was sent almost as soon as I had learned my letters." Another reminiscence, of a more painful kind, was that of the great fire which visited his native city in the year 1796. "The fire began," says Mr. Bolton, in giving an account of it, "on a Saturday evening, in the lower part of the city, and on a baker's premises. Our house was so far removed from the spot, that we thought little of it at first, but accounts of its spreading continually reached us. My father was engaged in preserving his warehouses by the water-side, which, by the aid of his black servants, he was enabled to do. About nine o'clock it reached our dwelling-house. We were left alone with my mother, and at that late hour of the night we had to set out for a friend's house further on; but soon finding that also in danger, we went quite to the outskirts of the city, called Carpenter's Row, and there rested for the night. When we came to look abroad in the morning, it was a melancholy sight; nothing was to be seen but heaps of smoking ruins and tall chimneys. My father removed to a comfortable house, afterwards the Planters' Bank, and then in the spring we sailed to New-York, where we spent the summer. Preparations were speedily made to rebuild the city, and my father determined to build the house which now stands further west and on the same lot. Our old one, in which we were all born, was burnt down. When we returned to Savannah from New-York our house was not ready, we therefore occupied one in Broughton street. The church was also burnt down, and indeed the greater part of Savannah. We were in the habit of leaving Savannah every summer on account of the heat, as it was not considered safe to continue there; multitudes who tried it, particularly persons from the North, and English people, fell sacrifices to the climate. My father bought a good airy situation at Washington, Wilkes County, Georgia, and for the last two or three years of his life, took his family there." Soon after the fire, and yet more calculated to teach a child the vanity of all earthly things, occurred the death of his father. "I perfectly recollect," he says, "his illness and death; it made a great impression upon my mind, and I had a singular dream, which tended to deepen the impression." It would seem that it was to his mother's influence, at this time, that his first decided religious feelings are to be traced. "She was rather small in person," says Mr. Bolton, speaking of her, "remarkably mild and gentle in disposition and manners. I can never speak of her without the deepest feeling, for to her I am indebted, under God, for any religious impressions I have. When she lost my father, she was heart-broken, and all my concern and endeavor was to comfort her. She removed into another part of the house, where I was much with her, my room adjoining hers. On a Sabbath morning, before going to church, she would get me to read hymns to her.

> 'Welcome, sweet day of rest,
> That saw the Lord arise,'

was a favorite one; and she used to say to me: 'What would I not give to see you a minister of Jesus Christ!' I know not whether my habits encouraged the hope, but I was fond of books, and I used to feel much under the preaching of the word."

He early served his generation by the will of God, making an open profession of religion at the age of twelve. He was peculiarly attached to the distinguished Henry Kollock, D.D., pastor of the Independent Presbyterian Church in Savannah, whose doctrinal views accorded so entirely with his own. It is pleasant to trace the goodness of God from generation to generation of such as love and honor him, and see the fulfilment of his gracious promise, "for the promise is unto you and your children, and to all that are afar off, even as many as the Lord our God shall call."

Some two years after the loss of their head, the whole household experienced an extraordinary deliverance, which, besides that we find an account of it written shortly after the event by Mr. Bolton, is of itself, as a display of Providential mercy, deserving of record. All along the coast from Charleston, as far south as the great Peninsula of Florida, extends a net-work of islands. One of these, lying at the mouth of the Savannah River, and called Tybee Island, was then the property of the family. It is some miles in extent, and washed on its southern and eastern sides by the Atlantic It seemed, therefore, to offer a cool retreat for the summer months; and, as a house had been erected on it in the course of the preceding summer, it was now proposed to remove thither, instead of taking the customary excursion to the North. "On Monday, September 1st, 1804," says Mr. Bolton, "our party started, consisting of my mother, three sisters, two brothers, aunt, three cousins, (one very ill,) three female and two male servants. The weather was fair when we left Savannah, nor was any thing unusual in the appearance of the atmosphere from the day we dropped down the river until Thursday, when the storm commenced by blowing very heavily from the northeast, directly from the sea up the Savannah River, which is about three or four miles wide here. What led us to take particular notice of the weather was, that we were expecting a boat from the city, seventeen miles above, with our regular supplies. We could see by the telescope that at length, finding it was impossible to get any nearer to our house, they had landed farther up, and drawn the boat on shore. The storm continued all that night. The next day we could see ships, and, indeed, every description of vessel, driving up the river, many of which became stranded in different places. But what alarmed us most was the height of the tide. We had never seen it above high-water mark before; but now we noticed first our bathing-house on the beach washed away, and then the water coming up to our dwelling, and the waves beginning to roll against it. We were thrown into the utmost consternation, for the tide was evidently rising higher and higher every moment. The negroes were consulted as to the possibility of getting to the house where the light-house keeper lived. Unfortunately, it was farther out upon the island, and more exposed to the wind, and at least a mile off; but it stood on an eminence, and was near the light-house itself, which could be a last resort. There was not a moment to be lost, as it became dangerous to stay in the house; so, wrapping ourselves up in what we could readily find, for it rained as well as blew with uncontrollable fury, we began our journey. I took my dearest mother, and each one had his charge, the negro servants carrying the invalids. We followed a path in the woods, staggering along through briars and thickets. The path to the house had usually been along the shore, but that was now covered by the ocean. Occasionally our way led us near the sea, and then we encountered the wind and rain in all their violence; it was like small sleet in our faces, so that we could not look up. Long before reaching our destination, hats, bonnets, shawls, blankets, or whatever we had thrown around us, were blown away. I recollect one place near the house where there was a depression, and some of us, in passing across, were up to our waists in the waves. Our progress sometimes was scarcely perceptible. Had no other than mortal's hand or a mortal's counsel guided us, we must all have perished!

"At length we reached the house; it was a very small one, but it seemed like Noah's ark to us. It was some time ere we could recover ourselves, and wipe our faces. We found the keeper of the light-house up-stairs, sick in bed; and upon our calling out to him to know what he meant to do, as the sea was still rising, he replied that, for his part, he might as well die where he was, for the attempt to move would kill him; but we might do as we liked. A large flock of goats, belonging to the island, had run up and taken shelter under the house, which was erected on piers, and added to our annoyance by the noise their horns made against the floor. Just at this time we observed a good-sized boat floating at a little distance, and one of the men offered to swim and fetch it. He did so, and presently brought it to the door, where already there was water enough to float it. We threw into it some biscuits and matches, and what we could get ready, and began to consider who should form the first set to endeavor to reach the light-house. Just at this moment I was standing at the window, watching the waves rolling towards the house—death full in view, and the prospect of life too small to be admitted—when I thought I saw some straw on a little hillock, indicating that the water was subsiding. I called those who were able to observe it, and we agreed to wait a little. And surely enough, God had begun to rebuke the sea and the wind, and not to let them go any further. From that hour the storm abated. Happy was it for us, for there was so deep a valley between us and the light-house, that, had the boat upset, we should inevitably have been lost. It now began to grow dark, and we watched the next tide, as may be supposed, with great anxiety, lest it should rise as high or higher on its return. But the wind had gradually subsided, and with it the waves. The next day was Saturday, and never shall I forget the calm of that day, not a breath of wind stirred; and as we were beginning to think of getting up to the city, we heard voices, and on opening the shutters towards the sea—they had been kept closed during the storm,—we perceived our friends come to look after us with a large boat. On seeing us, they fell on their knees, and gave thanks to God, for they had concluded we were lost. It had been reported that Tybee Island had been seen from the opposite shore entirely submerged. O, what a joyful meeting was that! The accounts from the city were mournful—docks washed away, ships sunk, every person in the Government Fort drowned; a hundred slaves on one plantation alone lost.

"As to ourselves, every thing was gone, save our lives. Our property was floating about in every direction. Doddridge's *Family Expositor*, saturated with sea-water, was found in one place, our clothes in another, some of them blown up into trees. As we approached the city, many ran to the wharf to greet us, and express their thankfulness for our safety. The church-steeple was blown down; ships had run their bowsprits into the warehouse windows; sea-fowl in abundance and many cormorants had been driven up to the city from the ocean; and it was said to have been so dark during the storm, that a star had been seen in the day-time. We soon entered our home with grateful hearts. What made it the more striking to me was that it was my birth-day, and so it seemed like a new lease of life to me. My mother, who, strange to say, though delicate, had not suffered from the exposure, reminded us all to make it at once a matter of praise and special thanks-giving to God."

On the 3d day of January, 1806, Mr. Bolton was called upon to resign this his remaining parent. She was struck with paralysis, and lingered a few days. "Her removal," he says, "had a very solemn effect upon us all." But there is another interesting circumstance in the formation of Mr. Bolton's religious character, which must not be overlooked here, especially as it was one to which he himself frequently and thank-fully alluded. The family coachman was a negro, named Andrew Marshall. He was not only a respectable, but a religious person; and, in the warmth of his zeal for the good cause, seems never to have lost an opportunity of speaking a word, in or out of season, to his young master. He might be cleaning down the horses in the stable, or driving his mistress out into the country, there was sure to be something for "Massa Robert," if he were but by his side. "Massa Robert must be a Christian," he would say: "I pray every day for young massa to be good Minister of Jesus Christ." These pious suggestions, offered with the utmost respect, and backed by a thorough consistency of character, told upon the youthful mind, and led, with other things, to an early establishment in grace. And may we not infer that in this way the philanthropy of the grandfather, who half a century before had befriended the efforts of Cornelius Winter, was bringing about, in the righteous arrangements of Providence, its own exceeding great reward? Whilst to others, who had despised the poor slave, and endeavored to keep him in darkness, that they might keep him in subjection, he became not unfrequently the source of uneasiness and alarm, here, converted and emancipated, he becomes the very instrument employed by Him who sometimes chooses to use " the base things of this world, and things which are despised," in the conversion of the future head of the family. Andrew was eventually elected the pastor of the first congregation of black people in Savannah; and Mr. Bolton, then in England, had the pleasure of assisting him, by sending him out Matthew Henry's *Commentary*, and a few other works, which were thankfully received and well used. Nor must we omit to mention that years after this, on revisiting his native place, Mr. Bolton found the old man, now with snow-white hair, holding on his way, having lived down much persecution, and regularly and efficiently serving a congregation of a thousand souls. Mr. Bolton, then an ordained Clergyman of the Episcopal Church of America, proposed to officiate for him, to which the venerable man, though himself a Baptist, humbly and gladly assented. The place of worship was crowded, and never was there a more attentive audience. At the conclusion of the service, an aged colored person, who had once been a servant in the family, was heard to exclaim, with the usual animation of her race: " Only to think of my hearing Massa Robert preach, and that to my satisfaction, too!"

Such were some of the circumstances that seem to have given a bias to Mr. Bolton's character; indeed, we have the means of knowing their immediate effect to some extent. He appears early to have experienced that true conversion of heart which the Holy Scriptures teach us to regard as the real and only entrance into the kingdom of God. He attended prayer-meetings, and, while yet a youth, took part in private devotional exercises.

In the spring of 1806, Mr. Bolton went to the North to

meet his eldest sister on her return from England, and spent part of the time in studying at Newark, New-Jersey, under a tutor. On his return South, he entered Mr. Waddell's Academy. "I began, however," Mr. Bolton writes, "to desire to travel, and hearing from my sister so much about England and a Mr. Jay she had become acquainted with, it seemed just what I wanted. We had a ship about to sail for Liverpool, and I embarked. I was the only cabin-passenger. After a passage of about thirty days, we arrived at Liverpool. I was pleased with every thing I saw. It was a state of society just suited to my taste. In a few days I set out for Manchester to deliver some letters of introduction to Mr. Spear, who had been one of my father's business correspondents, and whose agents for the purchase of cotton had frequently staid in our house in Savannah. I was much pleased with Mr. Spear and his family, and staid with him for a few days. He then asked me in what direction I thought of going, and strongly recommended me to go and hear and see Mr. Jay at Bath." He had also brought letters from his sister and brother-in-law, direct to Mr. Jay, whose acquaintance they had made while on a tour through England, a year or two previously. The circumstance, perhaps, is worth mentioning, as opening the way for Mr. Bolton, with his future father-in-law. We give it in Mr. Jay's own natural language, in his *Life of Cornelius Winter.* "Mr. and Mrs. John Bolton, from the United States, were travelling through England. They came to Bath, and were introduced to me by a letter from an eminent merchant in Manchester. Soon after their arrival, Mr. Winter called at my house, and upon my telling him that I was just going to see a gentleman and lady from America, he said: 'I love America dearly; I should like, if agreeable to you, to go with you.' We went, and what was his surprise and delight when, in the course of conversation, he found, not only that they resided in Savannah, but that this lady was the eldest grand-daughter of the excellent Robert Bolton, who acted so kind and noble a part, when, in his work and labor of love towards the negroes, almost all besides had opposed and despised him. Melting into tears, he arose, and immediately embraced them, and nothing could have been more interesting than to hear him relate the particulars of his American attempt and disappointment. Nor was this the whole of a remarkable event. Some time after this, the eldest grandson, worthy of such a grandsire, saw and espoused my eldest daughter, worthy of such a husband, and the providence is yet telling: 'Whoso is wise, and will observe these things, even they shall understand the loving-kindness of the Lord.'"

Upon arriving in Bath, Mr. Bolton thus describes his own feelings: "Every thing in Mr Jay's family pleased, and profited me. I saw religion in its loveliest form; and my mind already tending towards the ministry, it seemed to me what I should desire above all things I talked freely to Mr. Jay, who gave much kind advice. But just then, there being an appearance of war between England and America, my friends persuaded me to return. Accordingly, I took my leave of Bath, just caught a glimpse of London, and then reembarked from Liverpool for Savannah. We had a long passage of sixty days. The same ship was lost on a subsequent voyage, and never heard of. Oh! why was I thus mercifully dealt with? This was in the autumn of 1807. In the spring of the next year I went again to the North, and was introduced to General Moreau, still hoping that something would arise to carry me back to England. We travelled back to Georgia from New-York by land, and at Baltimore I determined to write to Mr Jay about my prospects and wishes for the ministry, and then about his daughter whom I had just seen on my last visit. I laid my heart entirely open to him. His answer came to me at Savannah. He replied encouragingly, stating that, if I were fixed in England, there was no one whom he would so gladly intrust his daughter to. I had not a friend I could talk to. Both my elder sisters were now married, but my brother James was younger than myself, and my youngest sister, Frances, was about ten or twelve. How should I leave them? I was at a loss to know what to do. But it seemed impossible for me to prepare for the ministry then. After much reflection, I concluded to go. On landing, I went to Mr. Spear's again, and for the first time spoke in public in his little chapel. I thought of entering myself at Cambridge, but was prejudiced against it on account of the tests. I came to the conclusion, however, to marry and reside in England. My family gave me up, knowing where and with whom I was, and I soon became reconciled to my new home." Mr. Bolton went to Hoxton, a dissenting academy, then under the able direction of Dr. Simpson, in order to prepare for the ministry. Here he attended lectures, and was sent forth into the neighborhood to visit and expound to the poor. Some time also was spent in Edinburgh, with the same object. In May, 1810, he was united to Miss Jay, at Walcot Church, Bath. Speaking of this event, more than forty years afterwards, he says: " Of course, I then found my earthly treasure " Indeed, there could not be a more romantic attachment, nor a wife that deserved it better. She seemed exactly suited to him, not by resembling him in character, but by being just the complement he needed, meeting his wants, sharing his burdens, and encouraging him in every good and holy enterprise.

The newly-married couple first resided at Frenchhay, near Bristol, where they found an agreeable society and made many friends Here Mrs. Bolton had an alarming illness. Her father and mother were summoned from Bath. " I well remember," says Mr. Bolton, " dear Mr. Jay coming in, and it seemed as if, the moment he entered the house, my dear Anne began to recover. He quoted the words of the prophet Malachi, as he entered the door: ' I will spare them as a man spareth his own son that serveth him.' " Shortly after this, they removed to the neighborhood of Glastonbury, in Somersetshire. Here Mr. Bolton officiated gratuitously as a lay-preacher. " Glastonbury," he says, speaking of this period of his life, " was recommended to me as a pleasant neighborhood, where I might do good in helping good old Mr. Major. I rented, therefore, a pretty place, called Edgarly, under the Tor, and preached almost every Sunday evening. I trust it was not without benefit; great numbers attended the chapel."

As Mr. Bolton had been constituted by his father's will a partner in a large commercial concern, and as some of his friends, with Mr. Jay among them, were averse to his entering the ministry, on the ground that there was a great need of pious laymen of wealth and influence, it was determined that he should establish himself in Liverpool as a merchant. A partner of experience joined him from Bermuda, to undertake the onerous part of the business. Mr. Bolton's leisure was occupied in "every good work." He assisted deserving persons by establishing them in business. Many years afterwards he had a pleasing acknowledgment, in his own time of need, from one whom he had thus benefited. It was whilst at Henley, that he received a letter enclosing a £5 note, with this appendage: "A like token of regard *you* kindly placed in my hands some years ago. It has ever been recorded by a thousand kind thoughts of you; and you will give credit to this by the acceptance of the enclosed"

Dr. Raffles, whose ministry Mr. and Mrs. Bolton attended during their residence in Liverpool, thus speaks of them to the family: "I cherish the memory of both your excellent parents with the warmest respect and esteem. My remembrance of your father is as a merchant in Liverpool. He resided in a house near my chapel, and, together with your mother, became a member of my church. It was my privilege, during his residence in Liverpool, to enjoy his intimate friendship. He was fond of books and autographs, in which I had a great sympathy with him. I remember that he greatly enlarged his house, chiefly, I believe, that he might have a room of sufficient capacity for his library, which was large and valuable. I recollect, at that time, the Rev. Dr. Kollock, of Savannah, being a guest with your father, when he (your father) took us in his carriage one morning to Dr. Adam Clarke; who then resided at Millbrook, near Preston, to breakfast, when Dr. Kollock presented the Doctor with the original manuscript of the Wesleyan Hymn-Book, in the handwriting, as I understood, of Charles Wesley.

"My recollections of your father while here, are now very vague and general. I remember well the seat in which he sat, and that it was always occupied by himself and family. He maintained his Christian character honorably while engaged in commerce. I believe that through the whole of his career as a merchant he lived habitually under the influence of Christian principle—lived near to God, and walked humbly with Him. He was a man of a meek and quiet spirit, and took his part liberally in the support of the great Christian institutions of the day. I felt much upon his leaving Liverpool; for he was a man exactly suited to my taste, and we never had a difference of opinion. And, then, his house being opposite my chapel, I knew where I could go myself at all times and find a welcome, and where there was ever a home ready for any Christian friend. The conversation was always profitable at his table. I regret that I can say so little on a theme so deeply interesting to me. I seem to have out-lived all my contemporaries, and your father and his history seem to me as matters of a long time ago."

Among Mr. Bolton's friends and correspondents at this time was the Rev. Rowland Hill. This holy and zealous man had received the mantle of Whitefield as an earnest evangelist. In 1772, while a curate, and only in deacons' orders, he preached to large crowds at Tabernacle and Tottenham Court Road Chapels, London, quite reviving the cause of "Methodism," as Gospel-teaching was then stigmatized. His labors are said to have been "immense in the metropolis." Captain Joss, his friend, writes to him: "We have taken above a hundred into our society, concerning whom it may be said you were the happy instrument of their conversion." To the same effect Lady Huntingdon writes: "The popularity of Mr. Hill, and the crowds that follow him wherever he is called to preach, overwhelm me with astonishment and gratitude to the God of all grace, who hath endowed him with such gifts. Excepting my beloved and lamented Mr. Whitefield, I never witnessed any person's preaching wherein were such displays of the Divine power and glory as in Mr. Hill's."

Mr. Bolton had been introduced to his notice by Mr. Jay. One or two of the letters of this good though eccentric man, while illustrating the character of Mr. Bolton's friendship, will also throw light upon his Liverpool life. From one we gather that Mr. Bolton preached even now occasionally, but not so frequently as his good Mentor wished.

"Humanity directs me," he writes, "to put these few lines into your hands. The bearer of them was once affluent. His father was a wealthy brewer in M——, and commanded the credit and respect of all that knew him But some persons who are rich by providence, want to be richer still This many aim at in a way of speculation, and thereby frequently bring themselves to ruin As I was frequently a guest at the father's house in my younger days, who hospitably entertained the ministers when they came to preach in that town, which was in those days in a state of darkness that might be felt, I could not refuse his request for a recommendation to you, that he might not appear quite a stranger. He hopes to provide for himself, and by his wife's industry, when he is known to be worthy of regard. While I am writing to you, I know you are on your accustomed visit to Bath, and that you will not receive this till your return We shall be happy to hear your return is attended according to the accomplishment of your own wishes. I think it may soon be said, that no one in Liverpool will be enabled to sing the 127th and 128th Psalms to a better tune than yourself. Well, well, the more the merrier, if they turn out to be of the same stamp with the parents! The Lord bless them with his grace, and they will be your glory It is a good thing to have the nation stocked, and no children can be brought up with the fear of the Lord, but by such parents as fear the Lord However, I confess I have but one fault to find with you, and that is, you are too like our modern Bishops—you don't preach enough. You must forgive the old hound that he still keeps barking upon the same subject, though he requests you to believe that he subscribes himself from the bottom of his heart,

"Yours, most sincerely and affectionately,

"ROWLAND HILL.

"January 30th, 1819 "

In another letter he thus counsels his young friend, half-seriously, half-playfully :

"I am truly glad at heart that you have taken again to the work of fighting It really concerned me when it was supposed you meant to step down from being an ambassador of Christ to be a mere trading-merchant in this world's goods. There is nothing more beneficial to the credit of religion than when persons of independent property can take up the sacred standard; that the world may be convinced there are some noble souls that can give themselves up to the work of God, for the sake of no other gain than the gain of souls In this work, my dear sir, may you go on and prosper, and may you have souls for your hire (and this will be honourable hire) in large abundance Down with the devil's kingdom as fast as you can ' While men-made Parsons do nothing, God-made Ministers shall do wonders Remember me to Mr R——. God keep him humble, that he may be useful Thanks for your attention to Mrs. ——; what sort of a woman she is I cannot tell, but every one should have their rights "

Mr. Bolton opened his house at Liverpool for the reception of Ministers and Missionaries. In this way he had the pleasure of entertaining Dr. Philip and his family, previous to their first embarkation for Cape Town. This eminent missionary frequently corresponded with his friend. Mr. Bolton was also fond of literature and the fine arts. He had the pleasure, at this time, of forming the acquaintance of the distinguished American writer, Washington Irving, who, with his brother Peter, was residing in Liverpool. They were both of them men of talent, cultivated tastes, and pure morals. With one, or both, Mr. and Mrs. Bolton took a summer excursion into Wales. Washington Irving, writing to his eldest son, many years after, on occasion of Mr. Bolton's death, says:

"SUNNYSIDE, December 11th, 1857.

"MY DEAR SIR: It is with great concern that I receive the intelligence of the death of your father; for I cherished the hope that we should meet again on this side of the Atlantic. He was one of the gentlest, purest, worthiest beings I have ever known, and he has gone to receive the reward of his goodness; for we are told 'the pure in heart shall see God'

"Yours very faithfully,

"My dear Mr. Bolton,   WASHINGTON IRVING.

"ROBERT BOLTON, Esq,

"Beekmantown.'

Etty, the artist, then rising into reputation, was a guest for some weeks in Mr. Bolton's house in Liverpool, painting family portraits. His likeness of Mr. Jay, placed in the Royal Academy Exhibition of the year, and engraved twice, was painted at this time

For three or four years Mr. Bolton was engaged in the mercantile life. when he was to be most signally tried. It was the year 1820—a period of great perplexity in the commercial world; and, of course, Liverpool was suffering: men went to bed rich, and rose up beggars Things began to look very threatening. The workmen of Manchester refused to work; thirty thousand paraded the streets for several weeks; all the manufactories were at a stand, and accordingly the supplies of raw material were not needed. The stock of cotton, on which Mr. Bolton's firm had advanced money, became at once depreciated in value to the amount of £20,000. America suffered equally, by sympathy Most of the persons who had sent them cotton, and drawn upon them, failed, so that the entire loss fell upon Mr. Bolton. Finding it impossible to go on, he, like many others, gave up his stock into the hands of creditors.

Collecting together the wreck of his fortune, secured by a marriage-settlement, and amounting to scarcely £300 a year, it will not appear strange that he now began seriously to contemplate what had all along been his own desire, namely, entering the ministry. His valued friend, Rowland Hill, stepped in here, and strongly encouraged him. The letters of this "Father in Christ" do such credit to the sympathy of his heart, and the singleness of purpose for which he lived, as well as to explain matters at the time with regard to the subject of this memoir, that we insert one of them :

"WOTTON, June 14th, 1820.

"MY DEAR SIR. I have been informed that times in America are even worse than with us , and yet, that we may be weaned from this present evil world, they are not worse than they should be Such is the carnality of our affection, that when things go well below, we are prone to forget better things above, though we are so positively told 'that to be carnally-minded is death, and to be spiritually-minded is life and peace.' If you and your family are the worse for these bad times, yet I trust the souls of men shall be the better for it. If, instead of being the rich American merchant, you should be the poor humble preacher of 'the grace of our Lord Jesus Christ, who, though He was rich, yet for our sakes became poor, that we through His poverty might be rich,' then the result will be a blessed one. One single soul called by your instrumentality, will ultimately prove a greater treasure than the possession of a thousand such poor worlds as this. I drop these hints, as you tell me how much you wish to have done with this troublesome world, and to resume your former occupation* as a preacher of the word of life. Though every year and every month now makes a considerable gap in my few remaining days, yet I know no one circumstance in my life that would give me greater pleasure than to find that your heart is inclined to retire into this neighborhood, that you may be near your relatives in Bath, and devote the residue of your days in your labors of love for the good of souls. Through infinite mercy, we have surmounted all our trials at this place, and prosper abundantly ; but about the neighborhood we have a sad dearth in many places of such ministers as are wanted, and truly devoted to God May the Lord of the harvest in mercy raise them up and send them forth."

---

* Referring to Mr Bolton's having assisted Mr Major, of Glastonbury, as a lay-preacher.

At this time, however, it was found necessary for Mr. Bolton to go to America for a time, to endeavor to settle his family affairs. He sailed for the United States in the spring of 1822, " in the ship Albion, Captain Williams, which was afterwards wrecked on the Irish coast, and all lost but one passenger and two or three seamen." " When we arrived," he writes, " at New-York, my own brother James received us into his house. I immediately set about business, to see if nothing was to be done." He soon found, however, the impossibility of bringing things to a settlement under his father's will. After some time, therefore, (" in which some pleasant acquaintances were formed in New-York, and employing his time in preaching on Sunday, chiefly at Brooklyn,") he returned to England, and rented a pretty place called Southdown Cottage, near Weymouth, in Dorsetshire, where he resided for the next year or two, occasionally supplying pulpits in Weymouth, or giving lectures to the poor in the neighboring villages of Sutton and Ashfield. Whilst residing here, (May 21st, 1824,) he received a call to become the pastor of the Independent chapel at Henley-upon-Thames, Oxfordshire.

It is not intended, in a brief memoir like this, to enter into all the particulars of Mr. Bolton's ministry at Henley. It was more than commonly effective, and owned of God; and yet, always disliking display and mere excitement, as he did, his influence was due rather to steady perseverance and simple dependence upon God, than to any extraordinary powers His was the credit of assiduously watching over and edifying his people :—

> . . . "A skilful workman he
> In God's great moral vineyard what to prune,
> With cautious hand, he knew, what to uproot,
> What were mere seeds, and what celestial plants,
> Which had unfading vigor in them, knew ;
> Nor knew alone, but watched them night and day,
> And reared and nourish'd them till fit to be
> Transplanted to the paradise above "

From A.D. 1829, for several years consecutively, Mr. Bolton became one of the regular supplies at the Tabernacle and Tottenham Court Road Chapels, London. He esteemed this a great privilege, as well as a pleasing circumstance, that he,

who in his early days had heard so much of George Whitefield, should now be called upon to stand up in his pulpit.
One of the chief gratifications of Mr. Bolton at this time, was
derived from the visits of his father-in-law.   Always a lover of
rural scenery, Mr. Jay now felt a double attraction to Henley.
Very pleasant and profitable must have been the discourse by
the banks of the Thames, or in the tasteful little parsonage.
Not only with Mr. Jay, but with many of the "excellent of
the earth," did Mr. Bolton at this time hold intercourse.   Together with Mrs Bolton and his eldest daughter, he visited
Hannah More, then residing at Clifton, and was much struck
with her parting remark: "Remember me in your prayers;
I think much of intercessory prayer."   The Rev. John Hughes
of Battersea, founder of the British and Foreign Bible Society,
used to visit and preach at Henley.   The late excellent Professor Scholefield, of Cambridge, when staying with his relatives in the neighborhood, seldom failed to look in at the parsonage—his early home;—and on one occasion conducted the
family worship.   From the United States, Mr. Bolton, neither
forgetting nor being forgotten by his countrymen,—had the
pleasure of welcoming Christian friends of all denominations.
Dr. Cox, the well-known and earnest Presbyterian minister
of Brooklyn, New-York; Bishop McIlvaine, the distinguished
and honored Bishop of Ohio; and Dr. Nettleton, who, it is
said, had been the means, under God, of awakening thirty
thousand persons during a revival of religion in the United
States, were visitors.   To the latter, Mr. Bolton opened both
his chapel and house for special services, and it was hoped
that some good was done.   The conversion of a servant in Mr.
Bolton's own household was one of the known fruits.

It may be mentioned here, that Mr. Bolton was very fond of
a garden, and displayed great taste in its arrangement. "I remember," says a friend, "how beautiful he made the minister's
residence at Henley in connection with the chapel."   Nor was
his taste a selfish one.   He suggested the formation of the
Henley Horticultural Society, which flourished for many
years, and not only improved the appearance of the cottagers'
gardens, but had another effect scarcely anticipated—that of
not a little increasing the harmony of the whole neighbor-

hood. It proved the means of introducing him to the Rector of Henley and some of the surrounding clergy, a circumstance very gratifying to Mr. Bolton, who through life observed, as far as possible, both as a man and a Christian, the rule: " Love as brethren, be pitiful, be courteous."

Mr. Bolton, whilst at Henley, assisted in carrying the Gospel into several neighboring hamlets. Such places were War-grave, Binfield Heath, Pheasants' Hill, Peppard, and Hurley, each of which was served by some occasional evangelist. Mr. Bolton was permitted to see, as the fruit of his labors, an organized church in each of those places.

The next position Mr. Bolton is found occupying, is that of a clergyman of the Episcopal Church in the United States. The largeness of his family and the difficulty of providing for his sons in England, had induced him for some time to contemplate a removal to America. He accordingly resigned his charge at Henley in April, 1836.

On reaching New-York—having had a merciful escape from fire at sea,—Mr. Bolton was advised to take his family into the interior, to see if any thing available presented itself. Having proceeded as far as Skaneateles, he became satisfied that the West was not the place for his family. He therefore took a house in New-York for the winter. A farm, at a distance of eighteen miles from the city, was soon obtained, and some of the family were sent out to take possession, and try farming-life. Mr. Bolton himself, however, remained in New-York, hoping to hear of some fresh sphere of ministerial duty. By some he was urged to unite himself to the Presbyterian body, one of the most influential denominations in New-York. Indeed, some steps were taken for placing him in a church in the upper and increasing part of the city. But just at this juncture the providence of God seemed to lead him in another direction. He went to pay a visit to his farm. "As we rode out," says Mr Bolton, "we had to pass the church of East-Chester, an Episcopal church, on the direct road from New-York, and four miles this side of our destination, when my dearest said: 'This is the place I should like to see you in.' Nothing, however, could be more improbable at the time, as there was a clergyman over it, and I had not been episcopally

ordained." In the course of a few months, however, Mrs.
Bolton's wish was literally fulfilled. It so happened in the
providence of God, that the clergyman of the parish was
about relinquishing his charge. The cause is immaterial; but
so it was. When Mr. Bolton and his family, therefore, came
to attend divine service at East-Chester, the nearest town,
they found the Clergyman absenting himself, and the people
becoming impatient. Meanwhile, an excellent Christian woman, who kept a school in East-Chester, hearing of Mr. Bolton's arrival in the neighborhood, at once recognised him as
coming from Savannah, her own native place. It seemed that
her father had been a carpenter there, but addicted to habits
of intemperance. His own resolutions, and every means that
his friends could devise, proved powerless to wean him from
this vice. He grew worse and worse. Mr. Bolton was then a
youth, but hearing of the case, and pitying the family, he
wrote out on a slip of paper some startling incidents relating
to a drunkard's end, and (doubtless, not without laying it first
before God) placed it beneath the door of the carpenter's
work-shop. It caught his attention, and led to a thorough reformation; and this was his daughter, who had married, and
removed to the North. How singular the coincidence, that
thus, after a lapse of so many years, and a thousand miles
from their native place, and in a retired country village, the
beneficiary and the benefactor should meet!

Not less singular was it, that this should be a link in the
chain of providence, by which Mr. Bolton was now to be
fixed in a new sphere of labor. This good woman was not
silent. She advised the church-warden that, in lack of a Minister, Mr. Bolton would, perhaps, officiate in the school-house.
An invitation arrived, and on the Sunday he addressed the
people in that building, the church remaining closed. On
the succeeding Sunday, as he approached over the fields, he
was surprised to hear the church-bell ringing as usual, and
still more to find the vestry and a large congregation waiting
to invite him to preach from the desk, as the school-house
could not accommodate the numbers that assembled. After
five or six Sabbaths, the vestry, "finding that their Clergyman
had entirely withdrawn, and left the parish destitute, and also

that Mr. Bolton was acceptable to the people, urged him to apply to the Bishop of the diocese for ordination, assuring him that, when so ordained, they would unanimously elect him to the vacant rectorship. On application being made to the then Bishop of New-York, Dr. Onderdonk, he very wisely and kindly supported the wishes of the people, and expressed his readiness to admit Mr. Bolton to holy orders in the Episcopal Church with the least possible delay.

He was accordingly admitted to deacons' orders in St. Paul's church, East-Chester, Sunday, 25th of July, 1837, and the same day was called as minister of that parish. He was ordained priest on Sunday, 12th of November, 1837. Mr. Bolton was the means of effecting good here. The number of communicants increased; the wealthy families of the neighborhood returned and assisted, and an efficient Sunday-school was established.

Besides the morning and afternoon services at East-Chester, Mr. Bolton undertook an evening-lecture in the vicinity of his estate. A spacious room was offered by a friend, and the immediate neighbors invited to attend a short service. It is interesting to find—showing that no effort made for the Lord is in vain—that even this temporary service was owned of God, and has led eventually to the erection of a place of worship, belonging to the Dutch Reformed Communion, upon the site of this room. And, further, it may be mentioned in proof of the liberality of Christian sentiment, as well as of natural disposition, which distinguished Mr. Bolton, that he gave two acres of land to this undertaking, and was delighted to hear of the prosperity of the little church, gathered in this place. As a testimony of regard, a funeral sermon was preached there on the occasion of hearing of Mr. Bolton's death in England, and particular allusion made to the circumstance by the Rev. Mr. Roosevelt of New-Rochelle.

It was now determined to settle on the shores of the East-River, or Sound—a broad and beautiful estuary, stretching in an easterly direction from New-York, and separating Long Island from the main land. By disposing of his property in Savannah, Mr. Bolton was enabled to purchase a small estate of thirty or forty acres, and to commence a handsome stone edifice, now well known as Pelham Priory. With infinite taste he selected a spot commanding an extensive view of wood, water, and islands, seen through a perspective of trees.

No sooner was Mr. Bolton established in his new abode, than he began to receive applications from Southern friends to allow their daughters to be educated with his own. One or two, and then others were admitted, but yet without interfering with the family character of the household, until it became, as it still continues to be, one of the most important educational establishments in the United States.

But we must follow Mr. Bolton more particularly in his pastoral work. He continued to serve East-Chester on the Sunday, and occasionally during the week. But being placed in a new locality, he began to consider what good might be done to those immediately around him. The population was a scattered one, consisting principally of fishermen, mechanics, and negroes. A few gentlemen of property also had villas in the neighborhood. Many of the people, as their names indicated, were descendants of the Huguenots, or French Protestant Refugees, who had fled from Roman Catholic persecution, after the Revocation of the Edict of Nantes, and found an asylum, side by side with the Pilgrim Fathers, in the New World. But, notwithstanding their descent, the poor among

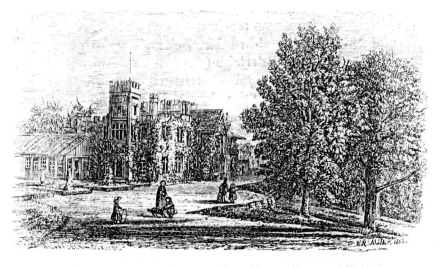

PELHAM PRIORY, ERECTED BY THE REV. ROBERT BOLTON, A.D. 1838.

them were, for the most part, ignorant and irreligious. Instead of "walking eighteen miles into New-York and back
again, to attend divine service," as their pious forefathers had
done, they went to no place of worship at all. The nearest
church was in New-Rochelle—named after old Rochelle, in
France; but that was at some distance. It was evident that
the spiritual provision must be brought closer to them. "Nature," says Dr. Chalmers, "will never go in quest of grace,
but grace must go in quest of nature."

A Sunday evening service, therefore, was opened in the
Priory. Many attended. Mrs. Bolton thus speaks of the circumstance in her Journal: "We have had about fifty respond
to our invitation. O, may good be done in bringing souls to
Jesus!" The numbers soon increased, especially during the
summer and autumn months, when the New-York families
seek some relief from the oppressive heat along the shores of
the East River. A few months subsequently, Mrs. Bolton
adds: "We are anxious to erect a little church here, but how
it is to be accomplished I know not, only I know that the silver
and the gold are the Lord's, and He can do it, whenever He
pleases to use us as instruments. We feel strongly the desire,
and would follow it up by effort, but we must be prudent. If
it is right, the way and the means will be made plain and
easy." At length, circumstances seemed to justify an appeal
to some of the gentry in the vicinity, and subscriptions soon

CHRIST CHURCH, PELHAM.

came in to the amount of one thousand dollars, or one third of the required sum; the rest was advanced by Mr. Bolton.

The corner-stone was laid Friday, the 28th of April, 1843. The edifice thus happily begun, was finished the same year, and on Friday, the 15th September, consecrated to the service of Almighty God, by the name of "Christ Church, Pelham."

Having held the cure of St. Paul's, East-Chester, for nearly nine years, Mr. Bolton at length found it necessary to resign that part of his charge, and to confine himself to Pelham; and, indeed, by this time he had accumulated work requiring all his attention.

There were many gratifying indications of the presence and blessing of God; and while the grounds and woodlands were being more and more cultivated and adorned under Mr. Bolton's eye, and became objects of admiration to visitors, among whom was frequently to be reckoned the genial and accomplished author of the *Sketch Book*, who, now residing on the Hudson River, renewed his acquaintance with Mr. Bolton, and took a lively interest in this specimen of English landscape gardening,—we say, while all this was being done, we are persuaded that nothing gave Mr. Bolton joy like the thought that he was also cultivating plants of God's own right-hand planting, and causing, invisibly indeed, but none the less really, the moral "desert to rejoice and blossom as the rose."

PAROCHIAL SCHOOL OF CHRIST CHURCH, PELHAM, ERECTED A.D. 1843.

Hitherto Mr. Bolton's own immediate family circle had never been broken into by death. It now pleased God to take his fifth daughter, Abby,[1] singularly like the mother in face and character, to Himself. She had been one of the most healthy-looking of the group up to the age of nineteen, when her strength began to decline. A voyage to England, her native air, was tried, but it proved only an alleviation, not a cure. She died at Pelham, June 16th, 1849. Mrs Bolton writes in her Journal: "*June 16th.*—The spirit of our precious child has left us; she has entered her rest. All blessed to the end—peace, perfect peace!"

This bereavement producing a shock from which he never entirely recovered, followed up by the desire of English friends, at length induced Mr. Bolton to think of returning once more to his adopted country. Accompanied by Mrs. Bolton and a part of his family, he landed at Portsmouth in the autumn of 1850. After a visit to Bath, he took up his residence in London, hoping to meet with a sphere of duty. It was found, however, that the law enacted in the reign of William III., relating to foreign orders, precluded Mr Bolton from holding a cure of souls in the Church of England. The Archbishop of Canterbury, with whom he had been acquainted while at Henley, kindly invited him to a personal interview, and stated the difficulty, regretting the effects of the law in such cases, and suggesting that the only remedy lay in a special act of Parliament, which, however, was not only expensive, but increasingly difficult to obtain. An Episcopal chapel in the north of Scotland was offered, but declined on account of the distance, one of the objects of the family in returning to England being to be near Mr. Jay in his declining years.

Just at this moment an opening appeared, so opportune and suitable in every respect, that it seemed made on purpose. The late Earl of Ducie had been compelled, on conscientious grounds, to withdraw himself and his family from the parish church, contiguous to his country-residence, Tortworth Court, and was, at this very time, engaged in looking out for a chaplain who could and would conduct the usual liturgical ser-

---

[1] A sketch of her last days has been given to the public, and received with much acceptance on both sides of the Atlantic, in a little volume entitled *The Lighted Valley.*

vices of the Church of England in a school-house, until a private chapel should be erected. Mr. Bolton was mentioned to his Lordship, and, after an interview or two, was offered this post, which he readily accepted. Had he searched England over, he could scarcely have met with any thing more to his wishes; for the work involved was enough, without being too much, for his strength; he enjoyed perfect freedom from all the shackles by which he might have been hampered in some places; and, above all, he found himself associated with a family—one of the "not many noble"—eminent for the simplicity and fervency of their piety. On the other hand, it may safely be affirmed that his patron could hardly have found a clergyman more acceptable to himself as to education, disposition, or manners, or one whose ministrations were more likely to prove beneficial to his tenantry. It is remarkable that Mr. Bolton thus became settled close to Wotton-under-Edge, whither his old and valued friend, Rowland Hill, long since dead, had invited him some thirty years before.

Mr. Bolton had been settled at Tortworth scarcely two years when Lord Ducie died. He remained two years longer, however, occupying the position of Chaplain to the present Earl, and officiating in the private chapel[u] attached to the New Court. But symptoms of failing health at length induced him, very reluctantly, to resign, and to remove with his family to Cheltenham. It may be mentioned here that he had resigned his church at Pelham during his residence at Tortworth. Mr. and Mrs. Bolton were much cheered by the Christian society they met with in Cheltenham; and it seemed providential that their steps should have been directed thither, just at a time when there was much of that with which they could fully sympathize. Many of these friends have since been removed by death, or scattered to different places; but the effects of such friendships extend to the heavenly world, where we may well suppose they will be renewed and spiritualized, never to be suspended any more.

---

[u] The Rev. William Jay preached, at the request of the Earl of Ducie and his mother, the Dowager Countess, on the occasion of the opening of this chapel, assisted by his son-in-law, the Rev. Robert Bolton, and his grandson, the Rev. Cornelius Winter Bolton.

Mr. Bolton seems, however, to have cherished to the last a lingering hope that he might again return to his native land. Here were the graves of his forefathers, the Priory, "his home," as he emphatically called it, built by himself; the little church, too, he loved so well, and which he had fondly hoped might be his last resting-place on earth. Is it any wonder then that he could thus write to one of his sons from

"CHELTENHAM, January 22d, 1857.

"MY DARLING R—— I forgot whether I acknowledged your letter, announcing the dear girls' arrival. I intended to do so, but left it to them to explain how we were situated. While they were with us, there was a probability of our accompanying them, for I saw that we must keep together But Providence seemed to separate us, and I saw that we must part and wait his will to bring us together again in the spring I quite long for the warmth of America"

One of his daughters writes concerning him: "He yearns quite too much after you all in America and after rest at home there." But God, in his wise providence, had determined otherwise. On the 21st of May, 1857, we find a short and hurried entry in Mrs. Bolton's Journal to this effect: "My precious husband, on rising this morning, had a severe seizure. O gracious God! be with us in this hour of trouble!" But there was a rallying again for a few months. Presently it is added: "The clouds seem gathering, but it has been so gradually broken to us—now for nearly two years—that we are in a measure prepared. And though it is indeed a trying dispensation, we do not repine. There is much mercy mixed with judgment—no pain. Lord, support the dear one! May we feel it a privilege to wait upon him in his hour of weakness. To-day we have begun a new medicine. Thou alone, O Lord, canst give it efficacy. We would begin and end every thing with thee."

At length the dreaded event occurred

"November 21st.—How little do we know what is before us! Since I wrote last, I am a widow. My precious husband has gone to his heavenly home. Precious, indeed, has he been to me in life, and death will not long divide us. I bless Thee for the husband he has ever been to me—for his bright example. What a married life have we passed—a happy one, indeed! He loved me with the purest affection, which never ceased, and I have the sweet feeling that it was the same on my part, now as forty-six years ago. I never left him but for a fortnight to nurse my dying father. My will, I can truly say, was his, and I gave up every thing for him For the last two years I have never left him, save on the Sabbath morning for the sanctuary I gave up visiting, and was ever at his side. He was never intrusted to servants, though we had faithful ones. O Lord! how shall I thank thee for the merciful kindness shown to him! So gently hast thou dealt with him in taking him to the rest prepared for him through a Saviour's love. All the circumstances have been full of mercy—many of our dear children round his bed—not a pang or groan even when the spirit was leaving its enfeebled tabernacle; and then to know that he is at rest! And now, Lord, what have we to do but to follow him? I have been sadly harassed with the thought that I may never reach that rest, yet, Lord, 'thou knowest that I love thee.' I come to thee in Christ, and thou hast promised that all who come to thee through Him shall enter in When I think of the sweet simplicity and purity of my precious husband's character, I feel thankful that thou hast set such an example before me. Oh! let me not trifle my short remainder of life away, but be preparing more earnestly for a reunion with the loved one."

Mr. Bolton's death, as the above extract intimates, was truly a falling asleep in Jesus. Rarely could that text have been more appropriately applied: "Mark the perfect man, and behold the upright; for the end of that man is *peace*."

He died on Thursday evening at ten minutes to seven o'clock, November 19th, 1857, at his residence, Vittoria House, Cheltenham, Gloucestershire.

To great gentleness of character, he united much firmness of purpose, and having laid the foundation of his faith on the Rock of Ages, he would "know nothing among men but Jesus Christ and him crucified." In him the warmth of Southern character was allied to great love of antiquarian research, and led him to delight in the land of his forefathers. An American in his feelings, he could justly appreciate the conservative tone of English society. A man of taste and of letters, he was in all respects the Christian gentleman.[v]

His remains were deposited in the cemetery at Cheltenham. A plain slab marks the spot, bearing the following inscription :

---

[v] There are excellent portraits of both Mr and Mrs. Bolton, by the celebrated Etty of the Royal Academy, in the possession of their grandchildren at Pelham Priory.

Beneath this Stone

Rest the Mortal Remains

of the

REV. ROBERT BOLTON,

Rector of

CHRIST CHURCH, PELHAM,

and Chaplain to the Earl Ducie.

Born in Savannah, Georgia, U. S.,

10th of September, 1788.   Died at Cheltenham,

19th of November, 1857.

He held forth the word of Life faithfully for forty years in many places.   Christ
was his confidence, and Christ his theme.   The last text which he preached
from, was: "He which testifieth these things," &c   Rev xxii.
20   His wife and family here record in thankfulness to
God his tender affection, prevailing prayers,
and pure example.

Also of

ANNE,

his tenderly beloved wife, eldest daughter and child of the

Rev. William Jay, of Bath,

who died September 27th, 1859,

aged 65 years.

Mr. Bolton's last will and testament bears date, Pelham,

seventh of August, 1850, and was proved at White Plains, nineteenth of January, 1858:

WILL OF THE REV. ROBERT BOLTON, RECTOR OF CHRIST CHURCH, PELHAM.

IN THE NAME OF GOD: AMEN. I, Robert Bolton of the Town of Pelham, in the County of Westchester, and State of New-York, clergyman, being of sound mind and memory, and considering the uncertainty of life, do make, publish, and declare this to be my last will and testament in manner and form following: That is to say, after all my just debts are fully paid and discharged, I give, devise, and bequeath all that shall remain of my estate and property of every kind and description whatsoever, and wheresoever the same may or shall be situated, unto my beloved wife Anne for and during her natural life, and at and after her decease, or immediately upon my decease, if she should die before me, I give, devise, and bequeath the said estate and property to my seven daughters, Anne, Mary Statira, Arabella, Rhoda, Adelle, Adelaide, and Georgiana,[w] or to each of them as shall survive one another, in equal shares, share and share alike, and as tenants in common as to any real estate I may leave; to have and to hold the same to them, their heirs and assigns forever.

And I do hereby constitute and appoint my said wife Anne and my said daughter Anne, (usually called Annette,) to be executrixes of this my last will and testament, hereby revoking and annulling all other wills by me at any time made.

In witness whereof I have hereunto set my hand and seal, this seventh day of August, in the year of our Lord one thousand eight hundred and fifty.

Robert Bolton

Signed, sealed, published, and declared by the Testator, as and for his last will and testament, in our presence, who have hereunto, at his request, witnessed, and have hereunto subscribed our names.

GERARDUS CLARK, Pelham, Westchester Co., N. Y.
H. W. CLARK, Pelham, Westchester Co., N. Y.

Upon the 11th of May, 1811, Mr. Bolton married Anne, eldest daughter and child of the Rev. William Jay, in Walcot Church, Bath. She was born at Lambridge, in the County of Somerset, November 15th, 1793, and baptized by the Rev.

---

[w] His five sons had been already provided for under the will of their grandfather.—AUTHOR.

Cornelius Winter. Her father, the Rev. William Jay, (only son of William[x] and Sarah Jay,) was born at Tisbury, in Wiltshire, on the 6th of May, 1769, and was the author of the *Morning and Evening Exercises*, which bear his name, and which have profited so many thousands of Christians. "He commenced preaching at the age of sixteen," "at Ablington Wilts, and made his first appearance at Surrey Chapel at the age of nineteen;" "but his regular ministry was confined to Bath, and was never interrupted until he resigned the charge of Argyle Chapel, January 30th, 1853. This venerable man, like a shock of corn, fully ripe, departed this life at Percy Place, Bath, at half-past six o'clock in the evening, on Tuesday, December 27th, 1853, in the eighty-fifth year of his age. Few men have lived to accomplish so much good or to leave behind them a name so honored and precious." His remains were interred on the 2d of January, 1854, in the cemetery at Snow Hill, belonging to Argyle Chapel.[y] Her mother Anne,

---

[x] "The family of Jay have been seated in Wiltshire for nearly three centuries. Many of the name of Jay have been baptized, married, and buried at Milton Listebon in Wilts. There is one marriage that may have been that of the Rev. William Jay's father and mother: '1751, May 13th. William Jay and Sarah Smith.' A Rev. Charles Jay was vicar of that parish in the year 1733, and died there 1761." The Jays are of French origin, and presumed to be of the family of Le Jay of Poitou. The arms of Le Jay are: D'azure au chevron d'or, en chef demi soleil splendant, entre deux étoiles de même en point, a roc propre surmonté par oiseaux. Crest, Deux cœurs unis. See also *Tresor Heraldique ou Mercurie Armorial.* A Paris, MDCLVII.

ARMS OF LE JAY.

[y] The following tablet was erected to his memory in Argyle Chapel, Bath:

was the eldest daughter of the Rev. Edward Davies, first Rector of Bengeworth, Worcestershire, and afterwards of Coy church, County of Glamorgan, by his wife, Anne, whose maiden name was Gauntlett, sister of the Rev. Mr. Gauntlett, Rector of Olney, Buckinghamshire, during the time the poet Cowper resided there. Mrs. Jay's step-mother was the celebrated Arabella Davies, whose letters to her children were published, and of whose character an account is found among Gibbons' *Pious Women*. Mrs. Jay died October 14th, 1845, in the seventy-ninth year of her age. Mr. Jay thus speaks of her in his autobiography: "It was she (for we always judge of the whole by parts, and chiefly by those parts with which we are most acquainted) it was she who contributed so much to give me that exalted idea of the female character which I have always entertained and expressed. She excluded perfectly the entrance of every notion and feeling of submission or authority, so that we had no rights to adjust, or duties to regulate. She possessed every requisite that could render her a helpmate. Her special qualities were admirably suited to my defects. She had an extemporaneous readiness which never failed her, and an intuitive decisiveness which seemed to require no deliberation. Her domestic virtues rendered my house a complete home, the abode of neatness, order, punctuality, peace, cheerfulness, comfort, and attraction. She calmed my brow when ruffled by disappointment or vexation; she encouraged me when depressed; she kept off a thousand cares,

---

Sacred to the Memory

of

THE REV WILLIAM JAY,

For more than sixty-two years the faithful and beloved Pastor of the Church and Congregation, assembling in this Place of Worship His distinguished gifts, his holy life, and his unwearied labours were crowned, by the Divine Blessing, with extensive usefulness, and he left a conviction of his inestimable worth, which this tablet, erected as a tribute of affection, is designed to commemorate He was born May 8th, 1769, ordained, January 30th, 1791, died, December 27th, 1851, in the 85th year of his age He was a good man, and full of the Holy Ghost and of Faith. Acts xi 24 and left me free to attend to the voice of my calling. She reminded me of my engagements when I was forgetful, and stimulated me when I was remiss, and always gently enforced the *present* obligation, as ' the duty of every day required ' "[z] "The writer of this can testify, from his own experience, that the husband has not over-painted the character of the wife to whom he had been united for the long period of fifty-four years."[a]

Mrs. Bolton was scarcely seventeen years of age at the time of Mr. Bolton's first stay at Bath, but mature in character for her years. " Her father thus speaks of her in his autobiography : ' My first-born was a daughter, and named Anne, after her mother. She seemed one of those who are sanctified from the womb ; and instead of being averse to any of the duties required of her in her training, she appeared naturally and without admonition to fall in with them. When she was only seven years old, and we went away from home for a few days, the little creature, not waiting for any intimation from us, read a chapter and a prayer every morning and evening with the servants. Here was the early manifestation of a sensitive conscience and a decision of character which distinguished Mrs. Bolton through life. Mrs. Hannah More, on seeing her as a child, archly pronounced her ' a little Independent.' This prediction was not verified in the direction of Nonconformity, for she finally became an Episcopalian by preference ; but in matters involving principle and essential truth, no one was more firm and uncompromising, or better fulfilled the apostolic injunction in both its particulars, ' speaking the truth in love.' For those who believe in the theory of the face being an index of the mind, there certainly was some confirmation in Mrs. Bolton's case. She had a thoughtful and beautiful countenance, but this seemed only the expression of what was within—a peculiar innocency of mind, truthfulness, serenity, and sensibility. Her natural character might be described as a blending of the exquisite feeling and simplicity of her father, and the quiet dignity and

[z] *Autobiography of Rev William Jay*, edited by Redford and James, vol 1. p. 103
[a] *Recollections of William Jay* By his son Cyrus Jay, p 208.

benevolence of her mother, with yet a certain loveliness all
her own. 'Noble creature,' Mr. Jay would say of her, his
eyes swimming with tears, when he heard of any of her acts
of devotion and self-sacrifice. And then to this was added—
like 'the crown' round the various articles of furniture used in
the tabernacle service—the grace of a genuine though retiring
piety. This had already so approved itself, that she had been
admitted to the Lord's table in Argyle Chapel; whilst at
home—perhaps the truest test—it had manifested itself in
such a choice of friends, in such sympathy with all, in such
patience and fortitude under some physical suffering to which
she had been called in this her early youth, as gave promise of
no ordinary kind.

Such was the wife destined, or rather provided, for Mr. Bolton. A few years after their marriage, and during their season of prosperity in Liverpool, we find Mrs. Bolton superin-
tending the affairs of her large household in the most conscientious manner. She was "in the world, but not of it."
Though moving necessarily in an extensive sphere of society,
she was not entangled by its snares, nor distracted by its turmoil,
so as to be rendered unfit for domestic and religious duties.
Indeed she seemed at this time rather to have grown in grace.
"God's goodness was leading her to repentance." Sometimes
affliction has to effect this; but it is not always so. God often
melts and draws by the bands of love. It was at the height
of earthly bliss, surrounded by every luxury, with a loving
husband and loving children, herself just emerging into the
world where she was only valued and admired—it was just
then that the results of a pious training told and the real
responsibilities of life began to be felt. It will be seen from
her diary or *Record of Mercies*, as she used to call it, that she
regarded this as the turning point in her religious history.
To those who knew her best, this would admit of a question.
The evidence of piety had already been too palpable to be
mistaken. But, at any rate, we may be sure that there had
been something hitherto wanting toward the establishment of
her Christian character—far deeper and more experimental
acquaintance with Gospel truth, and a more entire consecra-
tion of the body and soul as the living sacrifice, acceptable

unto God through Christ. To this, therefore, God was now leading her, and making every thing conducive. A single extract from the diary will best show this.

The first entry, made in the year 1815, when Mrs. Bolton was twenty-five years of age, is as follows:

"I have been reading a memoir of that devoted young Christian, Mrs. Newell, and trust it has been useful to me in leading me to examine myself. O God! forgive me! May I never cease wrestling with thee until I have an assurance that I am pardoned, and that I have an interest in the merits of Christ Jesus! My sins now seem as if they would overwhelm me. Where shall I go, what shall I do to get rid of them? I will lay them at the foot of the Cross. It was there poor Pilgrim dropped his, and was eased, and went on his way rejoicing. But shall I ever rejoice? It seems impossible. Even should God have mercy upon me, yet I can not but mourn for the rest of my days the iniquity that has abounded in me; and that, too, with all the light of a religious education; Lord, now assure me that I have an interest in thee I ask nothing else, that alone seems to me as if it would be more than I could bear What! Pardon one who has so often rebelled against thee, and been wrapped up in the world and the things of the world; always thinking how I should appear in the eyes of my fellow-creatures while my soul was naked before Thee? The more I look back, the more it seems an infatuation, a dream, that the cares of this life should have so engrossed my time and attention when eternity is before me! O Lord! how can I endure thine all-searching eye? Thou art merciful, full of compassion; have pity on me, the greatest of sinners!"

During the period of painful suspense and trial, which followed Mr. Bolton's losses in Liverpool, she writes, March 19th, 1821:

"Mr. R——'s text to-day was indeed most applicable under our present circumstances; it seemed a sermon of itself. 'The Lord direct your hearts into the love of God, and into the patient waiting for Christ.' He observed how much easier it was to be active than patient; that the confinement of some persons to a sick chamber required more fortitude than meeting a thousand perils When we have spread all before a throne of grace, we seem to expect necessarily an immediate answer to our prayers, and begin to feel discouraged if we do not perceive it But this is wrong—God's time is the best time, and we may safely leave all with Him He will answer us just when it will most conduce to His glory, and be of the most use He generally allows every expectation and hope of relief from man to fail, that His power may be the more apparent. So it was with the raising of Lazarus O my soul! under all difficulties, both spiritual and temporal, be content to wait God's time! Thy strength is to sit still. This I know, that, in His own good way and time, He will appear for us and bless us. Yes, in that God, who has done so much for us hitherto as a family, we may safely trust, leaving all to Him."

"*New-York, United States, March 3d,* 1822 —I feel ashamed that special mercies and deliverances alone seem to compel me to write. Am I not every day receiving mercies? It is because they are so common they are not recorded. May this renewed instance of thy goodness—a safe voyage— lead me to Thee, the Fountain of all good! I shall then feel it as difficult to restrain my pen, as I have done to use it in this solemn way; for solemn it is to converse between God and my soul. Am I not now in thy presence, O thou searcher of hearts? Accept my song of praise. The One hundred and sixteenth Psalm has always been dear to me, and speaks the feelings of my heart after such deliverances. But if so formerly, how much more now! 'Oh! that I may walk before the Lord in the land of the living!'"

On returning to England, she writes:

"*Weymouth, January 1st,* 1824 —This day twelve-month I was writing in my diary in America. How much has transpired since then! Life spared when brought to the borders of the grave; carried safely over the mighty deep, restored to those dear relations I left, without a breach having been made by death in the two years. Reflecting upon such great and continued mercy, I feel overcome with gratitude, and know not how to express my feelings. I never felt so much enjoyment in religion as I have done for this past year, so that, at times, I have said: 'This is no delusion, I must be interested in it, or I should not be thus happy.' I feel that I can leave *all* in the hands of my dear Redeemer and Saviour; and, though I serve Him with faltering step, and in much weakness, yet I do endeavor, I do long and pray to be more holy. This heart, though hard still, is, I trust, softened; *affliction* has not been altogether lost upon me."

Mrs. Bolton had a very tender and sensitive conscience, and it is interesting to observe how, while she grew in grace and in confidence in the finished work of the Saviour, she never lost this. Not the most encouraging doctrines or promises ever seduced her into presumption or Antinomian carelessness. The more she saw of the perfections and all-sufficiency of the Saviour, the more she seemed to feel the need of daily renewal by His Spirit. The secret of this completeness of her Christianity, we believe to have been, that by a simple faith she was kept close to the word of God, and to "the whole counsel of God" in that word. Every part of it, in its place and proportion of faith, found its reflection in her heart without prejudice and without partiality.

A few further reflections from the diary, made during her twelve years' residence at Henley, will serve to illustrate this point, and the *heart-work* of the Christian generally.

"*Henley*, 1825 —And have the desires of our hearts been so far accomplished, our wishes thus gratified? Without our seeking it, hast thou, O Lord! thus fixed the bounds of our habitation? When ready to sink, and to say where shall we go, what shall we do, thou hast directed and led us We can not doubt (so evidently has thy hand appeared in this event) but that thou hast placed us here. And if so, then it is to answer some good end. Oh! let it be accomplished Make us blessings to our fellow-sinners, and in watering others, may we ourselves be watered. I feel so unworthy of all—and this is no affectation, but the genuine feeling of my heart—that I long for some retired place in which to weep and pour out my soul. I long for a tongue unloosed to praise my God, and tell what the dear Saviour has done for me, one of the most unworthy of his children "

"*January 13th*, 1828 —Our ten little ones are now under our roof. Lord, bless them spiritually. As to temporal concerns, we would leave them I treat these as secondary matters, if thou wouldst only give them thy grace. Oh! how do my bowels yearn over them, and how earnestly do I desire that they may live before thee !"

"*Surrey Chapel House, London, July 6th*, 1835 —How remarkable that I should be visiting Surrey Chapel as the minister's wife, where I have so often gone as the minister's daughter ! Much might be expected from me, favored as I have been with such privileges. I can but exclaim · 'Why so barren, O my soul ?' "

Mrs. Bolton, with every child of her own, committed to her charge, seemed to hear God's voice saying : "Take this child, and nurse it for me " It was the truest of all philosophies, because taught by God Himself, that she should value the soul more than the body, the heart more than the intellect. She seemed at once to realize the precious but short period in which parental influence chiefly tells; and with the noblest solicitude she cared for nothing in comparison with seeing early manifestations of true and earnest piety. Mental acquirements, personal accomplishments, comfortable provisions for life, were not forgotten; but of what use would all be, unless sanctified and dedicated to God? It would be that danger which a merely secular education carries with it, of only giving greater power to do the greater mischief.

She began from the first, therefore, and she began in the right way, by continual agonizing prayer. Observe some of

12

her expressions: "Lord, hear the prayer of a mother!" And again: "What responsibilities do I feel in my children!" Is she absent for a few days from home? She writes: "I am absent from my dear children. Lord, teach them, by thy Holy Spirit on the morrow!" Does she return? She says: "I have been reading to my dear children an account of one of the loveliest of thy saints, Harriet Vivian, who was to glorify God by her early departure amidst all that could make life attractive." Does one of her sons go forth into life, she follows him with her prayers: "Our dear J—— has left the parental roof, and is now on the wide waters. May his fathers' God be his God! Lord, preserve him, and make him thine! Oh! the anxiety I feel about our dear children; but this is uppermost, that they may be thine!" On another occasion, when one is about to enter upon a situation which will bring him under his grandfather's ministry at Bath, she asks particularly that God would bless that faithful preaching to his conversion—and what she asks in faith is granted.

To one of her sons, on the anniversary of his birth, she writes:

"*April 17th*—This day brings you so vividly before us—the exchange of kisses before breakfast, etc., etc.—that I must for all wish you many happy returns of it. Another mile of your life passed. Oh! that, as your birthdays shorten your life *here*, you may be advancing for the heavenly. Let every year find you riper for heaven. What a mercy that our whole family are travelling the same road, though distant in *person*, yet one in *heart*, as it respects the best things, can go to the same Father, and to Jesus Christ, and I trust will all meet in our heavenly home. I often think what a *rich* family we are. Indeed it overcomes me at times that God should have dealt so with us; for what are earthly riches compared to the unsearchable mercies of redemption—to feel we are sinners, and that Christ has shed his precious blood to restore us to God. When we look around at the poor thoughtless world, we can not be too thankful that we have been led to make a better choice."

Another means made use of by Mrs. Bolton (we speak more of the mother just now, because to her belongs in an especial manner the early training) was the hallowing of the Sabbath. How much she loved and prized this holy day herself, her diary bears witness. Her feelings and desires can only find vent in the outpourings of the Psalmist: "How amiable are thy tabernacles, O Lord of hosts!" Her children well remember how she led them on in this way, and taught them to begin, even on Saturday evening, to anticipate the Sunday. "Saturday evening," she would say, "is the gate of the Sabbath." The garden-paths were to be swept; things were to be tidied and put away; the little hymn, "Safely through another week," was to be sung; Sunday lessons to be prepared; and altogether the hallowed atmosphere was to reach forward and pervade the mind, in the dismissal of earthly thoughts as much as possible, and in making "preparation for the Sabbath." On no account did any of that household go forth to a party on Saturday night. How vapid and uninteresting would God's courts and services have appeared immediately following upon scenes and dreams of worldly gaiety! And then, on the day itself, what a thorough entering into its spirit there was!—the father's thoughtful countenance, his faithful sermons, his delight in sacred music; the mother, sitting in the family pew, looking upon all with moistened eyes, her Bible-teaching in the afternoon, her spiritual fervor and conversation throughout the day. And yet there was nothing of Puritanical rigor about the Lord's Day at Henley or at Pelham. Cheerfulness and activity and healthy excitement were not wanting, only they were directed into their legitimate channels—God's service. No attempt was made—how miserable always is the failure where it is made!—to try and see just how much of the world, and how little of God can be brought into the Christian Sabbath. But it was honestly taken for granted that the day belonged to God and not to man, and therefore, that all its pleasures and occupations should be of a sacred character. The result was, that even before some could be said to be truly converted to God, they hailed the Sunday with delight; how much more when the real meaning and beauty of all those hallowed exercises broke in upon the mind, and the worship, and the praise, and the love of Christians were recognised to be the type and foretaste of joys above—

> " Where the assembly ne'er breaks up,
> And Sabbaths never end !"

One other special way of influence, blessed in this instance, was, the parents' own decision for God. Mr. and Mrs. Bolton did not weary the mind or harden the conscience by continual references to religion. It was always uppermost in their thoughts, but they knew the value of times and seasons. They lived, rather than talked religion. Much was done by a tear, a look, a smile of approbation, a pencil-note of warning or encouragement—still more by a holy and consistent example. Two simple instances of Mrs. Bolton's firmness and decision on the side of truth occur to the writer's mind here. She was staying at the house of a friend in England, who, though a godly person herself, was timid, and found it difficult to manage her sons. In the evening cards were produced. Mrs Bolton looked at her friend with surprise. The explanation was, that, while regretting it, she could not interfere. "What can I do?" she asked, with a mournful look. "What can you do?" said Mrs. Bolton promptly; "let me show you!" and very good-humoredly gathering up the cards, she deposited them in the fire. On another occasion, Mrs. Bolton and some of her family were ascending the Catskill Mountains. A number of the passengers, having alighted from the coaches, were toiling in company up the steep ascent. A gentleman, hearing one of the drivers using profane language very frequently, rebuked him, begging that he would not swear *so much.* Upon this, Mrs. Bolton, looking out of the window, remarked aloud: "My Bible teaches me: 'Swear *not at all.*'"

"Never was there a happier home than that of Mr. and Mrs. Bolton. In this, as in every respect, their children 'rise up to call them blessed.' They mingled and assisted in the family recreations as well as duties. No time was lost; studious habits were inculcated, and high attainments in every branch of study aimed at. History, the physical sciences, language, literature, art—nothing was neglected, but rather pursued with a sweeter relish, because interspersed with visits to the poor and sick, and with all the spiritual requirements of a daily walk with God."

Soon after her return to England, Mrs. Bolton writes:

"*April*, 1851 —God has indeed appeared for us, for, I may safely say, God only could have brought about so unexpected an event. The Earl of

Ducie has appointed my precious husband to be his Chaplain at Tortworth, in Gloucestershire. Lord! what are we that we should be cared for thus? May we enter upon this sphere with holy confidence, and enable us, O Lord, to do much good. Our evening of life is come, but thou canst make it the most useful."

The ninth volume of Mrs. Bolton's Diary commences thus:

"Permitted to open another record of my God's great goodness to me! Wonderful! Surely *this* will carry me to the brink of Jordan."

This anticipation was realized.

But first of all, there was work to be done. The activities of life, indeed, had nearly closed, but there had succeeded that higher and more difficult stage of experience when the Christian is called to be passive, and to do nothing but that great work of receiving more of the image of the suffering Saviour, in speedy prospect of receiving the image of the glorified Saviour.

Whilst yet at Cheltenham, she adds:

"I write under peculiar feelings, for we are thinking of a new home. I seem seldom well here, and, perhaps, need a more bracing air Brighton has been proposed, and some of my children have gone thither to see about it. Lord, condescend (for what right have we to ask such favors?) to let us see the pillar guiding us where thou wouldst have us to be Let us not follow our own inclinations."

The removal soon took place, and a house near to Christ church being secured, Mrs. Bolton usually worshipped with the congregation assembling in that place. The simplicity of the service, the congregational singing, as well as the earnestness of the preaching, were suited to her taste. Friends, new and old, soon gathered round, and she found such an abundance of Christian society as to make it appear no strange land. In her Bath chair she could enjoy the refreshing breezes without fatigue; and the sight of the ocean seemed ever to fill her with delight, not only as a sublime object in itself—the work of a God whom she loved—but because it appeared to be a link uniting her to the members of her family on distant shores. The ships slowly moving along the horizon were like winged messengers between her and America.

Her interest in literature and politics, and especially in the religious questions and movements of the day, by no means declined with advancing years, but continued unabated   She inherited a thirst for reading and for self-improvement from her father, whom, indeed, in many mental as well as moral endowments she much resembled. " Bridges on the One hundred and nineteenth Psalm" was a constant favorite with her.   The last books she perused were Prime's *Power of Prayer*, illustrated from the American Revivals, and the *I Wills* of Scripture, by an excellent clergyman of Worthing.   Upon the whole, her residence in Brighton, though a short, was a very happy one. For, whilst it was impossible not to perceive that her feeling heart was suffering intensely at times, yet, at the same time, those who were about her could not but perceive also the submissive and thankful spirit, rejoicing under the influence of Divine grace and cheerful society, not only in the prospects of eternity, but in all the incidents of daily life.

Here are a few reflections made during the years 1858-9, the "last thoughts" of one preparing for heaven :

"*September 19th.*—I feel this is a solemn day—my last Sabbath in Cheltenham.   I have been sitting in my pew at St Mary's for nearly three years   I have heard the most faithful preaching.   Ah! my soul, how little hast thou profited!   What should I do but for that most precious blood that cleanseth from all sin?   We had a solemn sermon from Mr. W——: 'Every plant, which my heavenly Father hath not planted, shall be rooted up'   Am I one of thine own planting?   I can only come to thee as a poor sinful creature!"

"*September 22d.*—I have visited my precious one's tomb.   I felt he was not there, but with his risen Saviour.   It is a severe struggle to leave behind even the dear body, and, indeed, all—so many kind, dear friends—I dare not dwell upon it   Lord, it humbles me to be made so much of by many. Ah! they know not this sinful heart; and yet it is open to thee!"

"*Brighton, October 4th*—Arrived safely in my new home, preserved from all harm through a kind providence, and with less fatigue than I expected."

On November 16th, the last anniversary of her birth-day, Mrs. Bolton writes :

"Another year—another birth-day!   Permitted to pass the day with my family.   Full of mercy—running over.   On the last my dear husband was with me. Though full of feebleness, and though I do feel bereaved and alone, still I would not recall him from his bliss. God, whose he *was*, and whom he *served*, has taken him to His own bosom, where nothing can ever hurt or annoy him any more. Now, in every pain, or disappointment, or trial, I can say, my dear one is safe. My text this morning was changed. It has been for many years 'Lord, it is thou who hast made my mountain to stand strong.' This morning it is: '*Arise, and depart hence, for this is not your rest.*'"

"*September 20th*, 1859.—Lord, I feel so *overwhelmed at thy goodness to me!*"

With this characteristic sentence, on a half-finished page, Mrs. Bolton's Journal of forty-four years closes. What a testimony to the faithfulness of God that goodness and mercy had indeed followed her *all the days of her life*.

It was written just a week previous to her death. On the following Sunday she attended Divine service in the morning, apparently in her usual health, but in the course of the day complained of sickness and fainting. Treated medically with the utmost skill and attention, it was thought at first that she might rally again, as she had done frequently before. But a closer examination served to show a want of action at the heart, symptoms of which had manifested themselves while at Cheltenham, and it became a critical case.

In the course of the Monday she asked her son, who resided near by, to pray with her, specifying the subjects of petition, and especially mentioning patience and submission under the hand of God. Some time after this, waking from sleep, she said, "Surely this must be death;" and calling one of her daughters to her side, she took her by the hand and said: "In all thy ways acknowledge Him, and He will direct thy paths." The physical prostration now became so excessive, that the mind began to wander. But even then, through all the storm, the compass of the soul kept pointing true; first, a text, and then a portion of a prayer, would be repeated over and over again.

About midnight a marked change took place for the worse, and she fell into a deep slumber, only to awake "before the throne!" Life gradually ebbed away, until just at the break of day, and as the clock of the neighboring church struck four, she ceased to breathe. Her children, sorrowful as they were, could not but recognise the drops of mercy mingled in the cup, and, amongst the rest, that the sensitive heart had been spared any thing like a formal parting, and kneeling down they were enabled to mingle praise and thanksgiving with their tears. The constantly reiterated expression, too, "*In all thy ways acknowledge Him, and He shall direct thy paths,*" came now like a sacred legacy, in the strength of which they could turn to the most painful duties.

It was indeed a mercy to have had such a mother, endued with so much humility, tenderness, devotedness, unselfishness, and largeness of heart as rarely falls to the lot of mortals. Truly her whole character might be summed up in the most perfect restoration of Christ's image in the sinful children of men. She was a very Jacob in prayer, a very David in fervor of piety, and a very John in love.

Anne Bolton

Mrs. Bolton died Tuesday, September 27th, 1859. Her remains were conveyed to Cheltenham, and interred with those of her beloved husband in the cemetery of that place. "They were pleasant in their lives, and in death they were not divided."

Children of Robert Bolton[20] and Anne Jay:

I. Robert Bolton[21] (writer of this) was born at No. 13 Paragon Buildings, Bath, in the parish of St. Michael, in the County of Somerset, England, on Sunday, the 17th of April, 1814,[b] and was baptized by his grandfather, the Rev. William Jay, in Argyle chapel. Married first Elizabeth Rebecca Brenton, (daughter of James Brenton of Newport, Rhode Island,) 8th of January, 1838, who was born at Pittstown, New-York, 2d of August, 1814, and baptized in Trinity church, Newport, 24th of August, 1824; died in New-Rochelle, Westchester County, 12th of March, 1852, and buried in the family vault, Christ church, Pelham.

He married secondly, 5th of January, 1854, Josephine, eld-

<hr/>

[b] Birth registered at Dr. Williams's Library, Redcross street, near Cripplegate, London, September 7th, 1814. Thomas Morgan, Registrar. Book E, No. 2107, D.

est daughter of Brewster and Elizabeth Woodhull, who was born in Patchogue, town of Brookhaven, Suffolk County, Long Island, on Saturday, 28th of November, 1829, and baptized March, 1844. The Woodhull family is said to be very ancient, and may be traced to Walter De Flanders, who came into England with the Conqueror, and held, as a feudal lord, at the time of the General Survey, considerable estates in the counties of Bedford and Northampton, of which WAHULL, (now Wodhull or Odhull,) in the former shire, was the head of his barony. To this Walter succeeded Walter De Wahull, whose descendant in the ninth generation was Thomas de Wahull, summoned to Parliament as a BARON on the 26th January, 1297, 25th Edward I. He died in 1304, seised of the Barony of Wahull, as also the manor of Wahull, in the County of Bedford, and Pateshill, in Northamptonshire, leaving by his wife, Hawise, daughter of Henry Pracrs, an infant son and heir, John De Wahull, who, although possessing the honor of Wahull, had no similar summons to Parliament, nor had any of his descendants. He died in the 10th Edward III , leaving two sons, Sir John, whose line terminated in heiresses, and Nicholas, whose descendant in the sixth generation was Sir Nicholas Wodhull, Knt., who, by his second wife, Elizabeth, daughter and co-heir of Sir William Parr, Lord Parr, of Horton, had Fulk Woodhull, ancestor of the Woodhulls of Thenford. He was Lord of the manor of Thenford in the reigns of James I. and of Elizabeth, and died in 1613. Under the upper window of the north aisle in Thenford Church, Northampton, is a monument erected to his memory. By his wife Alice, daughter of William Coles of Leigh, he had, with other issue, Lawrence Woodhull, whose son, Richard Woodhull, was born at Thenford, Northampton, September 13th, 1620. The precise time of Richard Woodhull's arrival in this country is not known, but it must have been as early as 1648. He is first known in the town of Jamaica, Long Island, where his name appears associated with the early settlers of that place. But disliking the policy and measures of the Dutch government, he left the western part of the island, and seated himself permanently at Setauket, then called Cromwell Bay, or Ashford, and became one of the most useful and valuable citizens of that place. His particular knowledge in surveying and drawing conveyances, rendered his services invaluable at that early period of the settlement, and his name is found associated with most of the transactions of the town during his life. His death occurred October, 1690, leaving issue, by his wife Deborah, Richard, Nathaniel, and Deborah. Richard, the eldest son, was born October 9th, 1649, and, like his father, was an intelligent and useful man. He was early chosen a magistrate, and retained the office till near his death, October 18th, 1699, having survived his father only about nine years. His knowledge and integrity endeared him to the people, and he died much lamented. His sons were Richard, Nathaniel, John, and Josiah.

By an original letter, now in possession of his descendants, it appears that a relationship existed with Thomas Crew, second baron Crew of Stene in the County of. Northampton, and the Rt. Rev. Nathaniel Crew, Lord Bishop of Durham.[c] This letter is as follows:

"SR. I was heartily glad to find by yr letter that it had pleased God to blesse and prosper your family, and that you received the small present," (crest and arms[d] of the family,) "I sent you some time since, wh I thought had been lost For our country news, take this account. My father departed this life Dec. 12, 1679, and as he lived well, soe he had great joye at his death, with a longing to leave this world. I have six children, but noe sonne, it having pleased God to take him in ye fifteenth yeare of his age, a

---

[c] He was forty-seven years Bishop of Durham, having previously held that of Oxford for three He died 1721

[d] This coat of arms and crest are still preserved in the old family mansion at Setauket It is nearly three feet square, in panel, and contains the following coats 1 Or, three crescents, gu Woodhull 2 Arg on a cross az five escallops, or, Foxcote 3 Quarterly, ar and gu a cross, formee, counterchanged Chetwoode, Or, fretty sa, a bar ermine, on a chief gu three leopards' faces, or Sounde, 5 Or, a fesse gu betw three lozenges of the last Hoccliffe 6 Ar a lion rampant, gu De Lyon, 7 Ar a cross, gu over all a bend az Newenham 8 Ar two bars, az within a bordure engrailed, sa Parr 9 Or, three water-bougets, sa, two and one Ros 10 Arg a saultier, gu fretty Or, Crophull 11 Or, a tret, gu Verdon. 12 Az three chev braced in base, or, a chief of the second Fitz Hugh 13 Barry of twelve, or and az an eagle, displayed, gu Gernegan 14 Gu a bend betw six cross crosslets, or Furneaux 15 Barry of six. arg. and az and over all on a bend, gu three martlets, or Grey 16 Vairy, a fesse, gu Marmion 17 Or, three chevrons, gu a chief vairy St Quintin 18 Gu a lion, rampant, or, between three crescents arg. Salusbury —Crest, two wings endorsed, gu issuing from a ducal coronet, over all a mantel for Woodhull.

man growne and very hopefull. God's will be done. My brother Walgrave hath left one sonne, who stands heire both to ye Bishop of Duresme (Durham) and myselfe for Thenford. Y^r cozen Wodhull lives very well, is a justice of peace, and very well beloved. The three brothers live all together with the greatest kindnesse that can bee. My uncle Sol died last year, and is buried at Hinton; my uncle Thomas a yeare before; my uncle Nathaniel is still living. I have inclosed the papers you desire. My service to all my cozens. I rest your loving friend and kinsman, CREWE.

"STEANE, Sep. 5, 1687.

"Ffor my Loving Kinsman, Richard Wodhull, Esq."

To his eldest son, Richard, who was born November 2d, 1691, Richard Woodhull devised his paternal estate in Setauket, now in possession of his descendant of the sixth generation. He, like his father, was a magistrate for many years, and was in all respects a useful and highly exemplary man. He married Mary, daughter of John Homan, by whom he had issue, Richard, Mary, Nathan, Stephen, Henry, and Phœbe. His death took place November 24th, 1767, aged seventy-six years, and his widow died in 1768. Richard, the eldest son, commonly called Justice Woodhull, took the paternal estate at Setauket. He was born October 11th, 1712, and died October 13th, 1788. By his wife, Margaret, daughter of Edmund Smith of Smithtown, he had, with other issue, Stephen Woodhull, born at Setauket, 1732, who, by his wife, Hannah, daughter of Abraham Cooper, had issue John Woodhull, who was born at Setauket, 1759, and died February 4th, 1804, the father of Brewster Woodhull, Esq.

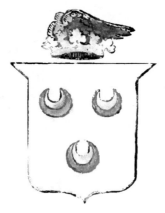

THE ARMS OF RICHARD WOODHULL, ESQ., OF THENFORD.

The children of Robert Bolton[21] and Josephine Woodhull:

I. ANNE JAY BOLTON, was born in Fulton street, Jamaica, Queens County, Long Island, Tuesday, November 21st, 1854, and baptized by her uncle, the Rev. Cornelius Winter Bolton, in Christ church, Pelham, December 25th, 1854.

II. ROBERT BOLTON[23], was born in New-Rochelle, Westchester County, Friday, November 30th, 1855, and was baptized by his uncle, the Rev. C. W. Bolton, in Christ church, Pelham, on Christmas morning, December 25th, 1855.

III. JOHN BOLTON[23], was born at the Irving House, Tarrytown, Westchester County, Tuesday, August 11th, 1857, and was baptized by his uncle, the Rev. C. W. Bolton, in Christ Church Chapel, Beekmantown, September 10th, 1857. His godfather was the late Washington Irving, Esq., of Tarrytown.

IV. JAMES ROBERT BOLTON[23], was born in Bedford, Westchester County, Saturday, February 26th, 1859, and baptized by the Rev. Edward Brenton Boggs, in St. Matthew's church, Bedford, May 8th, 1859.

V. WILLIAM JAY BOLTON[23], was born in Bedford, Wednesday, June 19th, 1861, and baptized by the Rev. Edward Brenton Boggs, in St. Matthew's Church, Bedford, Sunday, September 8th, 1861.

II. ANNE BOLTON was born at Paragon Buildings, Bath, Somerset, England, June 20th, 1815, and baptized by her grandfather, Rev. William Jay, at his house in Percy Place. She is still the principal of Pelham Priory, and the authoress of the *Lighted Valley; or, the Closing Scenes of the Life of Abby Bolton*, with a Preface by her grandfather, the Rev. William Jay of Bath. *Died Aug 6. 1884.*

III. WILLIAM JAY BOLTON[21] was born in Pulteney street, Bath, August 31st, 1816, and baptized by his grandfather, Rev. William Jay, in private. In 1849 he was entered as a fellow-commoner at Gonville and Caius College, Cambridge, where he graduated in 1853, and afterwards took his M.A. degree. He was admitted to deacons' orders, November 13th, 1853, and ordained Priest, November 12th, 1854, in Ely Cathedral, by Dr. Turton, Lord Bishop of Ely. He was appointed to the curacy of Christ Church, Barnwell, Cambridge, and thence to that of Rev. John Browne of Trinity Church, Cheltenham, at whose decease he removed to St. James's, Brighton, where he still continues to officiate. *Died May 28" 1884.*

He is the author of *The Evidences of Christianity, as exhibited in the Writings of its Apologists down to the Time of Augustine,* an essay which obtained the Hulsean prize for the year 1852 ; also of *The Footsteps of the Flock, being Memorials of the Rev. Robert Bolton, Rector of Pelham, U. S., and Chaplain to the Earl of Ducie, and of Mrs. Bolton;* and of *Fireside Preaching,* (Hamilton, Adams & Co.)

Mr. Bolton has been twice married ; first, September 26th, 1849, to Susanna, daughter of John Welch, Esq , London, who died at Cambridge, December 4th, 1851, leaving a daughter, Susanna Bolton, born November 29th, 1851, baptized in St. Paul's Church, Cambridge, by the Rev. G. Scott, grandson of the Commentator. Secondly, August 14th, 1855, to Margaretta Elizabeth Jones Wilkinson, daughter of Rev. Henry Watts Wilkinson, Incumbent of Sudbury, and Vicar of Walton cum Felixstowe, Suffolk, (eldest son of Rev. Watts Wilkinson, who for many years filled the office of Golden Lecturer at St. Bartholomew's, Exchange, London,) and of Sarah, his wife, daughter of Edward Walker, Esq., of Overhall, Guestingthorpe, Essex, and granddaughter of Rev. William Jones of Nayland.

By his latter marriage, he has had,

I. William Henry Bolton[22], born at Brighton, May 7th, 1859, baptized by Rev. C. D. Maitland at the Chapel Royal, June 17th, 1859.

II. Arabella Sarah Bolton, born at Brighton, October 6th, 1860, baptized November 16th, 1860, died at Farnham, Surrey, September 16th, 1861, (in the cemetery of which place she is buried,) and

III. Margaretta Grace Bolton, born at Brighton, November 14th, 1861, and baptized December 20th, by the Rev. C. D. Maitland, at the Chapel Royal.

IV. John Bolton[21], born at his grandfather's, Rev. William Jay's, house, No. 4 Percy Place, Bath, February 7th, 1818, and baptized by his grandfather, in public, at Argyle Chapel, on Sunday, March 8th, 1818. He was admitted to deacons' orders by the Rt. Rev. Horatio Potter, D.D., of New-York, in Christ church, Pelham, Saturday, November 10th, 1860, and ordained priest, Saturday, 25th of February, 1862. He was called Rector of the Church of the Redeemer, Morristown, New-Jersey, December, 1861. Upon the 21st of June, 1848, he was married, by the Rev. C W. Bolton, to Catharine, fourth daughter of Philip Schuyler, grandson of Major-General Philip Schuyler of Schuylerville, and Grace Hunter, and has issue,

I. ABBY BOLTON, born at New-Rochelle, April 5th, 1849, baptized by her grandfather, the Rev. Robert Bolton, in Christ church, Pelham, July 1st, 1849. *died*   *188*

II. CATHARINE SCHUYLER BOLTON, born at New-Rochelle, June 17th, 1851, baptized in Christ church, Pelham, August 31st, 1851. *died July 4" 1888*

III. PHILIP SCHUYLER BOLTON[22], born at Pelham Priory, December 13th, 1853, baptized in private, January 18th, 1854.

IV. NANETTE BOLTON, born at Pelham Priory, April 12th, 1855, baptized in Christ church, Pelham, July 8th, 1855.

V. CORNELIUS WINTER BOLTON[21], so named after the Rev. Cornelius Winter of Painswick, Gloucestershire, born at No. 35 Pulteney street, Bath, Somerset, June 3d, 1819, baptized at his father's house, No. 8 Great George street, Liverpool, England, by his grandfather, the Rev. William Jay. He studied divinity in the Theological Seminary at Alexandria, Virginia, and was admitted to deacons' orders in St. John's church, Richmond city, Virginia, March 21st, 1847, by the Rt. Rev. John Johns, Assistant Bishop of the Diocese of Virginia. He was ordained priest in St. Peter's church, New-York, April 16th, 1848, by the Rt. Rev. Alonzo Potter, Bishop of Pennsylvania; and was called to assist his father, March 29th, 1847; and resigned in 1850 to accept a call as assistant minister to Christ church, Baltimore, Maryland. In 1855 he was re-called as rector to Christ church, Pelham. On the 1st of May, 1858, was elected rector of South-Yonkers, from whence he was called as minister of St. George's Mission Chapel, New-York. September 11th, 1856, he married Cornelia, eldest daughter of Cornelius Glenn Van Rensselaer, Esq., of Greenbush, Rensselaer County, third son of General John T. Van Rensselaer, of Rensselaer Manor

The Rev. Cornelius W Bolton is the author of *The Shepherd's Call; Sunday-School Prayer-Book; Tender Grass for Little Lambs*, 1854; *Child's Heart;* and *Child's Shelter*, 1860. In 1854 he edited *Jay's Female Scripture Characters; Jay's Autobiography and Reminiscences.*

VI. MARY STATIRA BOLTON, (so named from her aunt Statira Jay, who died August 31st, 1820,) born at Bathampton Cottage near Bath, Somerset, November 6th, 1820; baptized by her grandfather, Rev. William Jay, April, 1821. She was married at St Mary's church, Cheltenham, Gloucestershire, by her brother, the Rev. James Bolton, B.A., July 14th, 1857, to the Rev. John Rooker, M.A., curate of Weobley, Herefordshire, now Incumbent of Holy Trinity, Runcorn, Cheshire. Their children are,

I. JOHN ROOKER, ⎫
II. ANNE ROOKER, ⎬ twin, born at Cheltenham, May 3d,
1858; baptized by their father at St. Mary's, Cheltenham, May 26th, 1858.

III. MARY STATIRA ROOKER, born at Runcorn, November 17th, 1859; baptized by her father at Trinity church, Runcorn, February 24th, 1860.

IV. JAMES JAY ROOKER, born at Runcorn, February 20th, 1862.

VII. ARABELLA BOLTON,[e] (so named from her beloved aunt, Arabella Jay, wife of Garfit Ashton, Esq., who died suddenly at her residence in Cambridge, on Sunday afternoon, February 19th, 1854,) born at her uncle's, James McClean Bolton's, residence, No. 490 Broadway, New-York, February 12th, 1822; baptized by her father, at the chapel Henley-upon-Thames. After much suffering, which she bore with Christian fortitude and resignation, this sweet saint rested in peace at her residence, 24 Montpelier Road, Brighton, Sussex, Thursday, June 28th, 1860, and on the 2d of July was buried at Hove church, near Brighton.

The following inscription is on her grave-stone:

---

[e] Her mother, Anne Jay, was the step-daughter of the pious Arabella Davies.

Here rests,

Awaiting the Morning of the Resurrection,

ARABELLA,

Third Daughter of the Rev. Robert Bolton, late Rector of Pelham, U.S.,

Born in New-York, Feb'y 12th, 1822.

Her life was one of singular Christian loveliness, and she was inexpressibly dear to all
who knew her. But her only trust was in the mercy of God, through Jesus
Christ. In her dying hour she said · "I have been an unprofitable
servant, but I hide myself in Christ" An abundant entrance
was ministered unto her out of much suffering into the
everlasting kingdom, June 28th, 1860. Reader,
has the same divine life begun in your soul?

VIII. James Bolton[21], born at Southdown Cottage, Weymouth, Dorset, February 11th, 1824; baptized by his father at the chapel, Henley-on-Thames, Oxon. He was entered at Corpus Christi College, Cambridge, 1844, where he took a scholarship in 1846, and his B.A. degree in 1848. In the same year he was ordained deacon in Ely Cathedral by the Lord Bishop of Ely, and appointed to the curacy of Saffron Walden, Essex. He was admitted to priests' orders, 1849, by the Lord Bishop of Rochester, in Archbishop Tennyson's Chapel, Regent street, London. In 1851 he removed to the curacy of St. Michael's, Pimlico, London; and from thence, in 1852, he was instituted to the Incumbency of St. Paul's Episcopal Chapel, Kilburn, London, where he still continues to officiate. June 30th, 1853, he was married in St. Michael's church, Pimlico, by the Rev. J. H. Hamilton, Incumbent, to Lydia Louisa, third daughter of the Rev. William Wollaston Pym, rector of Willian, Herts, descended on her paternal side from John Pym, the Puritan, and on the maternal, from the Gambiers, her great uncle, Baron

Gambier, being the founder of Gambier College, Ohio, United States.   Their children are, *Died apl 8" 1863.*

I. ROBERT GAMBIER BOLTON[22], born at Kilburn Lodge, Kilburn, August 24th, 1854, and baptized by his father, in the parish church, Hempstead.

II. FRANCIS JAMES BOLTON[22], born at Kilburn Lodge, Kilburn, August 23d, 1855, and baptized by his uncle, Rev. William Jay Bolton, at Leckhampton church, Cheltenham. Died at Kilburn, February 20th, 1858.

III. REGINALD PELHAM BOLTON[22], born at Kilburn Lodge, Kilburn, October 5th, 1856, and baptized by his father in St Mark's church, Hamilton Terrace, London.

IV. WILLIAM WASHINGTON BOLTON[22], born at Kilburn Lodge, July 3d, 1858, and baptized by his father in St. Mark's church, Hamilton Terrace, London.

V. MARY LOUISA BOLTON, born at Kilburn Lodge, April 29th, 1860, and baptized by her father in St. Paul's Episcopal chapel, Kilburn.

VI. JAMES BEAUCHAMP BOLTON[22], born at Kilburn Lodge, May 4th, 1861, and baptized by his father in St. Paul's Episcopal chapel, Kilburn.

The Rev. James Bolton is the author of *Addresses to the Young*, 12mo; *Fragments of the Great Diamond*, 12mo, *Brook Farm, a Record of American Country Life*, 12mo; *Life Lessons*, 8vo; and *Sermons on Special Occasions*, 1 vol. 12mo.

IX. RHODA BOLTON, born at Henley-upon-Thames, Oxon. September 20th, 1825, and baptized by her father at the chapel.   Now living at Brighton, Sussex. *Died at Brighton apl 25.*

X. ABBY BOLTON, so named from Abby Woolsey, daughter of Joseph Howland, Esq., of New-York, was born at Henley-upon-Thames, Saturday, February 3d, 1827, and baptized by her father at the chapel. This lovely flower, the subject of the *Lighted Valley*, was removed in the bloom of life, and transplanted to the heavenly paradise, June 16th, 1849, buried in the family vault at Christ church, Pelham, June 18th, 1849. There is a tablet erected over the vault, inscribed as follows:

Sacred to the memory

of

ABBY BOLTON,

Who slept in peace, June 16th, 1849.

She was the fifth daughter

of the

REV ROBERT BOLTON,

Founder and First Rector of this Church.

Loving purity from principle, she courted the shade   Her religion dwelt upon the

spirit, and was sweetly exhibited in the every-day duties of life   This is

pure and undefiled religion. "Her God sustained her in her final

hour—her final hour brought glory to her God"

This tablet is erected by her friends

XI. META BOLTON, born at Henley-upon-Thames, February 5th, 1828; died an infant.

XII. ADELLE BOLTON, } twin. Born at Henley-upon-
XIII. ADELAIDE BOLTON, } Thames, March 5th, 1830; baptized by their father at the chapel. The former living at Pelham Priory, the latter at Brighton, Sussex.

XIV. FRANCES GEORGIANA BOLTON, born at Henley-upon-Thames, Oxon, August 29th, 1831; baptized by her father at the chapel, Henley-upon-Thames, Oxon. Now living at Brighton, Sussex.

SECTION VI.

JAMES McCLEAN BOLTON[20], Esq., merchant, youngest surviving son of Robert[19] and Sarah Bolton, so named from his maternal grandfather, James McClean, was born at his father's residence in Oglethorpe Square, Anson Ward, Savannah, in the parish of Christ Church, Chatham County, Georgia, on Friday, July 6th, 1792, and baptized the same year. The death of his parents, while he was a boy, was a great grief to him, for he was just at an age to know his loss. He was constituted by his father's will a partner of the great commercial house of Robert and John Bolton, of Savannah. After his first marriage, in 1816, he removed to Philadelphia, and subsequently settled in New-York. He maintained an honorable character as a merchant, and took an active part in the support of the great Christian institutions of the day. He was an annual subscriber to the Deaf and Dumb Institution of New-York, from 1818 to 1823. Like his brother, he, too, was a man of a meek and quiet spirit, and so fond of private life, that he never appears to have desired any employment in public affairs. When his only brother, Robert, visited this country in 1822, for the purpose of settling their father's estate, he gladly received him into his own house, No. 490 Broadway. He loved this brother with the tenderest affection, and when he left New-York for England, the following year, seemed to feel the separation most keenly. In their case, it may be truly said, a cord had been snapped asunder which, in this world, could never be united again; but a few years swiftly pass, and the two brothers so meek, so good, so loving, and lovely in their lives, are now, we trust, reünited in heaven. He died at his residence in Fulton street, Jamaica, Long Island, Thursday, 12th of February, 1824. His remains were deposited in the Presbyterian burying-ground, at Jamaica, near the principal entrance on the east side of the path.

The following notice of his death appeared in the *Long Island Farmer* of February 19th, 1824 : " Died on Thursday last, in Jamaica, Mr. James Bolton."

James McBolton

James McClean Bolton, Esq., merchant, married first, April 30th, 1816, Mary Ann, daughter of Robert and Eliza Clay, who was born in Philadelphia, December 11th, 1802. Her grandfather was Curtis Clay, Esq., eldest son of Slater Clay, the first son of Robert Clay[f] and Ann Curtis, (who afterwards married Robert Bolton.) The Clays were an ancient family, formerly residing at Crich[g] in Derbyshire. Mrs. Bolton died on Monday, August 24th, 1818, and was buried in the Arch street cemetery, Philadelphia. On a neat marble tombstone is inscribed the following :

---

[f] Robert Clay, of Philadelphia, who was lost at sea in 1716, was the only son of Robert Clay, Esq., by his first wife, Hannah Slater. Robert Clay, Sen., Esq., who resided at Chesterfield, afterwards removed to Sheffield, Yorkshire, and died there in July, 1737. The will of Robert Clay, of Bridgehouses, in the parish of Sheffield, bears date 30th of September, 1736, and was proved in the Exchequer Court of York, 22d January, 1738. Among other items are the following: " I give unto my grandson, Slater Clay, and to my grandson, Thomas Clay, each of them five shillings a peece in full of what they may or can clame out of any part of my freehould, copyhould, or personall estate whatsoever." To his son, Joseph Clay, by his second wife, Joanna, he bequeaths " the residue of his lands and houseing at Walkley and Stanington," etc., " the smelting mill and house and lands at Dore, in the parish of Dronfield and County of Derby," etc., " his house at Bridgehouses, with all the land," etc., " and all his mines and personal estate." " His house and land at Tickell to be sould to the best bidder towards payment of his debts," etc. He appoints his wife, Joanna Clay and son Joseph, with others, executors of his will. Extracts from original will in York Registry Court of Probate. The following extracts are from the parochial registers of Chesterfield, Derbyshire: " January, 1687.—Robertus Clay et Hannah Slater nupt." " December, 1688.—Robertus filius Roberti Clay et Hannæ uxoris bapt."

[g] In the parish church of Crich are some monuments of the family of Clay, with quaint epitaphs, in which is a perpetual play upon the name. The following is from the monument of John Clay, Esq., who died May, 1632, and Mary, his first wife, daughter of William Calton, Esq., chief cock-matcher and servant of the

In memory

of

ROBERT CLAY,

Who departed this life July the 7th, 1804, aged thirty-four years.

ALSO

MARY ANN BOLTON,

Wife of James M. Bolton, and daughter

of

ROBERT AND ELIZA CLAY,

Who departed this life August the 24th, 1818, in the seventeenth year of her age

There is a good portrait of this lady in the possession of her son, Edward Clay Bolton, M.D.

Children of James McClean and Mary Ann Clay Bolton:

---

hawks to King Henry VIII, who died 31st August, 1583   His two sons were William and Theophilus:

> " Soules they are made of Heavenly spirit
> From whence they come ye heavens inherite.
> But know that body is made of Claye
> Death will devour by night or daye.
> Yett is her as her was, I saye.
> Ye livinge and dead remayneth Claye·
> His very name that nature gave:
> Is now as shall be in his grave
> Tymes doth teache, experience tryes·
> That Claye to duste the winde updryes·
> Then this a wonder coumpt wee must
> That want of winde should make Claye dust "

The arms of Clay are: Arg. a chev engrailed between three trefoils slipt sable Crest, two wings expanded, arg semée of trefoils slipped, sa. These arms and crest are engraved on a silver tankard, brought over to this country by Robert Clay, Esq, of Philadelphia, now in possession of the Booths of Newcastle, Delaware.

I. JAMES ROBERT BOLTON[21], Esq., merchant, of San Francisco, California; born in New-York on Friday, the 24th of January, 1817.

II. EDWARD CLAY BOLTON[21], M.D., of Poughkeepsie, Dutchess County; born in New-York on Saturday, 25th of April, 1818; married October 26th, 1859, Fanny R., daughter of Rev. Brozun Hoff and Caroline Clay, (daughter of Thomas Clay, Esq.,) who was born at Madison, Greene County, New-York, January 29th, 1837, and has issue, *fue*

1. MARY ANN CLAY BOLTON, born in New-York, August 7th, 1860; baptized by the Rev. Cornelius Winter Bolton, December 25th, 1860.

2. EDWARD CLAY BOLTON[23], Jr., born at Montclair, Essex County, New-Jersey, October 17th, 1861.

JAMES McCLEAN BOLTON[20], Esq., merchant, espoused secondly, March 14th, 1821, Honorah, daughter of Robert Richardson, Esq., who was born in Bermuda, May 19th, 1804, by whom he had issue,

I. WILLIAM HENRY BOLTON[21], Esq., of Far Rockaway, Long Island, born at 490 Broadway, New-York, Tuesday, January 8th, 1822; married, November 6th, 1845, Frances Howell, daughter of Thomas Hewlett, Esq., of Rock Hall, Far Rockaway, and Mary Halsey Howell, of Ketcheboneck, West Hampton, Suffolk County, Long Island, who was born at Rock Hall, May 30th, 1824, by whom he had issue,

1. SILVIE BOLTON, born at 53 Remsen street, Brooklyn, July 26th, 1846.

2. HONORAH RICHARDSON BOLTON, born at Far Rockaway, February 22d, 1849; died February 13th, 1854.

3. WILLIAM HENRY BOLTON[22], born at Far Rockaway, December 8th, 1850; died January 21st, 1857; buried at Rockaway, Queens County, Long Island.

4. MARY FANNY BOLTON, born at Far Rockaway, September 4th, 1853; died February 2d, 1857; buried at Rockaway.

5. THOMAS RICHARDSON BOLTON[22], born at Far Rockaway, August 31st, 1855; died January 21st, 1857; buried at Rockaway.

6. FRANCES HEWLETT BOLTON, born at 42 Smith street, Brooklyn, January 16th, 1858.

7. CATHARINE HEWLETT BOLTON, born at Far Rockaway, January 16th, 1860.

8. MARION BOLTON, born at Far Rockaway, October 5th, 1861.

II. JOHN BOLTON[21], second son of James McClean and Honorah Bolton, was born October 14th, 1823, and died at Jamaica, Long Island, September 8th, 1824. He was buried near his father in the Presbyterian cemetery at Jamaica.

THE ARMS OF ROBERT CLAY, ESQ., OF PHILADELPHIA, PENN.

It is a Reverend Thing to see an Ancient Castle or Building not in Decay, or to see a fair Timber Tree sound and perfect: how much more to behold an ancient noble Family, which hath stood against the Waves and Weathers of Time?—Bacon: Of Nobility

APPENDIX.

COPY of a letter from Rev Alexander Poe of Ohio to Rev. Robert Bolton of Pelham, respecting a volume of Rev Robert Bolton's works, entitled *Some Generall Directions for a Comfortable Walking with God*, printed at London, 1626, which contained a "Confession of Synns," written on the back of the last leaf This book has been handed down from parent to child for over two hundred years It was doubtless brought to this country by Robert Bolton of Philadelphia, as his wife Ann refers to it in her Journal; but appears, at the time the "Confession" was dated, to have been the property of Robert Bolton, the Divine and author, of Broughton, Northamptonshire, who died in 1671.

"To REV. R BOLTON: OHIO CITY, Dec 8th, 1849

"DEAR SIR: I have forwarded the book by express, according to your direction, and have to thank you for the receipt of Mr Jay's works I am much pleased with the work, and cordially thank you for the Jubilee exercises This is peculiarly interesting to me. Though I had heard of it, I had never before seen it Oh! I can not express to you how much I admire that *great* and *good* man.

"I exceedingly regret the fact that the signature of R Bolton to the temperance pledge has somehow been torn out When the work was rebound, it was trimmed too close. In 1834, when I copied it, that corner was a little torn, I wished to preserve it, but in removing and repacking from time to time, that was torn off before I knew it was done, and how, I am not able to say

"I believe my grandmother was of the same McLean family of your mother, her name was also Sarah. I shall make further inquiries when I again visit at my Father's "—"I shall be glad to hear from you often, and answer any inquiries you may wish to make, if I can. My grandfathers, on both sides, came to the western country in 1780 or perhaps '79 I have heard my grandmother speak of hearing Mr. Whitefield in Philadelphia. It was through the instrumentality of one of the tenants that she was converted, and to her death she retained the fervency in piety that strongly marked those excellent men

"Farewell,
"God bless you and yours,
"A. POE"

The following is a literal copy of the "Confession":

" Broughton, ... Confession of Synns.
1637.

"Ffrome this daye forward to the ende of my life, I will newer pleadge any health, nor drinke a whole Carrowse in Glasse, Cupp, Boule, or other drinking Instrument whatsoever, whosoever it be, or frome whomsoever it come, except the necessytie of nature doe require it Not my owne most gracious Kinge : nor any the greatest Monaike or Tyrant on earth, Not my dearest ffreinde, nor all the gould in the worlde, shall ever enforce me or alure me . Not an Angell ffrome Heaven (whoe I knowe will newer attempt it) should pswade me : Not Satan, with all his olde subtilties, nor all the powers of Hell itself shall ever betray me ; By this very synne (ffor a syne it is and not a little one) I doe plainely finde, that I have more offended and dishonored my great and gloriouse Maker and most mercifull Saviour, than by all other syns that I ame subject unto , And ffor this very syne I knowe it is that my God hath often bene stiange unto me And for that cause, and for noe other respect have I thus vowed ; And I hartely begg my good ffather in Heaven of his great goodness and infinit mercie in Jesus Christ, to assist me in the same and to be favourable unto me ffor what is past. Amen !

" Robert Bolton

"April 10, 1637."

Copy of a letter from Henry Bolton, of Blackburn, to Rev. Robert Bolton

"Dear Sir In reply to your letter, which I have just received, I hasten to give you all the information I can with respect to our family and the late Robert Bolton, the Divine. Robert Bolton, the Puritan, was born at Brookhouse near Blackburn, in the year 1572, and my father, who died about seven years ago, in the eightieth year of his age, always said he sprang from the same family, and from a brother of the Puritan, but the Christian name he could not find out. My father often said that some part of the family belonging to Robert Bolton, left the Kingdom and went to America. I can trace in our family Bible the birth of William, son of Henry Bolton, in the year 1683, of Little Harwood,[a] a place a few fields from Brookhouse, where the Puritan was born. The above Henry Bolton was my great-great-great grandfather. In the registers at the Blackburn Parish church, in 1609, there was Robert, son of John Bolton, baptized, and in 1622 Giles de Brookhouse, and again in 1632, John, son of Robert Bolton, of Brookhouse. I had a little book, containing about twenty pages in MS., on controversy, in the handwriting of the Puritan, and like the copy you have sent me, for which I kindly thank you , but the MS is lost If you have not already seen an account of the Puritan in the *History of Lancaster*, you may find it in *Baines*, page 326, 27, and 28, now publishing. I do not know the arms of our family, but the seal[b] on this letter is said to be the crest   I am, dear sir, your humble serv't,

"Blackburn, Sept. 25th, 1834.   Henry Bolton."

" P S —My father almost daily talking of Relations abroad and lamenting loss of MS of R Bolton "

---

a See Registers of St Mary's church, Blackburn, for baptism of William, son of Henry Bolton, of Little Harwood, 4th April, 1683 —Author.

b A falcon belle l and jessed on a wreath surmounting the letter B

Extracts from the Register Books for the Parish Church of St. Mary in Blackburn, Lancashire, from A.D 1568 to 1721, inclusive.

BAPTISMS

1568, Milo, fil Lawrentii Boulton, Aug 24.
  "   Elizabetha, fil Jacobi Boulton, Oct. 13
      N B —A blank in the Register.
1601, Agnes, fil Adami Boulton, Dec 7.
  "   Beatrice, fil Jacobi Boulton, Feb 24.
1602, Adamus, fil Esgidii Boulton, April 3
  "   Maria, fil Thomæ Boulton, Feb 23
1603, Maria, fil Thomæ Boulton, Feb 2.
1604, Jacobus, fil Jacobi Boulton, Nov 19.
  "   Jacobus, fil Alexandri Boulton, Nov 25
  "   Maria, fil Esgidii (Giles) Boulton, April 8.
  "   Anna, fil Milonis Boulton, Aug 15
1605, Jacobus, fil Jonæ Boulton, June 28.
  "   Elizabeth, fil Adami Boulton, Sep 2
  "   Jacobus, fil Georgii Boulton, Sep 27.
1606, Thomas, fil Esgidii Boulton, April 13
  "   Willmus, fil Thomæ Boulton, Oct 19.
1608, Henricus, fil Johannis Boulton, July 12
  "   Johannes, fil Georgii Boulton, Feb 18, De Blackburne.
1609, Elizabetha, fil Thomæ Boulton, April 9.
  "   Rosamund, fil Georgii Boulton, June 17, Bank
  "   Myles, fil Alexander Boulton, Jan'y
  "   Robert, fil John Boulton, 1st March
1610, Robert, fil John Boulton, June 4.
1615, Ann, fil Rouphe Boulton, Nov 13
  "   Thomas ⎫
      and   ⎬ fil Thomas Boulton, Feb. 16.
  "   Robert, ⎭
1616, John, fil Gyles Boulton, April 12, de Bruchouse
  "   Ellen, ⎫
      and   ⎬ fil Saunder Boulton, June 23
  "   Jane, ⎭
  "   William, fil John Boulton, 1st Nov.
  "   Ralph, fil Myles Boulton, Jan 26   Shoemaker
  "   Edmund, fil William Junr Boulton, Jan. 26.
1617, Thomas, fil William Boulton, Aug. 18
  "   John, fil George Boulton, Feb 1.
1618, William, fil Gyles Boulton, Nov. 4, de Forebank
1620, Marye, daughter of Henry Boulton, April 5
  "   Jane, daughter of Myles Boulton, Oct 8.
  "   William, son of Rouphe Boulton, Nov 8
  "   Joseph, son of Gyles Boulton, Dec. 12, de Forebank
  "   Gyles, son of Thomas Boulton, Jan 30.   Taylor
1621, Alice, daughter of George Boulton, May 28
1622, Grace, daughter of Henry Boulton, March 4.

1622, Gyles, son of Adam Boulton, April 27.
"   Robert, son of Robert Boulton, May 31.
"   Gyles, son of Robert Boulton, Feb 9, de Brookhouse.
1623, Gyles, son of Harry Boulton, Feb. 1.
"   Alice, daughter of Henry Boulton, Feb 18, de Mellor.
"   Margery, daughter of William Boulton, March 12, de Ramsgreave
1624, Alice, daughter of George Boulton, March 28
1625, William, son of Richard Boulton, May 19, de Bank-hey.
"   Ann, daughter of Gyles Boulton, June 6, de Shear-bank.
"   William, son of Robert Boulton, March 20, de Osbaldeston
1626, James, son of Gyles Boulton, April 7, de Brookhouse.
1627, Jenet, daughter of William Boulton, Sep. 5, de Ramsgreave.
"   Roger, son of William Boulton, Jan
1628, Joseph, son of Gyles Boulton, April 20.
"   Mary, daughter of James Boulton, Aug. 6.
1629, Agnes, daughter of Henry Boulton, April 26.
"   Hanna, daughter of Adamᶜ Boulton, Aug   Vicar of Blackburn
"   Alexander, son of James Boulton, Sep 23.
"   Jenett, daughter of Gyles Junr. Boulton, Jan 21.
"   Ellen, daughter of William Boulton, Feb. 21
1630, George, son of Richard Boulton, May 10.
"   Henry, son of Richard Boulton, Feb 27
1631, Myles, son of James Boulton, May 1.
"   James, son of Henry Boulton, Sep 4
"   Elizabeth, daughter of Adam Boulton, Nov. 27.   Vicar
1632, Robert, son of Richard Boulton, Oct 28
"   ᵈ*John, son of Robert Boulton, ——, de Brookhouse*
1633, James, son of James Boulton, May 5
"   John, son of Lawrence Boulton, July 28.
"   Henry, son of Henry Boulton, Nov 10.
"   Alice, daughter of Richard Boulton, Jan. 12.
"   Alice, daughter of Giles Junr Boulton, Jan 12
1634, Sara, daughter of Adam Boulton, April 6   Vicar.
1635, Adam, son of Richard Boulton, July 19.
"   George, son of Edward Boulton, Feb 7, de Ramsgreave
"   Elizabeth, daughter of Adam Boulton, Feb 14   Vicar
1636, Thomas, son of Richard Boulton, April 18, de Bolton
"   Thomas, son of William Boulton, Sep 4, de Ramsgreave
"   Ann, daughter of Richard Boulton, Nov. 23, de Bank-hey
"   Ellen, daughter of Lawrence Boulton, Nov. 30
"   James, son of Oliver Boulton, Jan 8.
1637, John, son of Edward Boulton, April 10, de Ramsgreave.
"   Elizabeth, daughter of Henry Boulton, July 23, de Lammock
"   John, son of Gyles Boulton, Feb. —, de Lane

---

c Rev Adam Boulton was appointed Vicar June 20th, 1628   In 1646 Mr Adam Boulton was minister of Third Classis of Lancaster, consisting of Blackburn, Whalley, etc , etc —EDITOR

d This entry was found by Mr Henry Bolton, of Blackburn, September 25th, 1834, but does not appear on the second examination, made in 1859 —EDITOR.

1638, Thomas, son of Henry Boulton, March 26, de Lane.

N B.—Blank in the Registers.[e]

1652, Mary, daughter of Thomas Boulton, May 8, de Mellor.

" Joseph, son of William Boulton, June 20, de Lane. Oppid.

" Jane, daughter of Thomas Boulton, July 8

1653, Elizabeth, daughter of William Boulton, Feb 13, de Mellor

1654, Elizabeth, daughter of John Boulton, May 28, de Brookhouse.

" John, son of James Boulton, March 18, de Ramsgreave.

1655, Jane, daughter of Oliver Boulton, March 25, Blackburn.

" William, son of Thomas Boulton, Aug 5, Blackburn.

1656, Ann, daughter of John Boulton, March 30, Blackburn

1657, Giles, son of John Boulton, Over Darwen, bapt at Tockholes.

" Mary, daughter of William Boulton, April 5, Blackburn

" Joseph, son of Thomas Bolton, Jan. 30, Blackburn.

1658, Mary, daughter of James Boulton, May 9, Ramsgreave Junr.

" James, son of James Boulton, Aug 23, Blackburn Butcher

" Richard, son of Mr Lancelott Boulton, Nov 7.

" William, son of Lawrence Boulton, May 16. Shoemaker.

" John, son of John Boulton, March 6, of Brookhouse. "Clarke of Blackburn."

1659, Joseph, son of Thomas Boulton, June 29, Blackburn.

1660, Giles, son of John Boulton, April 29

" Mary, daughter of James Boulton, May 2. Butcher.

" Elizabeth, daughter of James Boulton, Nov 4, Ramsgreave.

1661, Esther, daughter of John Boulton, Sep 11, Brookhouse

1662, Emma, daughter of Thomas Boulton, June 11, Blackburn

" Joseph, son of Lawrence Boulton, March 27, Cleyton le Dale.

" Ellen, daughter of James Boulton, March 29, Ramsgreave.

1663, Mary, daughter of John Boulton, Feb. 6, Blackburn

1664, Gyles, son of Thomas Boulton, Jan 15, of Blackburn.

1665, Catherine, daughter of John Boulton, ——, of Blackburn

1666, William, son of James Boulton, Aug 5, of Blackburn

1667, Richard, son of Henry Boulton, May 5, Lower Darwen

1668, James, son of John Boulton, May 17, Blackburn.

" Elizabeth, daughter of William Boulton, Nov. 1, Samlesbury

1669, Jenet, daughter of Henry Boulton, ——, Lower Darwen.

" Oliver, son of George Boulton, ——, Blackburn

" Ellen, daughter of William Boulton, Ramsgreave.

1670, George, son of John Boulton, May 1, Blackburn

" Roger, son of Thomas Boulton, May 15, Billington

" Richard, son of John Bolton, July 18, Blackburn

" Jane, daughter of Henry Boulton, February 3, Mellor.

1671, Elizabeth, daughter of Henry Boulton, Dec. 10, Lower Darwen.

" George, son of John Boulton, Feb 25, Blackburn

1674, Richard, son of George Boulton, June —, Blackburn

1675, Elizabeth, daughter of John Boulton, June 8, Blackburn.

---

[e] During the Usurpation no entries were made. The Presbyterian discipline was established in Lancashire in 1646, and continued until 1650, when the Independent plan began —EDITOR.

1676, Margaret, daughter of James Boulton, March 14, Ramsgreave
" Nicholas, son of Henry Boulton, April 16, Lower Darwen
" (John Bolton began Parish Clerk, July 9th, 1676)
1677, Edward, son of Henry Boulton, Oct 21, of Lower Darwen.
1678, Joseph, son of John Boulton, June 9, Blackburn
1680, Thomas, son of George Boulton, June 27, Blackburn
" John, son of John Boulton, Aug 15, Blackburn, (Ringer)
" Adam, son of Henry Boulton, Aug 22, Blackburn
" Ann, daughter of Robert Boulton, Nov 7, Wilpshire
1681, Alice, daughter of Henry Boulton, Jan 29
1682, James, son of Richard Boulton, Sep 18, of Osbaldeston.
" George, son of Richard Boulton, Feb 20, of Blackburn.
1683, William, son of Henry Boulton, April 4, of Little Harwood.
" John, } twin, sons of Robert Boulton, April 24, of Rishton
" Robert, }
" William, son of Henry Boulton, Feb 3, Lower Darwen
1684, William, son of Thurston Boulton, Sep 14, Blackburn.
1685, Margery, daughter of Henry Boulton, Feb 14, Blackburn
1686, Elizabeth, daughter of Henry Boulton, Dec 9, Blackburn
1687, Mary, daughter of Thurston Boulton, April 6, Blackburn.
" Ann, daughter of William Boulton, Feb 19, Blackburn
1688, Giles, son of Henry Boulton, March 17, Blackburn
1690, Lawrence, son of William Boulton, April 9, Blackburn.
" Ann, daughter of Giles Boulton, May 11, Blackburn
" Thomas, son of Thurston Boulton, July 13, Blackburn.
1691, James, son of Giles Boulton, Jan 14, of Blackburn
" Alice, daughter of William Boulton, March 6, of Blackburn
1692, Catherine, daughter of Henry Boulton, Sep. 4, of Blackburn.
" Joseph, son of Giles Boulton, Dec. 11, of Blackburn
" John, son of Elizabeth Boulton
1693, Mary, daughter of Richard Boulton, of Lower Darwen
" Thomas, son of Giles Boulton, March 18, of Blackburne.
1694, William, son of William Boulton, May 19
" Mary, daughter of Richard Boulton, Sep 30, of Osbaldeston
1695, Henry, son of Richard Boulton, April 7, Lower Darwen
" Robert, son of Giles Boulton, July 7
" William, son of William Boulton, July 14.
" George, son of Oliver Boulton, Sep 8.
1697, Thomas, son of Richard Boulton, May 2, of Lower Darwen
" William, son of William Boulton, July 25, of Blackburn
" Edward, son of Giles Boulton, Jan'y —, of Blackburn
1698, John, son of Richard Boulton, March 19, of Osbaldeston.
1699, James, son of Richard Boulton, May 28, of Lower Darwen
1700, John, son of Giles Boulton, Feb. 13, of Blackburn, Mercer
1701, James, son of Giles Boulton, March 15, of Blackburn, Mercer
1702, Henry, son of Richard Boulton, Jan. 24, of Lower Darwen.
1703, Giles
1704, Elizabeth, daughter of Richard Boulton, Oct. 15, of Lower Darwen Webster.

1705, Ellen, daughter of James Boulton, March 10, of Balderston.
1706, Jane, daughter of John Boulton, Oct —, of Blackburn   Butcher
1707, Joseph, son of James Boulton, April 7, of Blackburn.   Mercer
    "   Richard, son of James Boulton, March 3, of Blackburn   Mercer
1708, John, son of James Boulton, May 23, of Balderston   Weaver
    "   Richard, son of Richard Boulton, July 18, of Lower Darwen.
1709, Robert, son of Mr James Boulton, May 1, of Blackburn
1710, John, son of John Boulton, July, of Blackburn.
    "   John, son of John Boulton, Oct —, of Balderston.

MARRIAGES

1601, May, Richardus Hindle et Isabella Boulton
1603, May, Thomas Holde et Elizabetha Boulton
    "   Feb , Alexander Boulton et Letitia Broxuff.
1610, Mch , Rogerus Byrley et Cecilia Boulton.
1616, April, Myles Boulton et Mary Fielden
    "   June, Thomas Sounpner et Ellen Boulton
1617, Mch , Gyles Boulton et Elizabeth Dewherst.
1619, Jan , Ralphe Boulton et Susan Carre
1620, Oct , Henry Boulton et Jane Shorrocke
1621, July, John Lee et Ellen Boulton.
    "   Sep , John Foole et Elizabeth Boulton
1625, May, Robert Bolltoun et Jenett Beroun.
    "   Sep , Joseph Pomfret et Mary Boulton, vidua
1626, April, William Bolltoun et Jane Kyrkehew
1627, Feb , James Boulton et Lettice Aspinwall
1633, Oct , James Bolton et Mary Haworth
1637, June, Richard Bolton et Alice Ellel
1654, April, John, son of Richard Haworth, husbandman, et Ann Bolton, widow,
            of the Parish of Leyland
    "   April, Robert, son of William Bolton, husbandman, of Balderston, et Eliza-
            beth, daughter of Wm Walton, of Ribchester.
    "   June, Thomas, son of Henry Bolton, of Blackburn, et Margaret, daughter
            of Wm Collinson, of Huncoat
    "   Aug , Lawren, son of James Bullen, of Samlesbury, et Isabel, daughter of
            Robert Bolton, of Osbaldeston
1655, Oct , John, son of Robert Bolton, of Mellor, et Ann, daughter of John
            Lawson, of Balderston.
1656, May, William, son of Richard Barton, of Rishton, blacksmith, et Grace,
            daughter of Wm Bolton, of Rishton, spinster
1667, Nov , George Boulton et Jane Whitebay.
1672, Feb , John Sharrock et Elizabeth Boulton, both of this parish
1679, Dec , Henry Bolton et Alis Rothwell, both of this parish.
1685, June, James Holden et Mary Bolton, both of this parish
1686, Nov , William Bolton et Grace Marsh, both of this parish
1688, Oct , Ralph Longworth et Ellen Bolton, both of this parish
1689, April, Ralph Ludell et Elizabeth Bolton, both of this parish
1690, Feb , Richard Bolton et Ellen Dewhurst, both of this parish
    "   Feb , Randal Ffeilden et Mary Bolton, both of this parish.

1692, Feb., Richard Aspden et Elizabeth Bolton, both of this parish
1694, Oct , Oliver Bolton et Ann Foster, both of this parish
1696, April, James Johnson et Jane Bolton, both of this parish
 "   Sep , John Astley et Ann Bolton, married at Tockholes
 "   Feb , Nicholas Bolton et Agnes Thompson, both of this parish.
1700,   •
1702, June, James Dale et Elizabeth Bolton, both of this parish.
1704, July, Thurston Bolton, of Blackburn, et Elizabeth Ffeilder, of Rishton,
            widow
1705, Sep , James Bolton et Elizabeth Ireland, both of Balderston.
 "   Oct , James Longworth et Grace Bolton, both of this parish.
 "   Feb , Samuel Pickering, of Lower Darwen, et Mary Bolton, of Blackburn
1707, June, John Aspinwall, of Blackburn, et Martha Bolton, of Wethill, in Ley-
            land.
1710, Jan , John Piccop et Alice Bolton, both of Lower Darwen
1711, Aug , John Bolton et Jane Cottam, both of Blackburn.
1712, July, Samuel Fogg et Jane Bolton, both of Blackburn.
 "   Feb , William Bolton, of Lower Darwen, et Ann Edleston, of Little Har-
            wood
1714, Mch., Henry Bolton et Ann Whalley, both of Blackburn.
 "   Aug , William Yates et Elizabeth Bolton, both of Blackburn
1718, July, William Holden et Mary Bolton, both of Blackburn
1720, Feb , George Boulton et Mary Craven, both of Dinkley

DURIALS.

1600, Mar , Uxor Adami Boulton
1601, April, Wilhamus Boulton.
 "   Dec , Puer Milonis Boulton
 "   Mar., Jacobus Boulton, illeg.
1602, Jan'y, Jacobus Boulton.
 "   "   Daughter of William Boulton.
1603, June, filius Thurstani Boulton.
 "   Dec , Uxor Alexandri Boulton.
1604, May, Puer Johannis Boulton
 "   Feb , Uxor Richardi Boulton.
1605, Oct , Oliver Boulton
 "   Nov. 9, Adam Boulton.
 "   Dec. 29, Elizabeth Boulton.
1606, May 2, Uxor Adami Boulton
1608, Oct 10, John, son of John Boulton
1609, March 8, John Boulton
 "   June 20, Rosamond, daughter of George Boulton of Bank
 "   June 22, John, son of George Boulton.
 "   Nov 23, John Boulton
1610, June,   A child of John Boulton
1614, July,   A daughter of Thomas Boulton
 "   July 10, Uxor Milonis Boulton.
 "   Oct. 13, Uxor Oliver Boulton

1615, March 5, Robert, son of Thomas Boulton
 "   "   24, Margaret Boulton.
1616, May 10, Edward Boulton.
 "   Aug 5, Margaret Boulton.
 "   Jan'y 10, Elizabeth, uxor Thomas Boulton
 "   Jan'y 14, Thomas, son of Thomas Boulton
 "   Jan'y 25, Jane, uxor Richard Boulton, vidua
1617, June 22, Myles Boulton.
 "   June 24, James Boulton.
 "   Sep. 7, Uxor Thomæ Boulton.
 "   Sep 7, Jane, daughter of Alexander Boulton
 "   Nov. 26, Uxor Georgii Boulton.
 "   Jan 13, George Boulton de Bank.
1618, June 7, John, son of George Boulton.
 "   Nov. 24, Edward Boulton de Blackburn
 "   Dec 27, Jane Boulton, vidua
 "   March 2, John Boulton de Copthurst.
 "   Dec 13, Grace Boulton
1620, May 25, Henry (?) Boulton.
 "   Dec 4, Uxor Will'mi Boulton.
1621, Mch 12, Uxor Egidii Boulton
1622, April 17, Ann Boulton de Blackburn.
 "   July 19, Gyles, son of Adam Boulton.
 "   Nov. 6, A daughter of George Boulton
 "   Nov 24, Uxor John Boulton, Copthurst.
 "   Dec. 17, Thomas Boulton de Brookhouse.
f1623, Aug 4, George, son of Wm Boulton de Balderstone
 "   Aug 9, Launcelot Boulton
 "   Aug 13, Ann, daughter of Ralph Boulton
 "   Aug. 15, John Boulton de Bankhey.
 "   Aug. 18, Thomas Boulton, Ramsgreave   Tailor.
               Myles Boulton. Shoemaker.
               Gyles, son of Thomas Boulton   Tailor
               George Boulton, Blackburn
               William Boulton
               Thomas Boulton of Copthurst.
               Ellen, widow of William Boulton
1624, April, A base son of Ralph Boulton
 "   Dec , Thurston Boulton
 "   Mch , A daughter of George Boulton.
1625, April, Uxor Edward Boulton
 "   July, James Boulton de Balderstone.
 "   Sep , Ann, daughter of Gyles Boulton, a cripple
 "   Jan , William Boulton, oppidanus.
1626, June, Thomas, son of Henry Boulton
1627, Sep., Uxor Richardi Boulton, oppid.

---

f 1623 was the year of the plague in Lancashire —Editor

1627, Jan , Sara, uxor Thomas Boulton

1628, Aug , Mary, daughter of Gyles Boulton

  "   Sep , James Boulton.

1629, June, Alexander Boulton

1630, June, Uxor Robert Boulton.

  "   June, A child of Gyles Boulton

  "   Jan , John, son of Adam Boulton. Vicar.

1631, Dec , A base child of Richard Boulton

1632, Oct , William Boulton.

  "   Nov , Thomas Boulton

  "   Mch , Ann Boulton.

1633, Nov , Uxor Henry Boulton

  "   Jan , Robert Boulton.

1634, Mch , Elizabeth, daughter of Adam Boulton, Vicar

1635, June, Uxor Alexandri Bolton

  "   Oct , James Bolton

  "   Nov , Adam, son of Richard Bolton

  "   Feb , Uxor Will'mi Bolton.

  "   Feb , George, son of Edward Bolton.

  "   Mch , A child of Henry Bolton

  "   Mch , John Bolton.

1636, July, James, son of James Bolton

  "   Sep , James Bolton of Ramsgreave.

  "   Feb , James, son of Adam Bolton

  "   Feb , Alexander, son of James Bolton.

1637, May, Uxor Will'mi Bolton of Ramsgreave

           N B —Blank in the Registers.

1651, April, The wife of Lawrence Bolton of Mellor

1653, April, Thomas Bolton of Brookhouse

  "   Sep , Ann, uxor Thomas Bolton, Junior, oppidam.

  "   April, William, son of Robert Bolton of the Oaks.

1654, July, John, son of Edward Bolton, Ramsgreave.

1656, John, son of William Bolton, Ramsgreave

  "   April, Joseph, son of William Bolton of the Lane.

  "   Sep., Ralph Bolton, Ouseburn

  "   Dec , Henry Bolton of Samlesbury.

1657, June, Mary, uxor Jacobi Bolton, Blackburn, butcher.

  "   June, John Bolton, Blackburn, fustian webster

1658, Nov., Robert Bolton, Balderston.

  "   Jan , Catharine, daughter of Oliver Bolton, Blackburn.

1660, Oliver Bolton, Blackburn.

  "   Annas, widow of Robert Bolton, Ramsgreave.

  "   Mary, daughter of John Bolton, Blackburn

1661, Jenet Bolton, Balderstone

  "   Margaret, daughter of James Bolton, Jun , Ramsgreave

1662, James Bolton, Blackburn.

  "   Leonard Bolton, Ouzebooth.

1665, Adam, son of Lancelot Bolton of Cleyton le Dale.

1666, Mary, daughter of John Bolton, Blackburn.
" William Bolton, Blackburn
" Adam Bolton, Blackburn
" Henry, son of Thomas Bolton, Blackburn.
1667, Elizabeth, wife of Giles Bolton, Blackburn.
" Lawrence Bolton, Mellor.
" Robert Bolton, Ramsgreave.
1668, Mary, daughter of Lancelot Bolton, Clayton
" Thomas and } Bolton.
" his son }
" Elizabeth, daughter of Robert Bolton, Clayton.
" John Bolton, Over Darwen.
1669, Jane, daughter of Thomas Bolton
" George Bolton, Little Harwood.
1670, Em Bolton, Blackburn
" James Bolton, Ramsgreave.
" James Bolton, Ramsgreave.
" Uxor Thomæ Bolton, Blackburn.
" Uxor Thomæ Bolton, Blackburn.
" John Bolton, Blackburn.
1671, George, son of John Bolton.
" Richard, son of John Bolton
" Robert Bolton, Salesbury
" Elizabeth, daughter of Richard Bolton, Balderston.
" Launcelot, son of Launcelot Bolton, Copthurst
" Ann, daughter of James Bolton, Ramsgreave.
" Ann Bolton, Ramsgreave.
1672, James Bolton, Blackburn.
1674, Alice Bolton, Ramsgreave.
1675, Janett, daughter of Henry Bolton, Lower Darwen.
" Elizabeth Bolton, Blackburn
1676, William Bolton, Ramsgreave.
" Ann, wife of James Bolton, Blackburn.
1678, Ann, daughter of Lawrence Bolton, Blackburn
" Abigail, daughter of William Bolton, Blackburn.
1679, Alice, wife of Henry Bolton, Lower Darwen.
" Edward, son of Henry Bolton, Lower Darwen.
" John Bolton, Clayton
" Ann Bolton, Balderston.
" John, son of James Bolton, Ramsgreave.
" Janet Bolton, Blackburn.
" George Bolton, Salesbury.
" Ellen, wife of James Bolton, Ramsgreave.
" Alice Bolton, Mellor.
1680, Robert, son of John Bolton, Blackburn, clerk.
1681, Ann, daughter of Robert Bolton, Rishton
1682, Lawrence Bolton, Blackburn.
" Thomas, son of George Bolton, Blackburn.

1682, William Bolton, Over Darwen
1683, John Bolton, Blackburn, clerk
"   John }
"   Robert } twin of Robert Bolton, Rishton
"   Robert Bolton, Rishton.
"   Alice, daughter of John Bolton, Blackburn.
"   Alice Bolton, Blackburn.
"   Jane, widow, Bolton, Over Darwen.
1684, Ann Bolton, Mellor.
"   Ann Bolton, Over Darwen
"   Elizabeth Bolton, Dinkley.
"   Elizabeth Bolton, Lamock
"   Elizabeth, wife of Thomas Bolton, Billington.
1685, Richard Bolton, Bank-hey.
"   Margery, daughter of Henry Bolton, Blackburn.
1686, Mary, widow, Bolton, Blackburn
1687, Jenet, wife of Richard Bolton, Osbaldeston
1688, John Bolton, Brookhouse.
"   Margaret, wife of Lancelot Bolton, Salisbury.
"   James Bolton, Lammock.
1689, Henry Bolton, Lower Darwen
"   Elizabeth, daughter of Henry Bolton, Blackburn.
1690, Mary, wife of John Bolton, Blackburn.
"   Mary, daughter of Richard Bolton, Osbaldeston.
1691, James Bolton, Ramsgreave
"   James Bolton, Clayton le Dale.
1692, James Bolton, Blackburn, mercer.
1693, Joseph, son of Giles Bolton, Blackburn.
"   Alice, daughter of William Bolton, Blackburn.
1694, Lettice, wife of Henry Bolton, Salisbury.
"   Alice, widow, Bolton, Harwood Parva
"   Thomas, son of Giles Bolton, Blackburn.
"   James, son of Giles Bolton, Blackburn
"   William, son of William Bolton, Blackburn.
"   Ann, daughter of William Bolton, Blackburn.
1695, Elizabeth, wife of William Bolton, Ramsgreave.
"   Elizabeth, daughter of William Bolton, Blackburn.
1696, Roger, son of Thomas Bolton, Billington.
"   William, son of William Bolton, Blackburn
"   Mary Bolton, Blackburn.
"   Mary, daughter of Roger Bolton, Over Darwen
"   A child of Giles Bolton, Blackburn
"   William Bolton, Blackburn, shoemaker
1697, Adam, son of Thomas Bolton, Billington.
"   Edward Bolton, Blackburn
"   James, son of Thomas Bolton, Billington.
1698, Abigail, daughter of William Bolton, Blackburn.
"   Thomas Bolton, Billington, husbandman

1698, Ann Bolton, Blackburn, poor.
  "   Giles Bolton, Blackburn, fustian webster
1699, George, son of Oliver Bolton, Blackburn.
  "   Lawrence Bolton, Blackburn, poor.
  "   Henry Bolton, Blackburn, poor, and found dead.
  "   Elizabeth, wife of Thurston Bolton, Blackburn, husbandman.
1700, William, son of Thurston Bolton, Blackburn, fustian weaver.
  "   Ellen, widow, Bolton, Salisbury
  "   James Bolton, Blackburn, woolen weaver.
  "   Oliver Bolton, Blackburn, bailiffe
1701, Alice, widow, Bolton, Blackburn.
  "   Lancelot Bolton, Salisbury, yeoman
  "   Richard Bolton, Osbaldeston, husbandman.
  "   Henry, son of Richard Bolton, Lower Darwen, webster
1702, Ann, widow, Bolton, Blackburn.
1703, Robert Bolton, Harwood Parva, husbandman.
1704, Jane, wife of George Bolton, Blackburn, webster.
1705, Robert, son of Giles Bolton, Blackburn, mercer.
  "   Giles Bolton, Blackburn, mercer.
1708, Rosamond Bolton, Little Harwood
  "   Samuel Bolton, Blackburn
1709, Robert, son of James Bolton, Blackburn.
  "   Jane, daughter of John Bolton, Blackburn.
1710, John Bolton, Blackburn

The parish registers consist of several volumes. It is said that the old accounts of the Church Wardens and Overseers were removed with the ancient parish chest when the parish church was taken down in 1820, and have not since been found. No lists of Taxable Inhabitants can be found.—AUTHOR.

Extracts from the Minute Books of the "Governors" of the Free Grammar School of Queen Elizabeth, in Blackburn, kept by the Clerk, namely, Thomas Ainsworth, Esq., King Street:

> 1590, Wm. Bolton, a Govr, mortuus 1594.
>   Adam Bolton, a Govr, obiit 1593
> 1598, George Boulton, a Govr.

In 43 Eliz., certain persons "bestowed their benevolence towards the purchase of a yearly rent of £20 for the use of the Free Grammar School." Inter alios I find George Bolton of Bank Hey gave 6s. 8d.

In 1628, Adam Bolton, Vicar, a Governor
    1625, Gyles Bolton, 1641, still a Govr, of Brookhouse.
    1612, John Bolton, Ex'or of Mr. Browne, late School Master, pays £5 to Treas^r
    1647, Adam Bolton, a Govr.
      "   Launcelot Boulton, a Govr.

1653, Adam Bolton, Auditor, elected Govr for his great pains.
1660, Launcelot Bolton, Auditor.
1662, John Boulton of Brookhouse, gent , a Govr, and gave gratuity, 10s
1681, James Bolton of Blackburn.

———

1567, Robert Bolton, one of the original Gov^{rs} under the charter
      Alex. Bolton, one of the original Gov^{rs} under the charter
      Adam Bolton, one of the original Gov^{rs} under the charter.
1590, Gyles Bolton signs a deed as Govr.
  "   Adam Bolton, a Govr.
1630, Adam Bolton, servant to Sir Thos Walmsley, Knt
1697, Thos Bolton witnesses a conveyance of Estate in Mellor.
1714, Mr. James Bolton elected Govr.
1743, John Bolton elected Govr.
1744, Rev. Ed Bolton of Rochdale Govr.
  "   Mr James Bolton of Preston Govr.
1761, Thomas Bolton Govr
1766, Edward Bolton of Preston Gov.
1744, Thomas Bolton Govr.
  "   Edward Bolton Govr.

The Free Grammar School of Blackburn was founded 8 August, 9th of
Elizabeth, (1566,) and endowed with lands, etc , producing less than £128.

———

Genealogical Extracts from the Wills and Administrations, granted in the
District Registry, Chester, England, of the name of " Boulton or Bolton,"
from Blackburn and Neighborhood, from the year 1620 to the year 1700,
inclusive:

In the Will of MARGARET BOLTON, late of Blackburn, in the County of Lan-
caster, widow, (late wife of MYLES BOLTON, deceased,) bearing date the 22d of
March, 1620. Testatrix mentions her nieces, Letice Haworth, Margaret Walmsley,
wife of James Walmsley, Ann, wife of Thomas Sharples, Mary, wife of Ralph
Fish, Ann, daughter of the said James Walmsley and Alice Walmsley, and Cousin
John Walmsley Testatrix also leaves small legacies to James and Oliver Bolton,
(sons of George and Myles,) without giving their genealogy , appoints her niece,
Letice Haworth, sole executrix, and will proved by her in the Consistory Court of
Chester, on the 31st of July, 1621. Witnesses to will, Thurston Collinson, John
Gilibrand, and Roger Gilibrand

ADAM* BOLTON, late of BROOKHOUSE, in the Township of Blackburn, by his will,
bearing date the twenty-eighth of February, 1639, gave to his daughter, ELIZABETH
BOLTON, the whole of his property in the following words· "Also my will and mind
is, and I do give and bequeath unto my daughter, Elizabeth Bolton, all my goods
whatsoever, as much as I can, wch by law and right do to me belong; and I do
constitute and appoint my said daughter, Elizabeth Bolton, my true and lawful executrix." Witnesses to will, GYLES BOLTON and Richard Bradley. This appears to

---

* The eldest son of Adam Bolton, who died A D. 1596, and brother of Rev. Robert Bolton

be a nuncupative will, not being signed by the Testator, neither is there any seal attached. Proved in the Consistory Court of Chester, on the 8th of April, 1640, by Elizabeth Bolton, the sole executrix and only party mentioned in any way throughout the will

In the will of GYLES BOLTON, late of Shearbank, in the Township of Blackburn, yeoman, deceased, bearing date the 18th of February, 1640 Testator mentions his wife, Elizabeth, eldest son William, younger children Joseph, John, Henry, Lawrence, Ann, Jennett, Alice, and Elizabeth; appoints his wife and son William executors, and will proved by them in the Consistory Court of Chester on the 21st of April, 1641. Witnesses to will, George Tomlinson and Lawrence Holden

In the will of the Rev ADAM BOLTON,[h] late of Blackburn, Clerk, deceased, bearing date the 24th of September, 1646. Testator mentions his wife, Ann, son Samuel, daughter Hannah, sisters Margery Whalley, Alice Edge, Margaret Tomlinson, and Abigail Bolton, brothers James and Joseph, appoints his wife and brothers-in-law William Farrington and Henry Tomlinson executors, and will proved by them in the Consistory Court of Chester, in the year 1646 Witnesses to Will Thos Osbaldeston, Ralph Lindsay, Randle Sharples, and William Gates

In the will of JOHN BOLTON, late of Blackburn, Fustian-Maker, deceased, bearing date the 27th of August, 1657 Testator mentions his wife, Elizabeth, daughters Mary and Emma, brother Roger; appoints George Harobin of Blackburn. Felt-Maker, sole executor, and will proved, 25th April, 1661, by him in Consistory Court of Chester. Witnesses to will, Ralph Sumpner and Roger Pomfret

On the 5th of April, 1667, Letters of Administration of the effects of ADAM BOLTON, late of Brookhouse, in the Parish of Blackburn, deceased, were granted by the Consistory Court of Chester unto Robert Bolton, (genealogy not given.)

In the will of GEORGE BOLTON, late of Blackburn, husbandman, deceased, bearing date the 4th of January, 1669 Testator mentions his children and nieces, without distinguishing them, namely George Bolton, Robert Bolton, Kathrine Bolton, Ellis Bolton, Ann Bolton, Elizabeth Bolton, Ann Hoffman, brother Richard, appoints George Bolton sole executor to will; proved by him in Consistory Court of Chester 3d February, 1669. Witnesses to will, Roger Foster, Charles Blower, and Thurston Mawesley.

The will of ELIZABETH BOLTON of Blackburn, widow, dated the 12th day of July, 1675 Testatrix mentions her brother, James Horrabin, of Blackburn, and Jane, his wife, George, son of the said James Horrabin, Ellen Horrabin, daughter of Robt. Horrabin, nephew Wm Horrabin, one of the executors, Ellen Horrabin, daughter of the said James Horrabin, Margaret, wife of George Horrabin, and Wm Horrabin executors Proved at Chester on the 23d day of Feb'y, 1675, by both of the executors.

On the 14th September, 1682, Letters of Administration of the effects of LAWRENCE BOLTON, late of Blackburn, deceased, were granted by the Consistory Court of Chester unto Ann Bolton, the lawful widow and relict of the deceased

---

h The earliest record of a nomination to Blackburn, in the Bishop's Registry, Chester, is that of the Rev Adam Bolton to the Vicarage of Blackburn, on the presentation of the Archbishop of Canterbury, 20th June, 1628

On the 16th of May, 1683, Letters of Administration of the effects of John Bolton, late of Blackburn, deceased, were granted by the Consistory Court of Chester unto Ann Bolton, the lawful widow and relict of the deceased

On the 9th of November, 1692, Letters of Administration of the effects of James Bolton, late of Blackburn, Mercer, deceased, were granted by the Bishop's Consistory Court of Chester unto Alice Bolton, the lawful widow and relict of the deceased.

On the 26th day of September, 1696, Letters of Administration of the effects of Mary Bolton, late of Blackburn, spinster, deceased, were granted by the Bishop's Consistory Court of Chester to Thurston Bolton, lawful brother of the deceased

"In no instance in the foregoing genealogical extracts have the Testators given the locality of the Legatees, and the only will bearing a seal at all legible, is that of John, 1661, the impression upon it being a large water-bird."—Chas T. W. Parry, Registrar.

There is no record of the marriage of either Robert or John Bolton of Lancashire, in the Marriage License Registry Books at Chester, from 1684 to 1688.

In the York Registry is the will of William Bolton, of Kersey church, Lancashire, from which the following extracts are taken ·

"In the will of William Bolton of Kersey Church, deceased, bearing date 21st of June, 1593. Testator mentions his wife Isabel, his son Richard, his daughters Elizabeth and Agnes, his sons Roger and William, and his daughter Margaret"

The jurisdiction of the Archbishop of York, at that time, extended over Lancashire in matters testamentary.

Extracts from the Register Book for the Parish Church of St. John, in Wales, in the West Riding of Yorkshire, within South Division of the Wapentake of Strafforth and Tickhill, commencing A.D. 1580 [1]

BAPTISMS

Robert Bolton, son of John and Mary, his wife, baptized, July 3d, 1692.
Henry, son of Henry and Ann Bolton; baptized, 1708

The following entry also occurs in the Register Book.

Henry Bolton, Church Warden, A.D. 1700.

---

[1] "The registers at Wales commence at or before 1580, they are in a book previous to the one containing the Boltons. The outside leaves are unreadable from having been previously kept in the church In many places the color of the ink is gone, only sufficient remains to indicate it once was writing, (the early registers of Harthill are literally rotten) In the book containing the Boltons, from having been damp, some of the letters have run one in the other, the name of Robert Bolton could not well be made out at first sight Robert Bolt—the 'on' being very faint—Robert Bolt was very clear, but Mr Hawley, the incumbent, had no doubt as to the name The first book was produced on my second visit, on Friday, we examined the latter part, but no Boltons Robert Bolton was an early entry of the second book " "Another book contained the signature of Henry Bolton, Church Warden" "No entries of marriages or deaths of the name of Bolton." Communicated by Mr Thos Hinchliffe, Nov 27th, 1860 There are no Church Wardens' Accounts or Lists of Taxable Inhabitants of an early date

Extract from the Register Book of Tickhill in the West Riding of York

CHRISTENING

1698, Nov 9th, Robert, son of John Boulton.

Also twelve other entries of the name of Boulton.

There are some thirty names of Boulton in the Registers of Finningley, from 1672 to 1721. The two following are extracts therefrom:

MARRIAGE.

1673, Feb. 4th, Zacariah Boulton and Mary Taylor.

BAPTISM.

1698, July 28th, Henry, son of Zacariah and Mary Boulton.

Extracts from the Parochial Register of Christ Church, Philadelphia, Pennsylvania, from A.D. 1720 to 1748, inclusive, entitled " The Clark's buck of accounts of the Churg of Ingoland in philadelphia, Cept by him to pasifie and sartyfie, baptised, bands published, marreg and burialls from the year adomy 1710 for the publick good of the aforesad churg in Philadelphia in Amaraca by me Jonathan Ashton Clark of the curch of Ingoland in Philadelphia in pensilvania "

MARRIAGE IN FEB'Y, 1721

Robert Bolton, of Philadelphia, gent, and Ann Clay of ye same, widdow, ye 19th.

CHRISTENINGS IN JAN'Y, 1722.

Robert, son of Robert and Ann Bolton, gent, born ye first, and bapt'd ye 22d
1723, Feb 27th, Ann, daughter of Robert and Ann Bolton.
1724, May 8th, Mary, daughter of Robert and Ann Bolton.
1725, Mar. 28th, John, son of Robert and Ann Bolton, born ye 20th.

BURIAL.

May 20th, 1726, John, son of Robert and Ann Bolton, gent.

CHRISTENINGS.

1726, July 5th, John, son of Robert and Ann Bolton, born ye 20th.
1727, June 22d, Joseph, son of Robert and Ann Bolton, aged 2 days
1727, June 22d, Hannah, daughter of Robert and Ann Bolton, aged 2 days

BURIALS

1727, Oct 12th, Joseph, son of Mr. Robert Bolton.
1728, April 28th, By Robert Bolton's child, 4s. 6d —13 06.

CHRISTENING

1728, Sep. 2d, Joseph, ye son of Robert and Ann Bolton, aged eight days

BURIALS.

1729, April 28th, Hannah, the daughter of Robert Bolton.
1729, June 13th, Joseph, the son of Robert Bolton

CHRISTENING

1720, Dec 24th, Rebecca, daughter of Robert and Ann Boulton, aged four dayes.

BURIALS

1742, June the 25th, Robert Bolton.

Parish Clerk, MICHAEL BROWN

1747, May 7th, Ann Bolton
Acc't of breaking ground and use of pall, Widow Bolton, 1747, 4s. 6d.

1748, March 7th, Rebecca Bolton, youngest daughter of Robert and Ann Bolton

---

Extracts from the Register Book for the Parish Church of All Saints, in Rotherham, in the West Riding of Yorkshire, from the year of Our Lord 1666 to 1721, inclusive.

MARRIAGES

Richard Bolton and Martha Holt, Nov 9th, 1666
Elias Boulton and Mary Cutt, Oct 16th, 1709, of Sharpe.

BURIALS

Thomas, son of Mr John Bolton, Rotherham; buried—affidavit received, Dec 15th, 1669
William Bolton, Rotherham, buried April 4th, 1713.
Margaret, daughter of Richard Bolton, of Greasborough
Sept 7th, 1715, Mary, daughter of Richard Bolton, Greasbreaugh, buried
Esse, daughter of Johannes Bolton, Music-Master, buried 12th March, 1714
Johannes Bolton, of Rotherham, Music-Master, buried April 19th, 1716.

Extract from the Register Book of Treeton, in the West Riding of Yorkshire :

Jeremia Bolton, buried Feb. 28th, 1721

Extracts from the Register Book of Laughton, in the West Riding of Yorkshire:

BAPTISMS.

1699, Ann, daughter of Thurston Boulton, bap. Nov. 5th
1702, Thurston, son of Thurston Boulton, bap Aug 30th.
1705, Mary, daughter of Thurston Boulton, bap Nov. 11th.
1707, Thomas, son of Thurston Boulton, bap March 2d
1707, Joshua, son of John Boulton, bap Nov 11th
1709, Sarah, daughter of John Boulton, bap Sep 4th.
1710, Hannah, daughter of Thurston Boulton, bap March 4th
1709, Elizabeth, daughter of John Boulton, bap. Nov. 11th.
1713, Ann, daughter of Thurston Boulton, bap May 3d

J ,There are no entries of baptisms by the name of Bolton

1716, Qain, daughter of Thurston Boulton, bap June 3d

1722, Thurston, son of John Boulton, bap. June 14th.

BURIALS.

1709, Joshua, son of John Boulton, buried May 4th

1711, Ann, daughter of Thurston Boulton, buried April 24th

1714, Mary, daughter of John Boulton, buried July 20th

1715, Ann, daughter of Thurston Boulton, buried July 3d

1722, Ann, wife of John Boulton, buried Jan 7th

1722, William, son of John Boulton, buried Feb 2d

1723, John, son of John Boulton, buried Aug 22d

Extracts from the Register Books for the Parish Church of All Saints, in Chesterfield, Derbyshire, from A.D. 1672,k to 1721, inclusive

Jonas, son of Jonas Boulton, bap Aug 26th, 1676

Johe's, son of Jonas Boulton, sepul't Dec 26th, 1678

Elizabeth, daughter of Jonas Bolton, sepul't Sep. 24th, 1683

Alice, his wife, sep't

Johannes Fowler and Sarah Bolton, nupt Feb'y 2d, 169$\frac{4}{}$

Jonam Bolton Saram Calow, nupt May 20th, 1700

Margratia, daughter of Jonas Bolton, bap April 26th, 1701.

Grace, daughter of Jonas Bolton, bap Nov 29th, 1702

John, son of Jonas Bolton, Jn , bap Jan 30th, 1705

Alice, wife of Jonas Boulton, buried Dec. 11th, 1707

Sarah, daughter of Jonas Boulton, bap Jan 21st, 170$\frac{7}{}$

Sarah, daughter of Jonas Boulton, Junior, buried Sep. 19th, 1708.

Jonas Boulton, buried Nov. 8th, 1719.

Parochial Registers examined for Entries of Marriages, Baptisms, and Burials of Boulton or Bolton.

COUNTY OF YORK.	COUNTY OF DERBY.	COUNTY OF NOTTINGHAMSHIRE
Sheffield,	Killamarsh,	Worksop
Ecclesall Bierlow,	Beighton,	*Newark-upon-Trent,
*Rotherham,	Eckington,	Blyth and its chapelry
*Wales,	Stoney Middleton,	Bawtry,
Harthill,	Eyam,	Harworth
Thorpe Salvin,	Hathersage,	
Anston,	Balborough,	
*Laughton,	Whitwell,	COUNTY OF NORTHAMPTONSHIRE
Todwick,	Clown,	Broughton

---

k The registers were examined from 1672 to 1721, inclusive "The old Church Warden's accounts are in the possession (1857) of the present assistant overseer, and were found to be in such a state of confusion, that to obtain any thing like accurate information from them would entail much time and research."

COUNTY OF YORK.	COUNTY OF DERBY	COUNTY OF LANCASHIRE
Bradfield, and chapelries	Norton,	*Blackburn [1]
Bolsterstone and Mid-	*Chesterfield,	
hope,	Shirland,	
*Treeton,	North and South Wing-	
Whiston,	field,	
Wickersley,	Dronfield, with chapel-	
Maltby,	ries of Holmsfield and	
Aston,	Dore, including ham-	
Penistone,	let of Little Barlow,	
Stanington,	Beauchief,	
*Tickhill,	Staveley and Great Barlow,	
Auckley.	Finningley.	

The following Transcripts of Parochial Registers, belonging to Dean and Chapter of York, were examined for Baptism of Robert Bolton in 1688 · Slaidburn, Halifax, Kildwick, Broughton, Barwick in Elmet, Dinnington, Huddersfield, Elland, (part of the parish of Halifax,) and Garforth, all in West Riding of York.

———————

Extracts from the Marriage License Files in the Diocesan Registry and in the Registry for the Peculiar of Wales at York:

April 30th, 1685, Thomas Clarke of Long Preston, husbandman, and Elizabeth Bolton

August 19th, 1685, William Bolton of York, fell-monger, and Mary Smith

March 24th, 1686, Jonas Thomas of North Bierley, in the County of York, and Anna Bolton.

November, 1687, Timothy Bolton, of Wakefield, and Margaret Hattson.

There is no marriage-license of either Robert or John Bolton to Ann ———, from January, 1685, to December, 1687.

The Registry of Wills at York were searched for Wills or Administrations of John or Robert Boulton or Bolton, deceased, from 1688 to 1706· Also in the Registry of Lichfield, in which diocese Chesterfield is situated, without any good result. No John or Robert Bolton was found in the Lichfield registries, who resided in Derbyshire, nor will of Thomas Richmond, from 1717 to 1731, in York Registry.

———————

Wills and Letters of Administration found in Her Majesty's Court of Probate, Doctors' Commons, London. Search was made for Will or Administration of Robert or John Bolton or Boulton from 1688 to 1708:

John Bolton, February, 1691, late of Lambeth Surrey, Waterman, Pro. to Wm Kershue, sole exōr.

———————

[1] In all the parishes marked thus (*) the name of Boulton or Bolton was found

John Bolton, March, 1692, late of Cambridge, Pro to Boulton Rogers, sole exōr Property bequeathed to Elizth Dondson and Jane Clay

John Bolton, July, 1696, late of St. Olaves, Southwark Surrey, Pro. to Jane Bolton, w^d Property bequeathed to her

John Bolton, ——, 1698, Commander in the Navy, Pro to Daniel Bolton, (his father,) sole exōr, of East Smithfield, London, Cooper

John Bolton, April, 1700, late of St. Ann's, Westminster, admon to Ellen Bolton, w^d, the relict.

John Boulton, December, 1706, formerly of Stepney, in the County of Midd^x, but on board the ship "Bredah," admon. to John Cox, a creditor, Judith Isabella Boulton, w^d, the relict having renounced.

Et Patribus et Posteritate.

WILL OF JOHN BOULTON OF NEWARK-UPON-TRENT

In the Name of God: Amen I, John Boulton of Newarke upon Trent, in the County of Nottingham, Inholder, being weake in body but of pfect minde and memory, praised be to Almighty God for the same, and Whereas there is nothing more certaine then death nor more uncertaine then the houre of it, doe make and ordaine this my last Will and Testament in manner and forme following (that is to say) first and principally I comend my Soule into the hands of Almighty God, who gave it, and hopeing through the death and passion of his Son Jesus Christ to have free pardon and remission of all my sins, and my body to the Earth of which it was composed, to be decently buried at the discretion of my Executrix hereafter named And as for my worldly Estate, as hath pleased Almighty God to bestow upon mee, I dispose thereof as followeth First, I give and bequeath unto my sister Joan Wood One shilling, to be paid her imediately after my decease, being lawfully demanded And as for all the rest, residue, and remainder of my Estate undisposed of, I give and bequeath unto my loveing wife Anne Boulton, whome I make my sole Executrix of this my last Will and Testament, revoaking all former Wills by mee heretofore made. In witness whereof I have hereunto sett my hand and seale, this five-and-twentyeth day of March, Anno D'ni 168⅘.

[L S]   John Boulton.

Signed, sealed, published, and declared in the psence of Bernard Wilson, Thomas Jones, Hen. Newman

> This Will was proved in the Exchequer Court of York, 5th July, 1689, by the Oath of Anne Kilpatrick,[m] wife of Alexander Kilpatrick, (formerly Boulton, widow,) the sole Executrix therein named, to whom probate was granted, she having been first sworn duly to administer
>
> Wm Hudson,
> Jos Buckle

---

m Marriages solemnized in the Parish of Newark-upon-Trent, in the County of Nottinghamshire, May 25th, in the year 1689 'Alexander Kilpatrick and Anne Bolton " Copied from the Newark-upon-Trent Register of Marriages —Author

ERRATA.

On page 185, tenth line from bottom, after the word "issue" read "Michael Woodhull father of Fulke Woodhull, the father of," etc

Page 21, line 22, *for* Cascoigne, *read* Gascoigne
" 34, note h, line 13, *for* Henry III , *read* VIII
" 56, line 3, *for* June *read* May
" 62, " 6, *for* 1669, *read* 1668
" 86, " 11, *for* May, *read* April
" 87, " 8, *for* died 21st, *read* bur 20th.
" 90, " 11, *for* Ogeeche, *read* Ogeechee
" 137, note n, line 6, *for* ar *read* az
" 137, " n, " 7, *for* fesse *read* flags

ADDENDA.

Extracts from the Register-Book for the Parish Church of St. Andrew, Broughton, Northamptonshire.

BAPTISMS

Hannah Bolton, the daughter of Robert Bolton and Anne, his wife, baptized the 20th day of August 1615

Samuel Bolton, the sonne of Robert Bolton and Anne, his wife, was baptized the sixteenth of May, 16 , (these two last figures are torn out of the register They were probably 17, although Wood says 13)

Mary, the daughter of Mr Robert Bolton and Anne, his wife, was baptized the 22d of April, 1620, (or 21, the last figure being torn out)

Elizabeth Bolton, the daughter of Mr Robert Bolton and Anne his wife, was baptized the 7th day of March, 1622

Sarah Bolton, the daughter of Robert Bolton and Anne, his wyfe, was baptized the 12th day of March, 1625

BURIAL

Robertos Bolton, egregius ille concionator, idemque rector de Broughton, sepulchro compositus Decemb

MARRIAGES

Henry Pinedax and Elizabeth Bolton were married the 27th of November, 1619.

John Wiat, of Bugbroke, and Elizabeth Bolton, of Broughton, were married with a license the five and twentieth day of April, 1639

Early Notices of Boltons

Christopher Bolton, Vicar of Hatfield, 19th Dec 1507
John de Bolton, Vicar of Tickhill, 27th Feb 1361.
John de Bolton, Vicar of Sprotborough, Dec 1424
Thomas Bolton, Vicar of Hooton Pagnell 14th Oct 1406, party to a deed
4 Hen VI

CPSIA information can be obtained at www.ICGtesting.com
Printed in the USA
BVOW01s2203010814

361341BV00020B/181/P